Creation and Double Chaos

Creation and Double Chaos

Science and Theology in Discussion

Sjoerd L. Bonting

FORTRESS PRESS
MINNEAPOLIS

CREATION AND DOUBLE CHAOS
Science and Theology in Discussion

Library of Congress Cataloging-in-Publication Data

Bonting, Sjoerd Lieuwe.
   Creation and double chaos : science and theology in discussion / Sjoerd L. Bonting.
      p. cm.
   Includes bibliographical references and index.
   ISBN 0-8006-3759-3 (alk. paper)
   1. Creation. 2. Religion and science. 3. Chaos (Christian theology) I. Title.
   BT695.B58 2005
   261.5'5—dc22
                                                              2005018175

09   08   07   06   05   1   2   3   4   5   6   7   8   9   10

Contents

Preface

In this book I attempt to bring the science–theology dialogue, which has attracted so much attention in recent years, a step further. From the writing of my first book in this field[1] I gained the conviction that the 1800-year old *creatio ex nihilo* doctrine does not stand up very well in the light of our modern scientific insights and that it poses several other problems, not in the least that of evil. This led me to formulate a revised creation theology, which I called *chaos theology*.[2] Here I consider its usefulness for the science–theology dialogue and for obtaining new insight in some important theological topics. This means that I have come to abandon the traditional *creatio ex nihilo* doctrine, which was useful in the battle against gnostic dualism, but has contributed little to the further development of Christian theology.

My procedure is based on the premise that we have two worldviews, the theological and the scientific worldviews, both God-given. These two worldviews can, therefore, in principle not clash, but taken together they should give us a deeper view of reality, provided we keep in mind their limitations. The scientific worldview answers the How?-questions, while the theological worldview responds to the Why?-questions. In the dialogue each should be taken in its full integrity and—particularly in the case of science—with the use of the most up-to-date insights. Basic in the dialogue are in my opinion creation theology on the theological side, cosmic and biological evolution on the scientific side.

I have attempted to write for the non-specialist, the theologian who is not a scientist, the scientist who is not a theologian, and for all those who wish to deepen and strengthen their belief while living in a world that has come to be dominated by science and technology. So I avoid jargon from both disciplines as much as possible. For two matters I ask the reader's indulgence: the brevity of expression that is the fruit of a lifelong engagement with science, and the fact that I switch back and forth between science and theology, which some theologians may find a bit disconcerting. However, I have always tried to make it clear in the text from which discipline any particular statement comes.

Much of this book has grown out of the many discussions I have had over the past several years with theologians, scientists, and those who were neither. These have sharpened my thinking and helped me find new applications for chaos theology. Thus, readers' comments and criticism are welcome, for which purpose I include my e-mail address and website.

Sjoerd L. Bonting
s.l.bonting@wxs.nl
www.chaostheologie.nl

1

The Science–Theology Dialogue: How?

1.1 Three attitudes

Until the early nineteenth century, the Western world drew no clear distinction between science and theology. This ended after the publication of Darwin's *Origin of Species*, particularly after the public debate between Darwin's supporter Thomas Huxley and the bishop of Oxford, Samuel Wilberforce.[1] Their debate marked a turning point, inasmuch as science had declared its independence from theology. Since then, there are three possible attitudes toward the relation between science and religion: enmity, neglect, and dialogue.

Enmity is an attitude with a long history, as witnessed by the two-volume work of Andrew D. White, *A History of the Warfare of Science with Theology in Christendom* (1907).[2] In our time, enmity persists in groups of scientists and theologians as the result of misconceptions about the tenets and limitations of the two disciplines. On one side are fundamentalist Christians, who in a desperate attempt to hold on to a literal interpretation of the biblical creation stories, develop a pseudoscience (creationism; see section 1.5), which rejects all scientific findings that do not fit their beliefs.[3] On the other side are those scientists who maintain that science can explain all aspects of life (scientism); they reject all theological insights and replace some of them with misconceived scientific ideas. An example is French biologist Jacques Monod, who in *Chance and Necessity* firmly rejects a Creator God, maintaining that all natural processes are directed by a combination of necessity and chance, but not by purpose or design.[4] For Monod, "necessity" means the physical laws governing the universe. His idea of "chance" goes beyond mere absence of an assignable cause and acquires the status of a near deity, as is clear from his harsh assault on the Christian faith in the concluding chapter of his book.

Neglect is still the attitude of many, mostly continental European theologians. For instance, Reformed theologian Karl Barth does not discuss evolution in his massive *Church Dogmatics*.[5] Emil Brunner, another eminent Reformed theologian, appears to accept the evolution of the human body from animal origins but then poses without much argument the introduction of the human mind (*humanum*) "at some point."[6] Roman Catholic theologian Hans Küng devotes an entire chapter in his *Theology for the Third Millennium* to changes in theology and science without ever mentioning evolution.[7] Anglican theologian John Macquarrie also discusses creation without any reference to evolution.[8]

Neglect also occurs among scientists toward religion. For example, the late evolutionist Stephen J. Gould considered science and religion to be two "non-overlapping magisteria," which ask different questions and thus can neither conflict nor be integrated.[9] Moreover, whether believers or not, scientists generally need not bother nowadays with theological reflection for the successful pursuit of their scientific activities. After a survey of the history of the relation between science and theology, Belgian philosopher Mia Gosselin comes to the remarkable conclusion that the two disciplines are "eternally irreconcilable" unless one is willing to "water down" the Christian faith.[10] Unbelieving scientists lose the transcendental aspect of the scientific worldview, leaving only the materialistic aspect. For them, the benign Creator of pre-Darwinian scientists has been replaced by the twin deities of chance and reductionism. This may explain why the moral problems raised by modern science and technology, particularly in the biomedical area, have caught many scientists by surprise.

The divorce between science and theology has caused the cosmic dimension of the Christian faith to atrophy, shrinking that faith to a rather anthropocentric, individualistic belief for many of its adherents and contributing to the unchurching of western Europe.[11] Whether from enmity or neglect, the divorce between science and theology has caused harm to both camps. Thus, a dialogue between the two worldviews is greatly needed.

1.2 Dialogue between the two worldviews

Fortunately, in the last three decades, interest in this area has surged. Scholars who are qualified in both areas, including Ian Barbour, Arthur Peacocke, and John Polkinghorne, have played a leading role in this development. Before describing their positions on the dialogue, I shall summarize in six points the approach I have come to adopt:[12]

1. Science and theology provide two worldviews of a single reality, the cosmos in which we live. Both are God-given in the sense that God is revealed through human minds and hands not only in Scripture, but also in the scientific insight that God allowed us to develop through our senses and brainpower.

2. Both worldviews have limitations: Science cannot deal with the "beyond." It can tell us about mechanisms but not about purpose; it can answer *how* questions. Theology cannot properly deal with the scientific aspects of this world. It can tell us about purpose but little about mechanisms; it can answer *why* questions.

3. A dialogue between the two worldviews is possible, because the two disciplines have much in common. Both seek a rational explanation of basic data: biblical data in the case of theology and observational and experimental data in the case of science. Both have certain axioms in common, such as "Nothing can both be and not be at the same time and in the same respect."

4. Dialogue is needed in order to achieve a deeper understanding of the world in which we live and, hopefully, to solve some of the problems posed by it (for instance, bioethical problems).

5. Dialogue requires that each discipline be taken in its integrity. The two disciplines may challenge each other on a particular point, such as the virgin birth (see section 1.6). However, it is not permissible to reject a well-founded theory like the evolution theory in order to uphold a literal interpretation of the six days of creation in Genesis 1.

6. The meeting ground for the two disciplines is to be found primarily in creation theology on the one side and cosmic and biological evolution on the other side.

Ian Barbour's approach

In *Religion and Science: Historical and Contemporary Issues*,[13] Ian Barbour distinguishes conflict, independence, dialogue, and integration. He favors integration (p. 98), but this is an unfortunate choice, because it disregards the fundamentally different questions that the two disciplines attempt to answer.[14] Barbour says theological doctrines must be consistent with the scientific evidence, and in case of conflict, "some adjustments or modifications" of these doctrines are called for. This leads him to state that, because evolution appears to be a "trial-and-error" process, this must also be true for creation. Barbour's choice to make "religion," rather than theology, the discussion partner of science also is unfortunate, since religion includes, in addition to theology, such aspects as personal experience, spirituality, prayer, and worship, none of which have a counterpart in science.

The use of process theology (see chapter 5.3) and metaphysics leads Barbour to an insufficient treatment of the biblical data on creation (pp. 199–220) and keeps him from comparing these with present cosmology. He rejects *creatio ex nihilo* (creation out of nothing; see chapter 4), as I do, but does not explain why. (Neither do other process theologians.)[15] He emphasizes continuing creation, as I do, but fails to provide biblical evidence for this idea. He merely describes continuing creation as "a continuing struggle between order and chaos and . . . the persistence of evil and the fragility of creation" (p. 200). However, he doesn't make use of this insight when he treats the problem of evil (pp. 300–303). Finding earlier solutions wanting, he claims that process theology can explain evil: "God suffers with us in our suffering." But this can hardly be considered to explain the problem of evil, and it presents a picture of a rather powerless God, as is typical of process theology.

The weakness of Barbour's integration of science and theology by means of metaphysics is apparent in several places, including his treatment of quantum theory (pp. 165–77). Without adequately explaining what quantum theory really is all about, he opposes its metaphysical aspects to those of Newtonian physics. Hence, it doesn't become clear that quantum theory describes a transition of the Newtonian behavior at our level to the behavior of subatomic particles (chapter 7.2). Such a transition has recently been observed in laboratory experiments. Prematurely moving into metaphysics precludes a dialogue between science and theology, and integration is not achieved (section 1.4).

Arthur Peacocke's approach

In the introduction to his *Theology for a Scientific Age,*[16] Arthur Peacocke declares himself a proponent of "critical realism," which recognizes that no theory is an exact description of the world, yet the world is such as to bear interpretation in some ways and not in others. Critical realism acknowledges that language as used in science involves both indirectness of reference and realistic intent. For Peacocke, critical realism provides a valid and coherent philosophy of science, but he admits that it is still only the *aim* of science to depict reality (p. 12). He rightly notes that both science and theology use models and metaphors, and that this is inadequate but necessary

(p. 14). This is a fact of which we always need to be aware in carrying on the dialogue between science and theology. Peacocke says that in our language about God, we need to distinguish between referring to God and describing God (p. 15). In describing God, we need to practice "negative theology," recognizing that all we try to say about God will be fallible and inadequate, but we must also avoid speaking about an impersonal entity in the causal nexus, a First Cause. According to Peacocke, we need to be aware of religious experience, our own as well as that of others past and present, but he does not mention the biblical witness in this context.

Against the criticism that theology is less rigorous than science, Peacocke states that, like science, it strives for the best explanation, using criteria of reasonableness (p. 16) and religious experience (p. 18). Appeal to authority he finds not meaningful in view of the divided state of the church. More surprising is that he also rejects consensus as a reason for believing that a religious statement represents reality, yet in science, that is the common ground for acceptance of a theory. I would say that a basic requirement is agreement with the data—biblical data in theology, observational and experimental data in science. Peacocke rejects the sociological view of science that reduces science (and thus also theology) to an ideology. He asserts that the critical "winnowing" process in the development of a scientific theory or a theological position guards against ideology (p. 19). He sees the relationship between science and theology as an interacting approach to reality. Rather than dealing with two different realms (p. 20), science and theology deal with different domains of the same reality (p. 21). This agrees with my suggestion that they are two worldviews of a single reality.

John Polkinghorne's approach to dialogue

In *Scientists as Theologians*,[17] John Polkinghorne offers a useful comparative study of the approaches of Barbour, Peacocke, and himself. Polkinghorne first considers Barbour's four ideas about the relation between science and theology (conflict, independence, dialogue, integration). In contrast to Barbour, Polkinghorne opts for dialogue, because science and theology have things to say to each other (p. 5). He finds striving for integration (as by Teilhard de Chardin and process theology) undesirable. In view of the evident power of science in its own domain, theology is in danger of being assimilated into science (p. 7). Polkinghorne searches for "consonance," where the scientific and theological accounts of the world will fit together in a mutually consistent way with mutual enhancement and enlightenment. He rightly says that theology has particular subject matter that is not part of science, such as Christology, and refers to the chapter on this subject in his *Science and Christian Belief*.[18] However, for the science–theology dialogue, it is more useful to consider subject matter common to the two disciplines, while bearing in mind the different questions that they try to answer: the *why* and *how* questions.

Polkinghorne distinguishes his views from those of Barbour and Peacocke in the degree of consonance that can be sought, but he doesn't specify this.[19] Instead, he ends by listing what their approaches have in common, including a concern for critical realism (p. 9). Toward the end of his comparative study, he states that Scripture is very important to him and that he has written more about its role than the other two (p. 65). However, in two important cases, Polkinghorne does not come to a real confrontation between science and theology. First, in his discussion of the virgin birth,[20] he fails to mention the problems raised by science (contrary to Peacocke)[21] and the textual problems with the word *virgin* (see section 1.6), concluding, "The words 'born of the Virgin Mary' can be a proper part of the creed of a bottom-up thinker." Second, on eschatology, Polkinghorne describes first the somber cosmological prediction of full degradation of all matter to a chaotic cloud of photons and then adds the biblical idea of a new creation as the "transformation" of the old creation.[22] But can the creation of a new world from a cloud of photons be seen as a transformation? I return to this question in chapter 14.

In conclusion, I mention two further points of criticism. First, in the accounts of Barbour, Peacocke, and Polkinghorne, I miss the explicit recognition that creation theology must be the main topic for dialogue from the theological side (although Peacocke uses creation theology extensively in his *Creation and the World of Science*).[23] Second, Barbour and Peacocke mention "religious experience" as one of the criteria to use for verifying theological statements. Although biblical texts derive from the religious experience of author and community, data for the dialogue with science must be the canonical texts delivered to us. And these texts must be studied using the critical apparatus that has been developed by generations of biblical scholars.

1.3 Language and metaphors

Some theologians claim that a fruitful dialogue is impossible, because the disciplines of science and theology speak different languages. This perception probably has more to do with theologians' lack of knowledge of science than with a real language problem. Having worked for more than four decades in both fields, I feel that this problem does not arise as long as we use clear, direct, descriptive language with a minimum of jargon.[24] The realistic intent of language as used in science also applies to theology, as Peacocke emphasizes.

However, both languages frequently use models and metaphors. When such a model or metaphor is explained, this need not cause misunderstanding. But confusion and misunderstanding may arise when a writer on either side uses metaphoric language without mentioning it and without providing adequate translation. Two examples may make this clear:

1. Italian zoologist Ludovico Galleni relates the metaphoric concept of the Lorenz attractor to Teilhard's metaphoric and mystical idea of the Omega point.[25] In chaos theory (see chapter 7.3), the development of the equation for a nonlinear system can lead to the appearance of a set of ever-repeating figures that *seem* to be drawn to a single point, called the Lorenz attractor (after its discoverer, Edward Lorenz). Since there is no physical action involved, the Lorenz attractor is merely a metaphor. Teilhard sees biological evolution as converging to a perfected humanity, which he calls the Omega point (which is in conflict with the ever-widening evolutionary tree that biology shows us). The metaphor of the Lorenz attractor cannot enlighten us about Teilhard's equally metaphoric Omega point, and it certainly does not give the latter a scientific basis.

2. Australian philosopher Anthony Kelly launches the idea of an "evolutionary" Christ.[26] Without saying so, he uses evolution in a metaphoric, nonscientific way. Biological evolution is a serial process of gene mutation and selection, involving many individuals over many generations, by which a new species may develop (chapter 2.4). This cannot be applied to the life of a single individual. Kelly could at most speak about a "development" in the human Jesus of Nazareth, like that in every human from birth to death. But the transition of the human Jesus to the transcendental Christ is a unique event that defies both biological evolution and developmental psychology.

1.4 Is metaphysics useful for the dialogue?

In section 1.2, I commented on Ian Barbour's use of metaphysics in his treatment of the relation between science and theology ("religion" in his words). Here I present a critical analysis of the usefulness of metaphysics in this context. The word *metaphysics* comes from the Greek *Meta ta phusika*, which means "what comes after physics." It is the philosophical study aimed at determining the real nature of things, the meaning, structure, and principles of whatever exists.[77] The subject originated with Aristotle's treatise *Metaphysica*, which followed his work *Physica*. Aristotle explores the meaning of *being* and concludes that the primary meaning is having substance, determined by matter and form. He further believes in a divine Intellect, which doesn't create but functions as the ultimate Cause of the being of things. Plato believes in the existence of higher, eternal realities (the Ideas) behind the observable realities of our world. A divine Maker projects the Ideas into our observable world, but the Ideas world is the perfect world of true Being, accessible only to our thinking. The observable world is merely a world of appearance and change. Pythagoras, having discovered that the tone produced by lyre strings depends on the length of the strings, claims that number and structure—rather than matter—are the essence of existence.

Thus, metaphysics is the study of the existence of what is. It attempts to answer four questions: (1) What is it that causes a thing to be? (2) What is the meaning of the "being" of things; what is ultimate reality as opposed to appearance? (3) What is the world of all things as a whole? (4) And what are the first principles behind the observable world? A major problem encountered is to determine what is real. For example, are dreams, numbers, and lengths real? Are changing things real? If things that change are not real, this would leave few "real" things in our evolutionary world. This thought led A. N. Whitehead (1861–1947) in his process philosophy to make the notion of "process" central in his metaphysics. Another problem discussed till today is the mind-body relation. For Descartes, mind and body were entirely separate; for Spinoza, they were closely related. Modern neurobiology has convincingly shown that Spinoza was right, which also casts doubt on the relevance of metaphysical speculation on questions still being studied by science. The presently much-discussed problem of the difference between humans and machines is another example of the irrelevance of metaphysical speculation, in view of the ongoing developments in the field of artificial intelligence.

Metaphysics, theology, and science all study reality, but from different perspectives. For metaphysics, the perspective is the question of what "being" really is; for theology, it is the belief that all "being" is dependent on God; for science, it is the assumption that reality can be understood by means of observation and experiment. This in itself makes it unlikely that metaphysics can function as a bridge between science and theology. Its use in the science–theology dialogue contributes to a neglect of the biblical data, as by Whitehead and the process theologians, and of recent scientific insights (as I have pointed out in the case of Ian Barbour in section 1.2). However, these data should constitute the main source material for the dialogue. In addition, the metaphysicians indulge in the liberal use of unexplained terms like ontology, epistemology, determinism, and critical realism, producing a message that is unintelligible to the noninitiate reader. Finally, metaphysics is basically nontheistic, which renders it rather unsuitable to serve as a bridge between science and theology. Instead, the direct language of theological and scientific statements suffices without the use of a bridge.

1.5 Truth in science and theology

Both science and theology seek truth, but neither can claim to grasp it in an absolute sense. Science works from observations or experimental results, which lead in first instance to a supposition, a hypothesis. When further observations or experiments seem to confirm the hypothesis, it is accepted by the scientific community, and it becomes a theory. Such theory stands as long as no contradictory findings are obtained. It is then "truth" in a provisional sense: it remains open to revision or rejection on the strength of future findings. Scientists are not seeking Truth, but merely the best explanation of their observations.

Science is based on the assumption that we live in an orderly universe where physical laws and fundamental constants are always and everywhere the same. It is very difficult, if not impossible, to prove this assumption; trying to do so would stop the progress of science. Two further points place limits on science: (1) Science can only deal with natural phenomena within our universe, not with "supernatural" matters like the existence and activities of God. (Natural effects of God's activities can be treated by science without reference to God.) (2) Science cannot deal very well with unparalleled, unique events, like the biblical account of the resurrection of Jesus. The origin of our solar system is unique but not unparalleled elsewhere in the universe, so science can make claims about it.

Theology works with biblical accounts and religious experience (analogous to the observations and experimental results of science) and formulates from them doctrines (analogous to scientific theories). This involves logical reasoning, similar to that used in the formulation of a scientific theory. A doctrine needs to fit in with the body of doctrine of the church, much as a new scientific theory may not contradict the body of existing theories. And it must be accepted by the religious community in order to be considered valid, just as a scientific theory needs to be accepted by the scientific community. It then becomes a religious "truth" in a provisional sense, as is also the case for scientific theories. A religious truth only points to the absolute Truth to which Jesus refers when he says, "I am the way, the truth, and the life" (John 14:6). Our theology must remain open to revision in the light of new understanding of biblical texts and new insights like those deriving from science. And we should always bear in mind the words of Paul: "Now I know only in part; then I will know fully" (1 Cor 13:12), the "then" referring to the heavenly state to which we hope to attain.

We should also distinguish theology from spirituality. Theology pertains to the communal doctrines of the church; is intellectual, objective, and academic; and is based on reason. Spirituality, which concerns personal experience of God, results from a devotional attitude and is affective, subjective, and often mystical.[28] The former is concerned with belief, the latter with faith.

1.6 Dealing with conflicts

Mistaken positions

Mistaken positions on either side can lead to apparent conflicts between science and theology. Notable examples are reductionism and chance on the science side, creationism and Intelligent Design on the theological side.

(1) Reductionism
A characteristic feature of science is its hierarchical structure: biology < physiology < biochemistry < chemistry < physics < mathematics (in the direction of increasing depth).[29] For example, the biologist notes that sheep eat grass and describes the sheep's digestive tract. The physiologist then studies how the digestive organs do their work. The biochemist analyzes the grass components and elucidates the enzymes that help degrade these in the sheep intestine. Next, the chemist studies the molecular aspects of

these reactions and the mechanism of enzyme action in terms of structural dynamics of proteins. The physicist may then try to explain these molecular events in terms of quantum theory. Finally, mathematics can assist the physicist to express the physical explanation in a mathematical form at the deepest level of reduction. This process of reduction is a perfectly legitimate scientific procedure, which attests to the coherence of the natural sciences. It usually provides a greater depth of understanding of the phenomenon, with the possibility of predicting and even influencing it, as in the medicinal treatment of disease.

However, some scientists conclude from the success of this process of reduction that the original phenomenon is "nothing but . . ." They are guilty of *reductionism*, a materialistic ideology that does not necessarily follow from the scientific premise. For example, Francis Crick claims that so far everything we have found through biological research can be fully explained in chemical and physical terms, even human love.[30] What reductionists forget is that in going from one level to the next, there is always a loss of some aspect of the total phenomenon. In the preceding example, the vision of peacefully grazing sheep is lost by the time we descend to the level of protein structural dynamics. The whole is more than the sum of its parts! A growing number of biologists realizes that describing life as "nothing but . . ." is to lose sight of the meaning and essence of life.[31]

(2) Chance

How did humans arise? We can trace the process in considerable detail. We also know the mechanism of biological evolution as due to gene mutation and subsequent selection, yet we cannot explain why this process resulted at a given time in the appearance of *Homo sapiens*. Jacques Monod's answer is "by chance alone," by which he wishes to reject any divine purpose or design.[32]

However, a different view of the chance–law process is possible and may resolve this apparent conflict with theology. William Pollard speaks about a "fabric of turning points," from which nevertheless a path of remarkable coherence with great power and a sense of direction develops; he sees this as God's way of acting through chance in a world governed by scientific law.[33] Michael Langford concludes from various scientific studies that natural selection alone and "mere chance" might be insufficient to explain the overall course of evolution toward greater complexity, and that some form of "design" is needed.[34] He sees God steering nature without overruling it, although we cannot prove this scientifically. Arthur Peacocke discerns a creative process through which the full potential of matter comes to expression; the Creator is unfolding the potentialities of the universe, which he himself has given to it.[35] In chapter 7.3, I suggest that God may keep evolution under control through the influencing of "chaos events."

(3) Creationism

Those who hold to a literal understanding of the biblical creation stories obviously have difficulty with cosmic and biological evolution. This has led some of them to develop a "creation science" that can accommodate creation in six days and appearance of humans and other life-forms only six thousand to ten thousand years ago (based on the biblical genealogies).[36] Creation science makes several claims:

- All living beings were created recently in permanent basic forms with all subsequent variations occurring within the genetic limits built into them by God.
- The lack of transitional forms in the fossil record excludes evolution from a common ancestor.
- Evolution is *degeneration* of created complex organisms as a result of Adam's sin.
- The evidence from radioisotope dating is false, because the flood (Genesis 6) washed out decay products of uranium.
- The random mutations, assumed in the evolution theory, are usually detrimental and thus unlikely to contribute to the continuity of life.
- The law of conservation of energy and the second law of thermodynamics provide additional proof for an initial ordered state of the earth.
- Theories of origin and change are "fundamentally unprovable" due to quantum events.

By denying strongly supported and universally accepted scientific facts and theories, the creationists violate the integrity of science in order to support their questionable literalist understanding of the Bible.

Few theologians accept the literalist Bible interpretation of the creationists, and very few scientists subscribe to "creation science."

(4) Intelligent Design

Michael Behe and William Dembski claim that certain complex systems—for example, the immune system, blood clotting, the visual system, and the bacterial flagellum—cannot have arisen in time from a

Darwinian mutation-selection process and must be the result of "Intelligent Design."[37] They do not attempt to define the mechanism of Intelligent Design and scrupulously avoid using the term *God*, but claim that this is a scientific theory. If that were true, then the Intelligent Design hypothesis should be amenable to scientific research, but the adherents have not performed any.[38] Theologians will say that the hypothesis is basically a form of "God-in-the-gap theology," which is liable to disproof by scientific advances (see chapter 9.6).[39]

Science versus doctrine

More difficult to resolve is the case where scientific insight clashes with a generally held doctrine. Three examples are *creatio ex nihilo* (creation out of nothing), virgin birth, and eschatology.

(1) Creatio ex nihilo
Since its formulation by Theophilus of Antioch around 185 CE in his battle against the gnostic belief in an eternal evil matter, the church has generally affirmed and held that God created the universe out of nothing. Science, however, cannot explain an origin of matter out of nothing. Cosmology suggests that the state at $t = 0$ was an immaterial energy-rich chaos, but not a *nihil*. An appeal to the limitations of each worldview does not seem to help us here.

   To reconcile the conflict, some theologians have adopted a mitigated *nihil*: an "existing nothing" (Karl Barth) or "no thing" instead of "nothing" (Arthur Peacocke). However, neither of these is essentially different from assuming an initial chaos, whereas I think Theophilus intended a strict *nihil* in order to refute the gnostic belief in an eternal evil matter. This (along with three biblical-theological arguments discussed in chapter 4.5) has led me to reject *creatio ex nihilo* in favor of creation from an initial chaos, which is the biblical view (chapter 6).

(2) The virgin birth
The doctrine of the virgin birth is also in trouble from our scientific knowledge. It is biologically impossible to have a fully human male born without fertilization of the ovum by the sperm of a human father, as Arthur Peacocke has argued convincingly.[40] But already in the early church in the line of Justin Martyr (c. 150) to Athanasius (c. 350) to Gregory of Nazianzus (c. 380) to the Council of Chalcedon (451), the conviction

had grown that the Savior of humankind has to be fully human as well as fully divine.[41]

Actually, the biblical evidence for the doctrine has a weakness. The virgin birth of Jesus is mentioned only in the birth stories of Matthew (Matt 1:18-25) and Luke (Luke 1:25-36), but nowhere else in the New Testament. Matthew refers to the messianic text in Isa 7:14, which uses the Hebrew word *almah*, young woman of childbearing age, married or unmarried. But the New Testament authors used the much later Greek translation in the Septuagint, which translates *almah* with the word *parthenon*, young virgin. In addition, the virgin birth story (with the Holy Spirit as agent) clashes with the incarnation account in the prologue of John's gospel (with *Logos* as agent), which has served as the basis of the development of Christology in the early church.[42] Thus, it seems to me that we may consider the virgin birth story as not authoritative.

(3) Eschatology

The Bible offers a hopeful view of the future. The second Isaiah speaks about the new heaven and the new earth that God will make (Isa 66:22), and the first Isaiah associates this with the coming of the Messiah (Isa 11:1-9). The New Testament authors apply the title "the first and the last" used by Isaiah for God (Isa 44:6) to Christ (Rev 22:13), whom they expect to return on the last day for the definitive fulfillment of the creation. In stark contrast with this hopeful view is the somber prediction of cosmology of a complete degradation of all matter to a chaotic cloud of photons. John Polkinghorne and Ian Barbour describe the cosmological prediction without mentioning the sharp conflict with biblical eschatology, where even the apocalyptic writers (e.g., Daniel 7–12) do not predict a complete degradation.[43]

The creation of the new world from a fully degraded universe cannot be seen as a transformation, a fulfillment, of the old world. This would imply that the Creator failed in the initial creation. The contradiction can be resolved if we take into account that the cosmological prediction is based on the assumption of a thermodynamically closed system, but that in the biblical view, the Creator remains involved in his creation, making it a thermodynamically open system. This suggests to me that the transformation will come before full degradation of the universe can take place (see chapter 14).

1.7 A new approach: Chaos theology

In the preceding sections, I have argued that there is a need to confront science and theology in the form of an open but critical dialogue between the two worldviews. In this dialogue, the theologian considers the *why* questions: Why is there a universe? Why are we here? Why may we believe that this is the work of a loving Creator who works toward a final goal that makes it all meaningful? The scientist considers the *how* questions: How did the universe develop? How could life arise on Earth? How could this lead to the existence of humans? The scientist tries to formulate answers to the *how* questions without any theological premises, positive or negative. And the theologian attempts to embed the answers to the *how* questions in the answers to the *why* questions, while trying to remain loyal to the faith as delivered to us but willing to revise traditional formulations when scientific insight appears to make this necessary.

The great upsurge in such dialogue in the past three decades, particularly in Anglo-Saxon countries, has led to a large number of books. So why add another book in this field? For one reason, too much of the dialogue tends to lose itself in philosophical discourse on what we think about the relation between science and theology. Science is not looking for what we think, but for the best explanation of what is. So I like to confront traditional theology with the findings of modern science. This is what modern believers need, I feel.

As I was writing my first book in this field, *Creation and Evolution*,[44] I gradually came to the conclusion that the traditional doctrine of creation out of nothing (*creatio ex nihilo*) presents several problems. This led me to formulate a revised creation theology, "chaos theology," introduced in an article and a monograph.[45] Critical comments I received on this topic led me to further reading and thinking, the fruits of which are presented in this more comprehensive book, together with several applications of chaos theology.

Before describing chaos theology, I present a summary of the two worldviews (chapters 2 and 3), the origin and problems of *creatio ex nihilo* (chapter 4), and a critical summary of current thinking about creation theology (chapter 5). Chapter 6 presents the chaos theology, followed by the theory of chaos events (chapter 7). The remaining chapters offer applications of chaos theology on important aspects of theology (chapters 8 to 14).

1.8 Summary

Since the divorce between science and theology became complete after the publication of Darwin's *Origin of Species*, one can have three attitudes: enmity, neglect, or dialogue. Enmity persists through misconceptions about the tenets of the two disciplines. Neglect occurs among scientists, who can successfully pursue their branch of science without concerning themselves with ultimate questions, and among theologians, who fail to consider the relevance of important scientific insights, particularly cosmic and biological evolution. Since these two attitudes cause harm to both disciplines, we should choose dialogue between science and theology.

My approach to the dialogue differs to some extent from those of Ian Barbour, Arthur Peacocke, and John Polkinghorne. I see science and theology as two God-given worldviews of a single reality: the universe we inhabit. Since both worldviews are God-given, there should in principle be no disagreement between them. But we must bear in mind the limitations of each: science can answer the *how* questions, theology the *why* questions. Dialogue is possible because both disciplines seek a rational explanation of basic data: biblical data for theology and observational and experimental data for science.

The meeting point must be creation theology on the one side and cosmic and biological evolution on the other side. A language problem need not occur as long as direct, descriptive language is employed and any metaphors used are carefully explained to avoid confusion. Where conflicts seem to occur, we must look critically at the basic data and be willing to adjust earlier conclusions.

This has led me to the insight that the traditional doctrine of creation out of nothing (*creatio ex nihilo*) is flawed and to the formulation of a revised creation theology, "chaos theology," which the following chapters will explain and apply to some important theological questions.

2

The Scientific Worldview

In chapter 1.2 I claimed that the meeting ground for theology and science is to be found primarily in creation theology on the one side and cosmic and biological evolution on the other side. In this chapter I provide an overview of our knowledge of the latter two topics: how the cosmos came about and developed (part A) and how life may have originated and evolved (part B). Our extensive knowledge of both topics and the way this knowledge has been obtained constitute the scientific worldview.

A. Cosmic evolution

Understanding cosmic evolution (meaning evolution in the broad sense of "development") requires first an understanding of matter and forces.

2.1 Particles and forces

All matter in the universe consists of atoms with the same chemistry and obeying the same physical laws as on Earth. The atoms consist of a positively charged nucleus around which negatively charged electrons orbit. The nucleus is made up of positively charged protons and uncharged neutrons, both of which consist of three quarks (different types in protons and neutrons), held together by gluons. So there are three kinds of elementary particles: electrons, quarks, and gluons. Free quarks and gluons do not normally exist but have been briefly observed after collisions of gold atoms at extremely high energies in a particle accelerator, and they must have existed briefly (about ten microseconds) in the very early universe.

Four fundamental forces are operating in the universe. Their interactions with the elementary particles are described in the so-called Standard Model, according to which each force is thought to be carried by a particle:[1]

1. *Gravitational force*, the weakest of the four, is an attractive force acting over long distances. It is thought to be carried by gravitons, which have not yet been observed. They seem to be moving with the speed of light, in accordance with Einstein's theory of general relativity.[2]
2. *Electromagnetic force* interacts only with charged particles, such as quarks and electrons. It is 10^{42} times as large as the gravitational force (10^{42} means 1 followed by 42 zeros). The electromagnetic force is carried by photons, the light "particles."
3. *Weak nuclear force* is responsible for radioactivity; it acts on particles, but not on photons and gravitons. It has a very short range and is thought to be carried by W bosons.
4. *Strong nuclear force* holds the quarks together in protons and neutrons, and the latter in an atomic nucleus. It is carried by the gluons.

The Standard Model has two shortcomings. Although it describes elementary particles and their interactions with great precision, it does not explain the fact that particles have mass. Scientists have postulated an as yet undiscovered particle, the Higgs boson, that would confer mass. The Large Hadron Collider (LHC), being built at CERN, the nuclear research center near Geneva, will be looking for it.

Another problem of the Standard Model is that it does not provide for the unification of gravity with the other three fundamental forces. For this reason, scientists have for the past fifty years been searching for a Grand Unified Theory (GUT).[3] There are three approaches:[4]

1. *String theory* considers the elementary particles as vibrating strings. Its weakness is that it presents a ten-dimensional universe. The six extra dimensions (in addition to the four dimensions of space and time) are thought to be curled up. Although the model can fit in all existing particles, it predicts many additional particles that are not observed.
2. *Loop quantum theory* assumes quantized cubes of 10^{-99} cubic centimeters that incorporate space, time, and matter in the form of intersecting loops.[5] But it has to assume a second universe that runs

backward in time from $t = 0$. Another problem is that this theory cannot explain the observed polarization of gamma rays from distant explosions in the universe.

3. *Quantum-gravity theory* applies thermodynamics and information theory to black holes (section 2.2). This theory suffers from the virtual impossibility of ever detecting the gravitons it postulates.

Many physicists are still skeptical about these attempts to find a Grand Unified Theory.[6] Moreover, even if such a theory can be developed, it would only represent a deeper level of "reduction" of science. However, it certainly would not mean that, as Stephen Hawking claims, "Then we would know the mind of God."[7]

In the early twentieth century, it became clear that the Newtonian laws of motion, which govern the movement of bodies, fail at very large (cosmic) and very small (particle) scales. On the cosmic scale, this has led to Einstein's theory of gravitation, commonly called the general theory of relativity. It states that gravity curves the flat space-time surface. This can explain the bending of light from a very distant galaxy when passing a large body like the planet Jupiter. Earlier Einstein developed the special theory of relativity, which poses the equivalence of mass and energy:

$$E = mc^2$$

where m is mass, and c is the speed of light. The mass–energy equivalence is the basis of the nuclear bomb: the total mass of the fission products is slightly smaller than that of the parent nucleus of uranium or plutonium. The lost mass has been converted to energy—a very large amount because it is multiplied by c^2. In addition, the special relativity theory states that the mass of a moving particle increases with rising speed, such that at the speed of light, it reaches infinity. Thus, in our universe, nothing can move faster than the speed of light. But at speeds we deal with in daily life, the increase of the mass of the moving body is undetectable, and Newtonian law applies. Both of Einstein's relativity theories have been confirmed in numerous experiments and form the backbone of cosmology.

At the particle scale, Newtonian law's failure to explain the orbiting of an electron around the atomic nucleus led to the development of quantum theory, explained in chapter 7.2. Newton's theory has not been *replaced* by quantum theory and relativity theory; rather, it has merely been *adapted* for the extremes at the particle and cosmic scales. A gradual transition from quantum behavior to Newtonian behavior has been observed for somewhat larger systems (chapter 7.2). Quantum theory applies in the early stage of cosmic evolution, when the dimension of the universe was below or at particle scale. Since gravity played a crucial role in this stage, it is regrettable that the integration of quantum theory and relativity theory in a Grand Unified Theory has not yet been achieved.

With the physical laws that have been operating since the beginning of cosmic evolution comes a set of some twenty-five fundamental constants, including the speed of light, the gravity constant, constants of the other fundamental forces, and mass of the elementary particles.[8] Two questions arise: Why do these constants have the values they do? And have they really been constant all through cosmic evolution? I will address the first question, that of the "fine-tuning" of the fundamental constants, in chapter 9 (sections 9.4 and 9.5). The second question is not easily answered, since accurate measurements in the laboratory cover short times, and measurements by cosmic observations are rather inaccurate. Scientists have disproved a claim that the fine-structure constant (related to the speed of light) may have been 0.001 percent smaller in the early universe than at present.[9] A theory that the speed of light has been varying (formulated as an alternative for the inflation theory described in the next section) lacks any experimental and theoretical foundation.[10] So, for the time being, we may proceed on the basis of the constancy of the fundamental constants.

2.2 The big bang theory

Our universe is expanding. The nearly universally accepted explanation for this phenomenon is the big bang theory, which assumes an initial "explosion," forming galaxies that are flying away from each other.[11] The theory rests on four facts: (1) The spectral lines of the galaxies have a red shift, meaning the wavelength of their light waves is increasing, which happens when objects are moving away from us. (2) The ratio of hydrogen to helium in the universe is three to one, as the theory predicts. (3) There is a cosmic microwave background (CMB) radiation, which is explained as the afterglow of the explosion. (4) Very slight ripples have been observed in this radiation, a condition essential for star formation.

Extrapolating backward from the present gives a fairly precise picture of the development of the universe from the big bang to the present. Table 2.1 lists the stages of this development.

Table 2.1. Course of the Cosmic Evolution

Time Elapsed	Temp. (°K)	Energy (GeV)	Event
0	?	?	Big bang; not accessible to physical theory
10^{-43} sec	10^{32}	10^{19}	Gravity force separates
10^{-35} sec	10^{28}	10^{15}	Inflation takes place; strong nuclear force separates; photons produce quarks and electrons; steady expansion begins
10^{-10} sec	10^{15}	10^{9}	Electromagnetic and weak nuclear forces separate
10^{-4} sec	10^{12}	10^{3}	Protons and neutrons form from quarks and gluons
3 min	10^{9}	10^{-4}	Radiation dominates; protons and neutrons form deuterium and helium nuclei
300,000 yr	3×10^{4}	10^{-9}	Matter dominates; electrons bind to nuclei, forming atoms; transparent universe; ripples in radiation
1×10^{9} yr	10^{2}	10^{-11}	Formation of galaxies, stars, and chemical elements
9×10^{9} yr	10	10^{-12}	Formation of solar system
14×10^{9} yr	2.7	10^{-13}	Present universe

Explanations:
°K is temperature above absolute zero (−273°C)
1 GeV = 10^{9} electron-volts = 1.6×10^{9} joule
In powers of 10, the exponent equals the number of zeros: 10^{8} = 100,000,000; 10^{3}
= 1,000; 10^{0} = 1; 10^{-1} = 1/10; 10^{-3} = 1/1,000; and 10^{-8} = 1/100,000,000.

About the big bang itself, we can only say that it gave birth to time and space, the physical laws and fundamental forces, and all matter and energy the universe will ever hold. The theory doesn't permit us to reach time zero ($t = 0$), the precise time at which the explosion occurred 13.7 ± 0.3 billion years before present (BP). Rather, we can only go back to a fraction of a second after the explosion at the Planck time of 10^{-43} second (a fraction represented as 1 divided by 1 followed by 43 zeros). At this point, the gravity force separated from the unified force. A tiny fraction of a second later (10^{-35} second), a decisive event occurred: a very rapid expansion during which the universe grew in 10^{-30} second from 10^{-30} meter to 10 centimeters. This so-called inflation, originally assumed on theoretical grounds by Alan Guth in 1981,[12] has been confirmed by observations of the fine structure of the CMB. During the inflation, the strong nuclear force separated off, and the first particles—electrons, quarks, and gluons—were formed from very energetic photons. This marked the end of the inflation; from there on, a steady expansion has taken place.

At 10^{-10} second, the electromagnetic and weak nuclear forces separated, so from there on, all four fundamental forces have been operating separately. This permitted the formation of protons (hydrogen nuclei) and neutrons from quarks and gluons. At three minutes, protons and neutrons formed deuterium (heavy hydrogen) and helium nuclei, but radiation still dominated over matter. After three hundred thousand years, the temperature had declined enough to permit the formation of atoms of hydrogen, deuterium, and helium; matter then dominated. The universe had become large enough to permit photons to bounce around and exist long enough so that radiation began to stream in all directions: the universe became "transparent." This released the radiation we now observe as the CMB. The expanding gas cloud consisted of 73 percent hydrogen and 27 percent helium, as predicted by the big bang theory. Studies of the CMB have revealed the presence of tiny density differences in this gas cloud (ripples of 1:100,000), which are essential for the formation of stars and galaxies.

Further studies of the CMB power spectrum at large angles, observed with the Wilkinson Microwave Anisotropy Probe (WMAP), have led to the following conclusions:[13] (1) The universe is finite with a diameter of at least 78 billion light-years. (2) The inflation was nonchaotic, implying that there is only one universe. (3) The Einsteinian space-time surface of the universe is "flat," which means there is an exact balance between expanding force and gravity, so that the universe will neither undergo collapse (a "big crunch") nor expand forever. This requires that the ratio of the actual density Ω_0 (a density corresponding to five protons per cubic meter) to the so-called critical density Ω_c for the universe equal 1. In excellent agreement, the WMAP data yield a ratio of 1.013 ± 0.02.

Dark matter and dark energy

The visible matter of the universe accounts for only 5 percent of the critical density, and the still-undefined "dark" matter, which is indicated by the dynamic behavior of stars and galaxies, accounts for another 25 percent. For the remaining 70 percent of the critical density, scientists have found no explanation.[14] They now ascribe it to "dark energy," a form of negative gravity, which makes the universe expand at an accelerating pace. This accelerated expansion has been independently confirmed by observations of supernovas and by CMB analysis.[15]

What is the explanation for this mysterious negative gravity? At the time Einstein developed his original equation for the evolution of the universe, he believed in Fred Hoyle's steady-state model (a nonexpanding universe with continuous formation of hydrogen). To accommodate this model, Einstein inserted into his equation a term Λ (lambda) to prevent any expansion or contraction resulting from gravity effects. When Hubble discovered the expansion, Einstein removed Λ, giving the following equation:

$$\Omega_m + \Omega_k + \Omega_\Lambda = 1$$

For a flat universe, $\Omega_k = 0$, so the equation becomes:

$$\Omega_m + \Omega_\Lambda = 1$$

With the visible and known dark matter comprising 30 percent of all matter in the universe, $\Omega_m = 0.3$, so $\Omega_\Lambda = 0.7$. With the current value for the Hubble expansion constant (the rate at which the universe expands), this yields for the age of the universe 13.7 ± 0.3 billion years.[16]

The term $\Omega_\Lambda = 0.7$ represents the quantum vacuum energy, a fluctuating energy field that exists even in empty space and at absolute zero temperature. This energy is thought to arise from fluctuating electromagnetic fields and continuous formation and annihilation of particle–antiparticle pairs (for example, electrons that are negatively charged and their positively charged counterparts, positrons). In relativistic thinking, energy is equivalent to mass ($E = mc^2$), so the vacuum energy would represent the 70 percent missing dark mass. Dark energy is evenly distributed in the universe: the more it expands, the more space, the more energy, the faster the expansion.[17] It all fits, even though most of us don't quite comprehend such relativistic behavior.

All this means that in about 24 billion years, the universe will not collapse in a "big crunch," nor will it end in a stationary condition. Instead, it will fly apart in a "big rip."[18] One billion years before the rip (BR), the clusters of galaxies will drift apart; 60 million years BR, our galaxy will break up; a few months BR, our solar system will fly apart; 30 minutes BR, stars and planets will disintegrate; and a split second BR, molecules and atoms will break apart, followed by the elementary particles, leaving only a cold quantum vacuum. However, this scenario presupposes a closed universe, which is not subject to any external influence. The implications of this complete degradation of the cosmos for Christian eschatology are discussed in chapter 14.1.

Although the astronomical observations in recent years have provided a firm empirical footing for the behavior of the expanding universe, the big bang theory still has some uncertainties with regard to inflation, dark matter, dark energy, and symmetry breaking.[19] The last item refers to the fact that formation of particles from energy normally leads to equal numbers of particles and antiparticles, which then annihilate each other. For there to be a universe, this charge parity must have been lifted somehow, if only temporarily. Several attempts have been made to explain this mystery, but none has yet won general acceptance.[20] Garth Barber has developed an alternative cosmology that does not require inflation.[21] He combines general relativity with the principles of Mach and of mass-energy conservation, and treats gravitation as a negative energy. As the universe evolves, particle mass (but not the energy of photons) increases. Making measurements in a Jordan frame (which uses photons as a standard of measurement; named for Ernst P. Jordan, German quantum physicist, 1902–80), Barber finds a static and eternal universe. Making measurements in an Einstein frame (using atoms as a standard of measurement), he finds an initial explosion and a linear expansion rate without need for the ad hoc assumptions of inflation, dark matter, and dark energy. In the infinite past, according to the Jordan frame, all particles had zero mass and were like virtual particles. Quantum fluctuations allowed the mass of these virtual particles to increase from zero, so they became real particles that continued to increase in mass. The required energy came from the increasing negative energy of the gravitation field, which can explain the ripples in the CMB. The results of the ongoing Gravity Probe-B mission will provide a test of the theory.

Formation of stars and galaxies

The earliest stars were large (a few hundred solar masses) and appeared within 0.2 billion years after the big bang.[22] At a ripple with slightly higher density in the expanding cloud of hydrogen and helium gas, the combined effects of gravity and cooling make the cloud rotate and contract. The decreasing diameter of the rotating cloud leads to faster spinning and flattening, resulting in a hot, dense star in which nuclear fusion of hydrogen starts. The first galaxies, resulting from a similar process of contraction and rotation, appeared after 0.5 billion years. Galaxy formation peaked after 3 billion years. Clusters of galaxies began forming after 1.4 billion years.

There are now 30 to 60 billion galaxies in the universe. Our own galaxy, the Milky Way, has a diameter of 10^{18} kilometers and a thickness of 2×10^{16} kilometers at the center. Its formation appears to have taken 3 billion years, during which time star formation took place. It contains 10^{11} stars, which compose 98 percent of its total mass. The remaining 2 percent is made up of cool interstellar matter: gas clouds and dust. The interstellar gas has a density of 10^{-24} gram per cubic centimeter (one-millionth of the best vacuum attainable on Earth). It consists largely of hydrogen and helium with traces of heavier elements ejected from dying stars; these elements include calcium, sodium, titanium, iron, and potassium.[23] Galactic dust consists of ice, ammonia, methane, silicates, and silicon carbide, formed in the surrounding envelopes of stars.

In the galaxies, additional stars are formed (about ten per year in our galaxy alone) when a spinning cloud of interstellar gas and dust collapses under gravity. Accelerating rotation makes the cloud flatten to a disk with the highest density in the center, where the star begins to form. The interstellar gas, from which these stars are formed, is enriched by elements ejected from supernova explosions of early large stars.[24] There are some 10^{22} stars in the universe. Stars are the great factories of the universe; through nuclear fusion, they turn their hydrogen and helium, produced in the aftermath of the big bang, into all other known chemical elements. (Elements heavier than iron are formed through neutron capture during the explosion of the star.)

The final state of the star after depletion of its nuclear fuel depends on its initial size. Large stars (20 to 100 solar masses) turn into black holes. A black hole has such high density and therefore high gravitational attraction that light cannot escape from it. Hence, it appears black to the observer. At the center of the Milky Way are two black holes, one of 4 million solar masses and a smaller one of 1,300 solar masses. Stars swirl around them at 9,000 kilometers per second (3 percent of the speed of light). Medium-sized stars (8 to 20 solar masses) explode as supernovas, with ejection of the elements formed in them into the interstellar space. Then they turn into neutron stars (with a density 10^{14} times that of the sun) that end as cold, dark bodies. Small stars, like our sun, will swell into red giants (in about 5 billion years from now for the sun). After the red giants exhaust their last fuel, they become white dwarfs and finally turn into cold, dark black dwarfs.

Formation of the solar system
Our sun and its planets were formed 9 billion years after the big bang, 4.6 billion years before present (BP). The planets resulted from condensation of gas and accretion of dust particles present in the spinning disk around the sun. Their composition varies with the distance from the sun. The four inner planets—Mercury, Venus, Earth, and Mars—consist entirely of silicate rock and metallic iron or nickel. The four outer planets—Jupiter, Saturn, Uranus, and Neptune—are large and icy or gaseous. Our moon most likely resulted from a collision of Earth with a Mars-sized proto-planet formed elsewhere in the solar system. This formed a disk of debris from which the Earth-orbiting moon accreted.[25] The asteroids represent the remaining rocky debris in our solar system.[26]

2.3 Summary: Cosmic evolution

The universe is made up of three types of elementary particles governed by the four fundamental forces, as described in the Standard Model. The big bang theory describes cosmic evolution from a fraction of a second after the initial explosion, 13.7 billion years ago, to the present. The explosion was followed by a very brief and very rapid expansion, the inflation. This imprinted in the expanding fireball very tiny density ripples, which after 0.5 billion years led to the formation of stars and galaxies. The first elementary particles (quarks, gluons, electrons) appeared, and after three minutes, these formed hydrogen and helium. The heavier elements originated from nuclear fusion in the stars. When these stars finally exploded, the elements were ejected into the interstellar space as cosmic dust clouds. From these, the sun and Earth were formed 4.5 billion years ago by condensation and accretion. It now appears that a negative gravity, dark energy, is bringing the universe to a big rip, some 24 billion years from now, assuming that the universe is a closed system left to itself.

B. Biological evolution

Having described in part A our scientific view of the origin and development of the cosmos and of the tiny speck in it of our planet Earth, I shall now briefly describe the scientific answer to the question "How did life arise and evolve on Earth?"

2.4 Origin of life

In view of our detailed knowledge of biological evolution, it is logical to try describing the origin of the first living cells as an evolutionary process, usually called "prebiotic evolution." However, it must be admitted that our knowledge of prebiotic evolution is still very limited. In the absence of fossil evidence, the account of prebiotic evolution rests on model experiments in the laboratory and speculation. This account is summarized in Table 2.2.

Table 2.2. Tentative Course of the Prebiotic Evolution

Billions of Years BP[a]	Events
4.6	Formation of Earth
4.1	Beginning of prebiotic evolution:
	• synthesis of building blocks
	• organization in micelles
	• replication mechanism
3.5	Appearance of first living cells
2.7	Appearance of nucleated cells
2.4	Beginning of oxygenic photosynthesis
	• oxygen accumulation in atmosphere
2.0	Appearance of mitochondria
	• beginning of oxidative metabolism
1.7	Appearance of multicellular organisms
0.9	Present oxygen level reached
0.54	Cambrian explosion of biological evolution

[a]BP = before present

Toward the first living cell

The earliest evidence for living cells dates back to 3.5 billion years BP, in the form of microfossils observed in ancient rocks.[27] The primordial Earth atmosphere was formed from gases emitted by volcanoes from the hot, pressurized Earth's interior after an initial period of asteroid and meteorite impacts.[28] Hence, oxygen was virtually absent, so there was no ozone layer. Without an ozone layer, solar ultraviolet radiation could reach Earth's surface. This radiation can form biomolecules like amino acids,[29] but to be protected from the destructive effect of this radiation, these biomolecules must have been stored under water at a depth of more than ten meters. This requirement presents a difficulty for the original proposal that synthesis of biomolecules and their condensation to proteins would have taken place in warm, shallow pools. Attention has now turned to the hydrothermal vents in the ocean floor, which through volcanic activity release hot gas consisting of hydrogen, hydrogen sulfide, methane, ammonia, and carbon monoxide.[30] These gaseous substances, at the high temperatures near the vent and with clay or pyrite minerals serving as reaction catalysts, can form amino acids and nucleotides, the building blocks of proteins and nucleic acids. Drifting aside to cooler water, these molecules would have been preserved, allowing them to accumulate.

Nowadays, the synthesis of proteins in all organisms requires the nucleic acids DNA and RNA and several protein enzymes. This seems to present a chicken-and-egg problem! However, it is now known that RNA can act as an enzyme and can connect amino acids to form proteins.[31] This suggests that RNA appeared first and then caused the production of various proteins, some of which acted as enzymes. RNA can also form DNA, as still happens during virus infections. A molecular selection process, in which the formation of "successful" molecules is favored over that of "unsuccessful" ones, may explain the formation of ever more elaborate forms of DNA, RNA, and protein enzymes. These molecules provided a genetic system for protein synthesis and replication.

Encapsulation of these molecules in a vesicle (a membrane enclosing a microscopic amount of fluid) would further these molecular processes by concentrating the required molecules. Present cell membranes are made up of phospholipids. When these phospholipids are shaken in a salt solution, vesicles readily form. In a recent experiment, such phospholipid vesicles were prepared that contained a commercially available mixture of all biomolecules needed for protein synthesis and the DNA encoding for a fluorescent protein.[32] Production of the fluorescent protein then took place for some time. The production could be kept going for days, when the gene for alpha-hemolysin was added. Alpha-hemolysin inserts itself into the membrane and creates pores through which additional nutrients and ATP (the energy substance of living cells) could enter the vesicles. In the prebiotic period, ATP may not yet have been present, but carbonyl sulfide, released by hydrothermal vents, may have provided the chemical energy for such protocells.[33]

Photosynthesis and oxidative metabolism

The next important step in the development of life must have been the initiation of photosynthesis, the process plants use to convert carbon dioxide and water into carbohydrates and oxygen by means of solar energy. The blue-green algae *Cyanobacteria*, originating 2.7 billion years BP, could do this, owing to a photosynthetic system with chlorophyll, which gives them a green color. In a relatively short time, the seas must have turned green through the rapid growth of these cells. This had three important consequences for the further development of life:

1. The large quantities of oxygen produced by the *Cyanobacteria* changed the original virtually oxygen-free atmosphere into the present oxygen-rich atmosphere between 2.4 billion and 0.9 billion years BP.[34]
2. The action of solar ultraviolet radiation on oxygen in the upper atmosphere led to the formation of the ozone layer, which has ever since protected life on Earth from the solar ultraviolet radiation, eventually allowing plants and animals to emerge from the water and inhabit the land.
3. The presence of oxygen prompted the development of oxidative metabolism, which provides the cell with much more energy than the earlier anaerobic metabolism (about nineteen times as much per molecule of glucose utilized). Oxidative metabolism enabled the formation of multicellular organisms, opening the way to more complex life-forms.

An intriguing question is how the biomolecules, such as amino acids and nucleotides, acquired their stereospecificity. All but the simplest one of the twenty naturally occurring amino acids can have two mirror images, the L- and D-forms. Only one of these, the L-form, is present in natural proteins. When we synthesize amino acids in the laboratory, we get a mixture of equal quantities of the L- and D-forms, whereas the proteins of living organisms have only L-amino acids. The selection of the L-form must have occurred early in the prebiotic process, since without this stereospecificity of the biomolecules, there would be no viable replication system, no workable enzymes, no metabolism. Life would not exist. Amino acids found in the Murchison meteorite, which come from the asteroid belt between Mars and Jupiter, are predominantly in the L-form. This suggests that the preference for L-amino acids already existed in the universe before life on Earth originated.[35] Circular-polarized electromagnetic radiation from a spinning neutron star can have selectively destroyed the D-form. The remaining L-form would then have been brought to Earth by an early meteorite. This could have transferred its chirality to ribose, building block of RNA, by its synthesis from the amino acids.[36]

Eukaryotic cells
Cells also acquired a nucleus (site of the genetic apparatus) and mitochondria (site of cellular energy production). The nucleus probably was acquired through the fusion of an *Archaea* cell and a bacterium, the latter incorporating the DNA from both cells and becoming the nucleus of the new cell, the eukaryotic cell.[37] Mitochondria probably resulted from the incorporation of alpha protobacterium.[38]

Together, these developments—oxygen atmosphere with ozone layer, oxidative metabolism, eukaryotic cells, and multicellularity—led to the sudden appearance of all phyla of animals and plants about 540 million years BP in the Cambrian period. This established the carbon cycle, with its equilibrium between conversion of carbon dioxide to oxygen by plant photosynthesis and conversion of oxygen to carbon dioxide by animal respiration. The carbon cycle equilibrium, essential for the maintenance of life on Earth, is now being disturbed by the large-scale release of carbon dioxide through fossil fuel combustion and extensive destruction of tropical forests. The ironic fact is that the most intelligent creature resulting from 4 billion years of prebiotic and biological evolution is now endangering all life on Earth (see chapter 14).

2.5 The further biological evolution

Following the prebiotic evolution came the biological evolution from microbe to mammal over the past 3 billion years.

Evidence and mechanism
The evidence for biological evolution comes from several disciplines:

- *Paleontology*—the study of fossils. The fossils were first dated from the geological age of the sedimentary rock formations in which they were found, and later by means of radioactive dating methods.
- *Comparative anatomy*—the comparison of the structure of living animals and plants.
- *Comparative embryology*—the study of similarities in embryonic development of organisms that range from fish to humans.
- *Geographic distribution* of species, which played a key role in Darwin's formulation of the theory of evolution.
- *Molecular biology*, which has unraveled the genetic system and, by comparing DNA and proteins from different species, has confirmed the evolutionary tree constructed from the fossil evidence.

Table 2.3 lists the main biological events thought to have taken place in each geologic period.

In 1858 Charles Darwin presented a theory for the mechanism of evolution in his book *On the Origin of Species*. He suggested that evolution takes place through variation in an existing species followed by natural selection on the basis of "survival of the fittest." Dutch biologist Hugo de Vries proposed in 1900 the existence of genes as the hereditary units in cells and in 1901 mutations as sudden, inheritable changes of genes. If the mutant survives the process of natural selection, a new species will be established. The process has been produced in the laboratory in rapidly reproducing *Escherichia coli* bacteria[39] and observed over many years in nature in vertebrates, including guppies[40] and Darwin's finches.[41]

Genes and mutations
Genes consist of DNA (deoxyribonucleic acid), the molecule of heredity in all living organisms. Via a related molecule, RNA (ribonucleic acid), DNA produces in two steps, called transcription and translation, a protein that carries out a specific function in the cell. During cell division, replication of DNA is carried out with the aid of specific enzymes. These three processes are summarized in the following scheme:

$$\begin{array}{ccccc} & transcription & & translation & \\ \text{DNA} & \rightarrow & \text{RNA} & \rightarrow & \text{protein} \\ replication \quad \downarrow & & & & \\ \text{DNA} & & & & \end{array}$$

Table 2.3. Course of Biological Evolution

Millions of Years BP[a]	Geologic Period	Main Events
	Paleozoic Era	
540	Cambrian	Explosion of phyla, first chordates[b]
500	Ordovician	Sudden diversification of metazoa[c]
430	Silurian	First vascular land plants, insects
395	Devonian	First amphibians
345	Carboniferous	Scale trees, seed ferns, first reptiles
270	Permian	Major extinctions; diversification of reptiles
	Mesozoic Era	
225	Triassic	First mammals, first dinosaurs
190	Jurassic	Diversification of dinosaurs; first birds
135	Cretaceous	First primates
65		Extinction of dinosaurs
	Cenozoic Era	
65	Paleocene	Diversification of birds, mammals, primates
53	Eocene	More advanced primates
36	Oligocene	Primitive apes
26	Miocene	*Ramapithecus*
6	Pliocene	*Australopithecus*
2.6		*Homo habilis*[d]
2	Pleistocene	*Homo erectus*[e]
0.3	Holocene	*Homo sapiens*[f]

[a]*BP = before present*
[b]*Animals with dorsal stiffening rod*
[c]*Multicellular organisms*
[d]*Dwelling human*
[e]*Standing human*
[f]*Intelligent human*

The DNA molecule consists of two identical strands of thousands of four different nucleotides, code-named A, C, G, and T. The strands lie along each other head-to-tail, held together by nucleotide interactions (A with T, C with G). In nonmicrobial cells, the two strands are coiled up in the shape of the well-known "double helix." During cell division, the two strands split apart, and along each strand, an identical but opposing DNA strand is formed from free nucleotides arranging themselves through interaction with their opposite. In this way, each DNA molecule forms two duplicates (replication), one of which goes to each daughter cell. During transcription, an RNA copy of the DNA molecule is formed in a similar way. This messenger RNA (mRNA) leaves the nucleus for the site of protein synthesis, where it acts as a template for the protein to be produced (translation). In RNA, the nucleotide T is replaced by one called U, and the sugar component is changed from deoxyribose to ribose.

Proteins are made up of twenty different amino acids. The genetic code ensures that a given gene produces only one specific protein. For each amino acid, there is a codon of three adjacent nucleotides (for instance, AUG for the amino acid methionine). This code is identical for all existing organisms, from bacteria to humans, and has remained unchanged throughout the entire biological evolution. It also happens to minimize errors in replication and transcription, and thus maximizes the chance that a given mutation will be beneficial.[42]

Mutations are due to changes in the base sequence of DNA by spontaneous replication errors, radiation (ultraviolet light or X-rays), or mutagenic chemicals (as in smoking). The error rate in replication is very low—one error per 1 billion to 10 billion nucleotide pairs copied—owing to the operation of so-called repair enzymes. Most mutations are nonbeneficial, and no evolutionary change occurs. The few beneficial mutations lead to changes in the nucleotide sequence of a DNA gene and thus in the amino acid sequence of the protein for which this gene codes. These changes are passed on to a new species developing from it. When a human protein (or its gene) is compared with its counterpart in other species, more differences in amino acid (or nucleotide) sequence in an earlier species are seen than in a later-appearing species. From such data, it is possible to develop an evolutionary tree that turns out to be virtually identical to that derived from fossil studies.

Gene play

The genome is the collection of all genes of an organism. The genomes of over 170 species are now known, so comparisons among species are possible. The striking conclusion is that so few genes are species-specific. For instance, in the mouse, only 1 percent of its thirty thousand genes are mouse-specific, while 77 percent of its genes are shared with all other mammals, 62 percent with all vertebrates, 56 percent with all multicellular organisms, and 29 percent with all microbes. For humans, this means that what makes us human is not so much the genes we have in our genome, but the activity of each of these genes. This situation resembles the phenomenon of cell differentiation: our kidney, liver, and bone cells have the same genome, but in each cell type, a different set of genes is switched off.

Gene activity is regulated or affected in several ways:

- *Transcription factors*—These are proteins that switch genes on and off. Each cell has many of these factors, which regulate transcription. They form a complex network, because one factor can bind to several genes. For example, yeast has 141 transcription factors, of which 106 bind to 2,300 locations in the genome. Humans have 1,700 transcription factors.
- *RNA interference*—Short stretches of RNA (siRNA) are formed that inactivate the mRNA formed by the gene.[43]
- *Junk DNA*—This consists of stretches of noncoding DNA in the genome that do not produce proteins but produce RNA that can silence or regulate neighboring coding genes.[44] Since junk DNA sequences are strongly conserved (for as long as 300 million years), they are now called "conserved non-genic sequences" (CNGs).
- *SUMO-protein*—SUMO (small ubiquitin-like modifier), bound to a protein, controls traffic between nucleus and cytoplasm, including movement of transcription factors, thus influencing gene activity.[45]
- *Histone*—The histones, proteins closely associated with the DNA double helix, appear to regulate gene activity by detaching themselves from the gene every minute or so, allowing the gene to sample from the mix of transcription factors and other regulatory proteins present in the nucleus.[46]

Two other points illustrate the complexity and flexibility of the gene play. First, many genes occur in doubles (in yeast, 25 percent of its genes),[47] a condition that accelerates evolution by having one gene maintain the function while its double is free to evolve a new function. Gene doubling also offers better protection against harmful mutations. In mice, these doubles are involved in important functions, including reproduction, immunity, detoxification, and smell.

Second, hox genes direct cell differentiation during embryonic development.[48] An example is the pac-6 gene that controls the development of all three eye types: the facet eye of insects, the "reversed" eye of cephalopods like squid (visual cells turned toward the lens), and the mammalian eye (visual cells turned away from the lens).[49] When the mouse pac-6 gene is inserted in the fruit fly *Drosophila*, many facet eyes (not mouse eyes!) are formed on its wings and legs. This suggests that the pac-6 gene is at the head of a set of genes that form the eye. Hox genes must have arisen in a mutual ancestor that emerged from the Cambrian explosion, 540 million years ago. The hox genes hox-10 and hox-11 control skeletal development in all vertebrates.[50] Another hox gene, the twist gene, plays a role in the dorsal–ventral (back–front) orientation occurring in early embryonic development.[51]

Course of evolution
It is now generally recognized that evolution is progressive and has a direction.[52] Major evolutionary changes appear to be due to changes in gene regulation, as in the appearance of all present body plans in the Cambrian explosion. Since physical laws impose constraints on the variety of forms that can be produced in evolution, we see a repetition of similar forms. This is called convergence, the emergence of similarly shaped organs in widely different species. Swimming animals (ichthyosaur, whale, dolphin, walrus, seal) developed limbs adapted to swimming, which have similar skeletal structures although derived from widely different ancestors (in dolphins from a dog ancestor, in the ichthyosaur from an early lizard).[53] Convergence makes the course of evolution to some extent predictable.

It is estimated that only about 0.1 percent of all species that arose during the course of evolution persist today, suggesting that all possible life-forms have been explored in the evolutionary process. For the first 3 billion years after the origin of life, there were only microorganisms, except for multicellular brown algae that arose 1.7 billion years BP and a few primitive animal organisms from 1.2 billion years BP (see Table 2.3).[54] At 540 million years BP, a veritable evolutionary revolution took place, the so-called Cambrian explosion, which produced in a mere 5 million years all of the current animal phyla.[55] Life emerged from the sea to the land— plants and insects during the Silurian period (430 million to 395 million years BP), and amphibians during the Devonian period (395 million to 345 million years BP). During the Carboniferous period (345 million to 270 million years BP), dense forests of large trees and ferns developed and provided food for the large herbivorous dinosaurs. However, the largest dinosaur was the carnivorous *Tyrannosaurus rex*, which weighed up to 5,600 kilograms.[56] The finding that some dinosaur species had feathers suggests that birds developed from them about 150 million years BP.[57] The first small and primitive mammals appeared 215 million years BP. These findings are summarized in Table 2.3 above.

At the end of the Permian period (250 million years BP), the greatest mass extinction in history took place: 80 percent of marine species and 70 percent of terrestrial species were lost. It may have been due to an asteroid impact, which led to massive volcanic eruptions in Siberia, followed by global cooling, acid rain, and oxygen depletion of the ocean through the large discharge of carbon dioxide.[58] In the Triassic period (225 million to 190 million years BP), ammonites (known for their spiral shell) dominated the ocean, while insects and reptiles, particularly dinosaurs, became the dominant land animals, and the first mammals appeared. Another asteroid impact at the end of the Cretaceous period (65 million years BP) led to the extinction of the dinosaurs and 75 percent of marine animals, but small insects, reptiles, birds, and the early mammals survived.[59]

The extinction of the dinosaurs was followed by a diversion of species, leading to the development of birds and mammals during the Cenozoic era (beginning 65 million years BP). This was assisted by a gradual warming of Earth's climate, possibly due to a giant release of methane from the sea floor over a ten-thousand-year period. During this period, primates appeared 56 million years BP.[60] They diversified to various tree-dwelling kinds, from which the hominid line split off in the Miocene period (26 million to 7 million years ago). Human evolution is discussed in section 2.6.

Some critical questions
Although this understanding of evolution is widely accepted, some questions remain to be answered. First, how can new species arise when mating of members of different species (interbreeding) leads to sterile offspring, like the mule resulting from the mating of horse and donkey? In fact, interbreeding does occur in many plants and animals, and it actually accelerates evolution.[61] Sexual reproduction also accelerates evolution, because a favorable mutation present in both parents will always be passed on to the next generation, as shown for the green alga *Chlamydomonas*, which has both sexual and asexual reproduction.[62] In addition, sexual reproduction reduces copying errors.

Another question is, Where are the transitional forms in the fossil record? When careful search is made, they usually can be found.[63]

Finally, how can the development of organs of extreme perfection and complexity, like the eye, be explained by a simple sequence of mutation-selection steps?[64] As described earlier in this section, gene play is much more complex and flexible than suggested by this interpretation of evolution. In chapter 9.5, I return to this issue in my discussion of the Intelligent Design hypothesis.

Such questions, even in the absence of a satisfactory answer, do not invalidate the evolution theory. Rather, they indicate that our knowledge of the mechanism of the process is still incomplete because it is much more complex and flexible than a simple linear mutation/selection process. Much unnecessary confusion and polemic about the evolution theory could be avoided if we take into account the progress in our scientific understanding, distinguish ideology (as in speaking about "Darwinism," "neo-Darwinism," and "selfish-gene theory") from scientific theory, and abandon a literalist Bible interpretation like that of the creationists (see chapter 1.4) in considering the theological implications of evolution.

2.6 Human evolution

Since humans are anatomically and physiologically mammals, it was inevitable that they would be considered as a product of biological evolution. By the time Darwin's *Origin of Species* appeared, ancient human skeletal remains had already been found in three places in Europe, the best known being Neandertal man, found originally in the Neandertal. In 1867 the Cro-Magnon caves in Dordogne, France, yielded remains of the more advanced Cro-Magnon people. In his second book, *The Descent of Man* (1871), Darwin proposed that humans descended from the apes, but all current evidence points to a common ancestor, rather than to a missing link.

This common ancestor may have been *Pierolapithecus catalaunicus*, of which a 13-million-year-old skull and other bones were recently found in Spain.[65] Studies of the molecular evolution of cytochrome c (an enzyme playing a vital role in energy production in all animal cells) indicate that gibbons, orangutans, gorillas, and chimpanzees split off from the human line 12 million, 10 million, 9 million, and 5 million years BP, respectively. Its successor, *Australopithecus* (from 6 million years BP), particularly *Ardipithecus ramidus* (found in Ethiopia, from 4.4 million years BP),[66] is considered the common ancestor of chimpanzees and humans, which differ in only 0.8 percent of their genes. The term *hominid* is used for all bipedal ancestors of humans. The development of the human species, as now understood, is summarized in Table 2.4.

Table 2.4. Main Stages in Human Evolution

Thousands of Years BP[a]	Species	Characteristics	Skull Capacity (cubic cm)
65,000	Primates	Lemur/tarsier-like tree dwellers	
13,000	*Pierolapithecus*	Beginning bipedalism?	400
6,000	*Australopithecus*	Hominid; bipedalism	440–520
5,000		Split between chimpanzee and human lines	
2,600	*Homo habilis*	Dwelling (hut); making and using tools	640
1,900	*Homo erectus*	Advanced tool production; fire	800–1,100
1,000	*Pithecanthropus*	Cave dweller; fire	880
460	*Sinanthropus*	Cannibalism?	1,040
195	*Homo sapiens*		1,200–1,600
150	Neandertal	Burial rite; advanced tools	1,490
40	Cro-Magnon	Refined tools, ornaments, murals	1,510

[a]*BP = before present*

The East African origin

East Africa has played a prominent role in hominid development from *Australopithecus* to *Homo sapiens*. That region's prominence has been ascribed to a tectonic event some 8 million years BP that formed the present Rift Valley with a mountain range to the west of it.[67] This turned much of the eastern area (now Ethiopia, Kenya, and Tanzania) into a dry, open savanna with few trees. The changing environment drove the primates out of the trees onto the ground, leading to the development of bipedal hominids in this particular area.

After several *Australopithecus* species (some of which were sidelines), *Homo habilis* appeared around 2.6 million years BP. That species seems to have been the first hominid making tools and constructing dwellings. They spread out over Africa, Asia, and Europe between 2 million and 1 million years BP.

Two conflicting theories arose about the origins of the successors of *Homo habilis*, which were *Homo erectus* and *Homo sapiens* (modern humans). The multiregional-origin theory claims that *Homo erectus* developed from *Homo habilis* on all these continents, and similarly with *Homo sapiens*. In other words, there was only a single migration, that of *Homo habilis*. The single-origin theory maintains that all three species originated in East Africa and then migrated to Asia and Europe in three successive waves of migration. Recent fossil findings and studies of DNA from living human races and the chimpanzee all support the single-origin theory.[68]

Further development
After *Homo habilis*, *Homo erectus* arose in East Africa 1.9 million years BP with a skull capacity of 800 to 1,100 cubic centimeters (versus 640 cubic centimeters for *Homo habilis*). *Homo erectus* is distinguished by the use of fire (at 790,000 years BP) and the mining of flint (300,000 years BP).[69] The consumption of cooked food led to smaller teeth and jaws. The use of fire and of animal skins for clothing and shelter, allowing survival in colder climates, facilitated migration to Asia and Europe around 1.75 million years BP.[70]

Next in line was *Homo sapiens*, appearing around 195,000 years BP in Africa and migrating to Asia, the Near East, and Europe around 160,000 years BP.[71] A single origin for *Homo sapiens*, as now seems likely, requires that there was no significant interbreeding between that species and *Homo erectus* in Asia and Europe. The skull of *Homo sapiens* has a larger brain capacity than that of *Homo erectus*, with a more rounded top, broader face, and smaller jaw with chin and smaller teeth. Hands and arms are adapted to making and using tools.

The Neandertals, now considered to be a dead-end sideline in the development of *Homo erectus* to *Homo sapiens*, lived as cave dwellers from 150,000 to 30,000 years BP in Europe and the Near East. They developed an advanced tool-making technique, used throwing spears, and hunted in small groups for mountain goats. They produced simple animal figurines from baked clay, but virtually no ornaments.[72] The Neandertals are the first hominids known to bury their dead with ritual, indicating a beginning of religious belief.[73] There is also evidence that they developed speech and made music on a bone flute. They disappeared abruptly between 40,000 and 30,000 years BP after the invasion of the technically and socially more advanced Cro-Magnons, without evidence of interbreeding.[74]

The Cro-Magnons lived in Europe and the Near East from 45,000 to 11,000 years BP. Compared with the Neandertals, they have higher, more vertical foreheads, reduced brow ridges, smaller faces and teeth, and a chin. Their average height was 1.70 meters, with a body weight of 67 kilograms and brain capacity of 1,510 cubic centimeters.[75] They dwelled in caves, under overhanging rocks, and in huts on stone foundations. They were skilled hunters, using spears, harpoons, bow and arrows, traps, snares, and fishing nets. They made sewn garments, decorated with beads, and produced ornaments, including necklaces of animal teeth and pierced shells, ivory pendants, ivory figurines, and beads.[76] Best known are their beautiful cave paintings of animals. Numerous burial sites attest to various ritual activities. Language and speech existed. They disappeared rather abruptly 11,000 years BP, but some Cro-Magnons may persist to this day in isolated areas—for example, the Dal people in Dalarna, Sweden, and the Guanches of the Canary Islands.

The next phase in the development of *Homo sapiens* took place in the Near East and Egypt around 10,000 years BP. This phase was marked by new societal forms, but without the appearance of a new species. Instead, coinciding with the end of the last glacial period and the advent of agriculture, there was a population explosion that ended the bottleneck of fewer than 10,000 individuals that had existed for about 200,000 years.[77] The most important consequence of this persistent bottleneck is that genetically there is only a single human race. This conclusion is supported by a study of 377 stretches of DNA in 1,056 individuals from 52 populations worldwide.[78] In view of the low evolutionary rate of *Homo sapiens*[79] and the elimination of natural selection through modern medicine and technology, it seems that human evolution is ending or has already come to an end. We are now developing nongenetically by adaptation through learning and the use of tools like the computer and the Internet.

From the comparison of the human and chimpanzee genomes, we know that they differ in only 0.5 percent of their coding genes, particularly those involved in smell, hearing, and protein breakdown.[80] These differences can hardly explain the stark distinction between us and our nearest cousin. More likely, differences in the activities of many genes, and not only of the 0.5 percent different coding genes, are responsible for the different phenotypes (visible characteristics). However, at present, gene activity or expression is determined as the rate of mRNA production, but this rate does not measure the effects of all forms of gene regulation described in section 2.5.[81] A systematic search for sequence differences in the genes on chimpanzee chromosome 22 and its human counterpart, chromosome 21, has not uncovered changes that might explain the phenotypical differences between humans and chimpanzees.[82] More promising is the finding that 2.4 million years BP, a mutation of the myosin gene MYH16, which is responsible for the massive jaw muscles in primates, weakened these muscles in humans and not in the chimpanzee.[83] Since animal experiments have shown that changes in jaw muscles can radically alter craniofacial bones, it is possible that this mutation may have led to the large size of the human brain relative to that of the chimpanzee.

Moral evolution

There is evidence for moral behavior in higher animals, particularly primates. In extensive studies of monkeys and apes, Frans de Waal[84] has observed five forms of such behavior:

1. *Kin concern*—Males will defend females and young against predators, food is shared, and often sick or injured animals are supported.
2. *Reciprocity*—Unrelated animals share food but refuse the next time around if the favor is not returned.
3. *Sympathy*—A mongoloid rhesus monkey was continuously assisted by its mother and sisters. A chimpanzee placed an arm around an animal that had lost a fight.
4. *Norm behavior*—Stingy animals in food sharing are rebuffed at a later meal. Two chimpanzees who were late for dinner and thus delayed the feeding of all others were later beaten up and were the first for dinner next day.
5. *Inequity aversion*—Capuchin monkeys lay down tools if they see another monkey get a bigger reward for doing the same job.

Differences between monkeys and apes are noted: only apes show consolation behavior, punish violation of norm behavior, and accept other benefits, such as grooming, in exchange for food.

More advanced forms of these traits are observed among peoples such as the Melanesians. They display kin concern in their elaborate rituals of gift giving; they regard reciprocity as "right" and cheating as "wrong," leading to sanctions against the cheater. The question of how far reciprocity should extend—to members of the group, of the tribe, or even beyond the tribe—has led humans to establish moral codes. These findings suggest that moral behavior is also subject to evolution. Yet a case can still be made that human altruism is unique in the animal world and that gene-based evolutionary theory cannot explain important aspects of this phenomenon.[85]

Cultural differences have also been noted among primates.[86] Six groups of orangutans in Borneo and Sumatra show different behavior that cannot be attributed to differences in environmental ecology and thus must be culturally transmitted. Examples are yelling with hands before the mouth, "riding" on falling branches and jumping off just in time, kicking over decayed wood stumps to eat emerging insects, making sputtering sounds when building a nest, using tools for sexual self-stimulation, and using small sticks to obtain seeds from Neesia fruits (done by only one of four groups with access to these fruits). These observations suggest that the genetic roots for cultural behavior have been operating in primates and humans since the split between the orangutan line and the chimpanzee–human line 12 million years BP. A critical difference between humans and primates is that the latter do not improve upon a previous invention, whereas humans have been doing so for over a million years. Also, human children can imitate a demonstrated skill more readily than primates.

The nature–nurture problem

Is a complex property like intelligence determined by genes or by environment and teaching? Studies of single-egg human twins have shown that both "nature" (genes) and "nurture" (environment, education, etc.) play a role. In the case of intelligence, nature and nurture each account for about 50 percent.[87] Similar results have been obtained in a study of the titmouse (*Parus major*), of which there are two types: active and timid birds.[88] When males and females of the same type are mated in captivity for many generations, the active line shows increased activity, and the timid line increased timidity. When foster parents rear mixed nests, an estimate of the genetic component of behavior is 54 percent in captivity, but only 30 to 40 percent in the field. The smaller genetic effect in the field is ascribed to the more variable conditions as compared to those in captivity. Studies with bacteria have shown that the environment not only plays a major role in natural selection, but also may induce mutation and thus speed up evolution.[89]

However, it is now becoming clear that the nature-versus-nurture question is a false dilemma. Rather, our genes are both inherited and environmentally influenced. Gene expression in the brain is influenced by the environment during a lifetime, as found for bonding, foraging, and offspring care in animal studies with a detailed analysis of gene expression.[90] This evidence calls into question the idea of genetic determinism. It also explains why patients with exactly the same type of gene mutation may show a very different course of the disease.[91] For example, among patients with a kidney disease called Nagel-Patella syndrome, some remain virtually symptom-free, some show a nonprogressive urinary protein loss, and others develop chronic kidney failure. It is now becoming clear that searching for gene mutations in patients with a particular disease may lead to false results in two out of three cases.[92]

2.7 Summary: Biological evolution

The near absence of oxygen in the primordial Earth's atmosphere and ocean permitted the formation of amino acids and nucleotides (building blocks of proteins, DNA, and RNA), from hot gases released by hydrothermal vents in the ocean floor. Primitive RNAs were probably first formed, aided by catalytic action of clay minerals. These RNAs acted as enzymes to form proteins that could serve as enzymes in the formation of the first DNA molecules. Spontaneous formation of micelles by bipolar molecules such as phospholipids kept DNA, RNA, and proteins together, permitting the formation of enzymes for metabolism in the first living cells.

Over the course of more than a billion years, photosynthetic production of oxygen by *Cyanobacteria* established our present oxygen-rich atmosphere covered by an ozone layer. This produced oxidative metabolism, which allowed formation of multicellular organisms, plants and animals, that could crawl ashore.

Biological evolution is a process of variation within a species by gene mutation, followed by natural selection of the more successful variant, which then forms a new species. The hereditary system consists of a large number of genes, DNA molecules, each of which encodes for a protein with a specific function. The synthesis of a specific protein occurs in two steps: transcription (making an mRNA copy of the DNA gene) and translation (the synthesis of a protein molecule from the mRNA template governed by the genetic code). This code is identical for all organisms and has remained unchanged throughout the evolution from microbe to human. The genome, the collection of all genes in a cell, has now been sequenced for a great number of species. This permits us to know which mutations have taken place during evolution, and even when. The evolutionary tree constructed from these data is virtually identical to that derived from fossil studies.

The course of biological evolution has continued in human evolution. Four primate species first split off from the human line between 12 million and 5 million years BP. From *Australopithecus*, the probable common ancestor of chimpanzee and human, arose in succession *Homo habilis* (2.6 billion years BP; tool and tent maker), *Homo erectus* (1.9 million years BP; advanced tools, use of fire), and *Homo sapiens* (300,000 years BP; more advanced tools, primitive art). It seems these species all originated in Africa and from there emigrated in three waves to Asia and Europe. The Neandertals (150,000 to 30,000 years BP; probably a dead-end sideline from *Homo erectus*) lived as cave dwellers in Europe and the Near East, buried the dead with ritual (suggesting a beginning of religion), and may have developed speech. They were displaced by the more advanced Cro-Magnons (belonging to *Homo sapiens*), who lived from 40,000 to 11,000 years BP in Europe and the Near East. The development from Cro-Magnon to modern human seems to be through cultural advance rather than genetic evolution. Cultural differences and moral behavior are already observed in primates. All this shows that there is a continuous evolutionary progression from microbe to human, both in body and mind.

3

The Theological Worldview:
Creation Stories

3.1 Origin or creation

The preceding chapter summarized how scientists go back to the beginning of the cosmos and to the beginning of life. Their theories and equations have no place for a creator, and they speak about "beginnings" or "origins," usually avoiding the term *creation*. Science deals with physical, rather than metaphysical, processes. It attempts to answer the *how* questions: How did this object develop from something else? It cannot answer the *why* questions: Why is there something rather than nothing? Furthermore, although science has done remarkably well in unraveling cosmic and biological evolution, cosmology cannot tell us about conditions and events at or before $t = 0$; its story begins at 10^{-43} seconds after time zero.

Long before our scientific worldview was formed, humans have wondered where the world comes from and where we come from. This has resulted in stories of origin in all cultures and ages. The biblical creation accounts in Genesis 1 and 2 also belong to this category of stories. Common to all of them is the assumption that a supernatural agent, a god or gods, is responsible for bringing this world and ourselves into being in a purposeful act, which we call creation. In the next section, I review the nonbiblical stories for their accounts of who was acting and what was there at the beginning. I make use of the valuable compilation of creation stories by Ellen van Wolde,[1] following her arrangement by continent. Although she offers a selection of all existing creation stories, she has not chosen them for their likeness to the biblical creation stories and tells them without reference to these. References made to the Genesis stories are mine. It will become clear that there is a common theme to all these creation stories, namely, that creation is an imposition of order on an initial chaos by divine agency. The second part of this chapter (sections 3.3–3.7) deals with the biblical concept of creation.

3.2 Nonbiblical creation stories

Stories from Asia

The *Rig Veda*, written in India 4,000 to 3,700 years BP, begins, "There was neither non-existence nor existence then; there was neither the realm of space nor the sky which is beyond. What stirred? Where? In whose protection? Was there water, bottomlessly deep?" The reply to these questions reads, "Darkness was hidden by darkness in the beginning; with no distinguishing sign, all this was water." A later (2,500 years BP) account, the *Brihadaranyaka Upanishad*, says that in the beginning, the cosmos was self alone (*atman*), in the shape of a person. This self split in two: husband and wife.

One of the many Chinese creation stories is that of the giant Pangu. This story tells us that in the beginning, only dark chaos prevailed in the universe. This darkness took the form of an egg, and in this egg Pangu, the first living being, was born. After many years he awoke, stretched himself, and thus broke the egg. The lighter, purer part formed the heaven, the heavier and impurer part became the earth.

Also from China, the Taoist story of Lieh-tzu says, "From what were heaven and earth born? I answer, there was a primal simplicity, there was a primal commencement, there were primal beginnings, there was a primal material . . . things were not yet separated from each other; hence the name 'confusion.'"

Stories from Australia and Polynesia

Australian aboriginal people believe that their ancestors created themselves from clay, thousands of them, one for each totemic species, including animals, plants, stones, rain, or wind. Every one of these species was sung to life and became a totem, the emblem of a clan.

For the New Zealand Maoris, Io is the Supreme Being, the creator of the universe, of the gods, and of humans. Their story says, "The Universe was in darkness, with water everywhere. There was no glimmer of dawn, no clearness, no light. And he [Io] began by saying these words: 'Darkness, become a light-possessing darkness.' And at once light appeared." The story continues in remarkable analogy to the story of Genesis 1.

The Maoris also have a story that bears remarkable resemblance to the story of the fall in Genesis 3.[2] Baime, the creator of everything, created the first humans, Beer-rok-boorn and his wife, and gave them a good place to live. It had a yarran tree with a bee swarm in it. Baime told the humans, "You may eat of everything, except from this tree which is mine. If you eat from it, you and your descendents will suffer much misery." The wife of Beer-rok-boorn came upon the yarran tree while gathering wood. At first she was afraid, but she saw that there was much wood around the tree. Since Baime had said nothing about wood, she began to gather it. Then she heard the buzz of the bee swarm above her head and saw honey drip along the stem of the tree. She had once before tasted honey and knew that it was good. She could not withstand the temptation and climbed into the tree. At that moment, a cold wind came from above, and a dark figure wrapped its large black wings around her body. It was the bat Narahdarn, which Baime had stationed there to guard the holy tree. The woman fell from the tree and ran to her hole, where she hid herself. But it was too late; she had brought death into the world. Now all descendents of Beer-rok-boorn suffer from the curse of Narahdarn. The yarran tree wept bitter tears over what had happened. The tears ran along the stem and stiffened, and therefore one now finds red gum on the bark of the yarran tree.

The Hawaiian story begins this way:

> In the time of deep darkness, before the memory of man, the great gods (four) came out of the night. . . . The God of creation picked up a vast calabash floating in the sea, and tossed it high into the air. Its top flew off and became the sky. Two great pieces of the calabash broke away: one became the sun, the other the moon. The seeds scattered and became stars. The remainder of the calabash became the earth and fell back into the sea.

Then follows the creation of humans, animals, and plants. There are two similarities to the Genesis 2 story. The first man is called Red Earth Man, which is also the meaning of the name Adam in Genesis 2. The woman was created from his shadow while he slept, resembling the creation of Eve in Genesis 2.

Stories from America

From Guatemala comes the Mayan creation story, named *Popol Vuh* (Book of the Community). It begins as follows:[3]

> Once there was the resting universe. Not a breeze. Not a sound. Motionless and silent was the world. And the heavenly expanse was empty. This is the first message, the first word.
>
> There was not yet a human or an animal. Birds, fish, turtles, trees, rocks, caves, ravines did not exist. No grass, no forest. Only the heaven was there. The face of the Earth was not yet unveiled. Only the silent sea and the wide expanse of heaven.
>
> Nothing yet was connected. Nothing gave sound, nothing moved, nothing disturbed or broke the silence of heaven. Nothing yet had raised itself. Only the resting water, the silent sea, lonely and soundless. Nothing else. Motionless and silent was the night, the darkness.
>
> But in the water, shone about by light, they were: Tzakól, the creator; Bitól, the former; Tepeü, the conqueror; and Gucumátz, the green-feathered snake; also Alóm and Cathalóm, the begetters.

So the primordial universe consisted of an empty heaven and water, silent and motionless, a resting universe. Water is the primordial element, to which the world and all living beings owe their existence. *Popol Vuh* also has a story of a flood.

From Native Americans in what is now the United States comes the story of Father Earthmaker. The initial being awoke to consciousness, wondered what to do, and finally began to cry. His tears formed the waters. He thought again and wished for the earth, and the earth came into existence. Then he made a being like himself from a piece of earth. He talked to it, but it did not respond, so he made a mind and a tongue for it. He talked to it again, and it very nearly said something. Then he breathed into its mouth and talked to it, and it answered. This story bears a striking resemblance to the Genesis 2 story.

Stories from Africa

When the French missionary priest Loupias was told the story of the Rwandan Tutsis, he said to his informer that it was an interesting story. The latter replied, "It may be a story to you, but we Batutsis know that this history is true." So stories of the beginning are not fiction, but true stories for those concerned.

The Rwandan story relates that in the beginning, the Creator created two lands: the land above clouds, sun, and stars, and the land below, which he made in the image of the land above but without beauty and happiness. The land below is the earth we inhabit, a land of misery, suffering, and hard work. Before this double creation, there was nothing; only the Creator existed.

Other African stories are mainly concerned with creation of men and women and with their relationships.

Stories from Europe

The Greek poet Hesiod (2,800 years BP) left a creation poem, which tells us that at the beginning of everything was Chaos. Out of it came earth, gods, and humans amid much violence.

From Iceland comes the *Edda*, a collection of songs of heroes and gods, written down in the thirteenth century and influenced by Christianity, which was introduced around 1000 CE. The idea of an initial chaos, the great void, may therefore derive from the Genesis story. Nevertheless, various gods arise from the initial chaos.

The ancient Finnish *Kalevala* epic has an upper God Ukko, a Fair God ruling the air, a Wild God in the water, and a Dark God in the realm of the dead. In the beginning, there was only the foaming sea with clouds hanging over it (resembling Gen 1:2).

Stories from the Middle East

Creation stories from the Middle East are of particular interest, because they may have been known to the authors of the biblical creation stories. An Egyptian creation story, preserved on a temple wall, presents the image of a primeval hill emerging from the primeval flood (*Nu*) and bearing the first life.

In the Memphite story of creation (4,700 years BP), the god Ptah conceives the elements of the universe with his mind and brings them into being by his commanding word, anticipating by nearly 2,200 years the Genesis 1 idea of creation by the Word of God.

In the Babylonian creation story *Enuma Elish* (3,400 years BP), named after the opening words "When on high," the beginning state is described as a chaos without heaven and earth, without the reed marshes along the lower Euphrates.[4] Only water exists, without separation between the saltwater of the Persian Gulf and the freshwater from the Euphrates. Then the gods arise from the primeval waters, and a fateful struggle begins between the chaos induced by the evil goddess Tiamat (deity of the sea) and the cosmic order created by the benign god Marduk (god of Babylon, deity of thunder and rain). The Mesopotamians experienced this fateful struggle every year in the flooding of the land by the saltwater of the Persian Gulf.

3.3 The early Genesis story

Turning now to the Bible, the first book of the Old Testament, Genesis, has two creation accounts. The first account (Gen 1:1—2:4a) is the later (around 500 BCE), and the second account (Gen 2:4b-25) is the earlier (around 900 BCE).

The second account is characterized by the use of the name *Yahweh* for God (against *Elohim* in Genesis 1) and is attributed to the so-called Yahwist author (J). It contains relatively primitive ideas set forth in a simple narrative style.[5] It is followed by the story of the fall, the first human rebellion, indicating that J sees creation and the fall as closely related. My comments are based on Claus Westermann's commentary.[6]

J begins with God: "In the day that the Lord God made the earth and the heavens" (v. 4b). It is left open whether "in the day that" refers to the beginning of creation or to a later stage. Next J poses an initial chaos, an arid, lifeless desert, a devastation: "when no plant of the field was yet in the earth and no herb of the field had yet sprung up" (v. 5). The central topic is the creation of man, preceding that of plants (v. 9), animals (vv. 18-20), and even of woman (vv. 21-24). Yahweh, like a skilled potter, models a man from clay moistened by water: "a stream would rise from the earth and water the whole face of the ground—then the Lord God formed man from the dust of the ground" (vv. 6-7). The "rising stream" (probably an insertion of Akkadian origin) is also translated as "cloud" or "mist." J repeats here an ancient fertility idea that is found in many ancient creation stories.

Although the idea that man consists of earthly elements happens to be in agreement with our present scientific ideas about the origin of life (chapter 2.2), J's purpose is to express human frailty and mortality. That idea is also indicated by the later text "You are dust, and to dust you shall return" (Gen 3:19).

Then Yahweh "breathed into his nostrils the breath of life; and the man became a living being" (Gen 2:7). "Breathed . . . the breath of life" is to be taken as receiving God's life-giving spirit. This reflects the Hebrew belief that a living person is an inseparable unity of body and mind, made alive by God's life-giving spirit, in contrast to the Greek idea of humans as embodied souls. J indicates that the human creature requires more than mere physical life. Rather, God also provides the means of existence (v. 8), work (v. 15), community (vv. 18-24), and speech (vv. 19, 23).

J does not try to give his creation story a "biological" twist, as indicated by the creation of the man Adam before plants, animals, and even woman. He simply uses a familiar, ancient mythical form to present his message: Humans receive their existence from God, and human existence is nothing but a created, dependent existence, like that of all living beings on earth. Eden is not Paradise or Utopia, but an oasis in the desert, a fertile garden, provided and intended by God for human use, work, and care (v. 15). The work of "tilling and keeping" refers to all human work. Human existence includes work; life without work is not worthy of human beings. The aspect of care (keeping) is relevant in the context of our present ecological crisis (chapter 14).

Having created man, given him means of existence, a commission, and work to perform, Yahweh realizes that man needs a companion: "It is not good that the man should be alone" (v. 18). Cattle and birds are created (vv. 19-20). Again, the story may have a primitive form, but the thought behind it—the need for humans to live in community—shows a deep understanding of human nature. Animals cannot fill this need. So Yahweh creates woman (vv. 21-24) to satisfy man's need for companionship, rather than for the purpose of human procreation. Creation of woman from the rib of man expresses how man and woman belong together, how they are attracted to each other. Help is meant in the fullest sense: not only at work and in procreation, but in conversation, in silence, and in activity (cf. Eccl 4:9-12). Only now has the human creature become truly human.

3.4 The later Genesis story

Influence of Enuma Elish

The creation story in Gen 1:1—2:4a is attributed to the Priestly author (P), who wrote shortly after the Babylonian exile (about 500 BCE) and presumably knew the Babylonian creation story *Enuma Elish*. It seems likely that P has borrowed the concept of a "watery" chaos from *Enuma Elish*, but in all other aspects the Genesis 1 account is radically different and unique:[7]

- While *Enuma Elish* has the chaos at the beginning, P places God at the beginning. The Creator does not issue from primordial matter; there is no creation of gods as in *Enuma Elish*. The Creator in Genesis 1 is outside and above the process of creation. God is absolute and timeless, in the words of Isaiah: "I am the first and I am the last; besides me there is no god" (Isa 44:6).
- God in Genesis 1 is not limited or controlled by the chaos, as the gods are in *Enuma Elish*. The wind (*ruach*) in Gen 1:2b only superficially resembles the winds by which Marduk overcame Tiamat in *Enuma Elish*. God's sovereign Word turns uncreated chaos into created order.
- The presentation of creation in six days plus a day of rest is not found in *Enuma Elish* or any other ancient creation story.
- Another unique feature of Genesis 1, not found in *Enuma Elish*, is the separation of time and space. First there is the creation of light and with it day and night (time), then the creation of the firmament (space). P sees time, our clock time, as created with the universe, and light as preceding stars and galaxies, a prescientific intuition of our current cosmology (chapter 2.2).
- God's creation of sun and moon rejects the divinity with which these bodies were endowed in *Enuma Elish* and other ancient Near East religions, and thus eliminates the many lesser gods and astral cults of those religions.

Primordial chaos

The Hebrew language contains no definite article, so the first words of the story, "In the beginning" (v. 1) literally read "in beginning," or "before all beginnings." This implies that God creates time but remains outside time. Time begins when God's commanding Word calls forth light on the first day.

The remainder of verses 1 and 2 poses the problem that Hebrew does not have subordinate clauses. Older versions (KJV, RSV 1953) translate these verses as "In the beginning God created the heavens and the earth. The earth was without form and void." This translation would suggest that in creating the earth, God brought forth chaos. This is not very likely, as already noted by the prophet Isaiah in his saying "He did not create it a chaos, he formed it to be inhabited" (Isa 45:18). Claus Westermann[8] inserts the word *still* in verse 2: "The earth was still a desert waste, and darkness lay upon the primeval deep." Later versions (NEB, 1970; Living Bible, 1971; NRSV US, 1989; NRSV UK, 1995) make verse 1 a subordinate clause: "In the beginning when God created the heavens and the earth, the earth was a formless void."

The English word *create* is a translation of the Hebrew *bara*, which means to build, make, call forth. This word is exclusively used for divine creation (Job 10:9; Ps 119:73; Isa 29:16). It is applied to the creation of heaven and earth (Gen 1:1; 2:3; Isa 42:5), of stars (Isa 40:26), animals (Gen 1:21), and humans (Gen 1:27; 5:1-2; 6:7; Deut 4:32; Isa 45:12).

The phrase "formless void . . . darkness covering the face of the deep" is the Hebrew *tohu wabohu*, also used for the "pathless waste" (Job 12:24) and the earth "waste and void" (Jer 4:23). The expression implies a primordial chaos that was ominous and sinister to the Israelites. God creates by turning uncreated chaos into created order, in line with the Genesis 2 story and all nonbiblical creation stories.

In verse 2b, the Hebrew *ruach* has in the past been translated as "spririt," rendering the phrase "God's spirit was moving over the face of the waters," which was thought to imply a creative action of the Spirit. However, the Hebrew *ruach* has three meanings: wind, breath, and spirit. The associated verb must indicate which meaning applies.[9] In this verse, the verb is *merachefet*, which means to flutter, flap, or shake, suggesting that in this case, *ruach* means wind rather than spirit. With *ruach* stands the adjective *elohim*, normally the plural of *god*. The term *ruach elohim* occurs nowhere else in the Old Testament and is thought to signify a superlative of *ruach*: "a mighty wind." Thus, the more likely translation of verse 2b would read, "While a mighty wind swept over the face of the waters." This makes it part of the primordial chaos.

Separation and ordering

The process of creation is described as three acts of separation (light and darkness, water and heaven, earth and sea; vv. 4, 7, 9), followed by five acts of ordering (filling earth with plants; firmament with stars, sun, and moon; sea with animals and air with birds; earth with animals; human creation; vv. 11-31). Separation presupposes a primeval chaos.[10] Each act of creation, except that of humans, is preceded by the command "Let there be" or its equivalent (vv. 6, 9, 11, 14, 20, 24). This means that all events have their origin in God's commanding Word (Hebrew *dabar*, Greek *Logos*). These commands are not addressed to a person, which emphasizes the absolute transcendence of God, the Creator.

In "God saw that it was good" (vv. 10, 12, 18, 21, 25, 31), the Hebrew word *tov*, translated as "good," means functionally good rather than actually good—good for the intended purpose. Hence, we may not deduce from this repeated phrase that the initial creation was complete and perfect.

"God blessed them" (vv. 22, 28). The blessing confers fertility, the power to propagate ("be fruitful and multiply"). The fact that both humans and animals are blessed indicates P's awareness of the basic similarity between humans and animals. However, only humans are said to be created in God's image and thus set apart from the animals. A difference with the Genesis 2 story is that here the animals are created in their own right, rather than merely to serve humans as in Genesis 2.

Six days

P compresses the three acts of separation and five acts of formation into six days of creation, followed by a day of rest. This device strongly suggests that P intends to give an explanation for the Sabbath law. Therefore, we need not consider the "days" literally as human-made calendar periods, but rather as periods of undetermined length. This understanding suggests a process, a continuing creation (*creatio continua*), that moves through time toward its goal, the fulfillment of creation.

The extensive sequence of creative events in Genesis 1 shows that author P profoundly reflected not only upon the theological aspects of creation, but also upon what we would now call the scientific aspects. His sequence reflects a prescientific intuition of what we now know as the cosmic and biological evolution (with only one mistake: plants appear before the sun, indicating that P was unaware of photosynthesis). Theodor C. Vriezen says, "It is certainly the most 'modern' of all cosmologies known from the ancient East."[11]

3.5 Creation elsewhere in the Old Testament

Creation and history

Although creation is frequently mentioned in the Old Testament, the emphasis is more on the mighty acts of God in the history of the Jewish people, particularly the exodus from Egypt.[12] The creation stories were added later as an earlier part of the history of Israel rather than as the beginning of everything. This is shown by Jeremiah, who begins a message to the kings of Israel's neighbor countries with the words "It is I [the God of Israel] who by my great power and my outstretched arm have made the earth, with the people and animals that are on the earth" (Jer 27:5; cf. Jer 32:17). Israel's understanding of creation and its understanding of history are inseparably related. A fuller treatment of creation is found in the second Isaiah (chapters 40–55), written about the same time as Genesis 1. The author appeals to faith in Yahweh's power and wisdom as Creator in order to teach the despairing exiles that Yahweh is sovereign over history and therefore can and will save his people (Isa 40:12-31; 43:1-7; 45:9-13; 48:12-13).

The sovereignty of God, displayed in the works of creation, is the basis for adoration, trust, awe, and obedience (Isa 40:27-31; Ps 95). This is expressed in the image of the divine potter (Genesis 2; Isa 45:9-13), as well as in the more advanced idea of a transcendent Creator who creates by the commanding word (Genesis 1; Ps 33:6-9; 148:5). The Bible has no equivalent for the Greek idea of *cosmos*, the universe as a coherent, self-sustaining unity. Instead, it speaks about the relationship of the Creator with the created as a covenant (Isa 44:24-28; Psalm 8). The Old Testament doctrine of creation is primarily an affirmation of the sovereignty of God and the absolute dependence of all creatures.

Order of creation

The order of creation is not the rational order of the Greek cosmos, but a divinely decreed harmony in which every creature fulfills the will of the Creator (Job 38:33; Ps 104:9; 148:6; Jer 31:35-36). The celestial bodies are not independent deities who control human life, as in other ancient religions, but servants of God who designate the seasons and separate day and night. Earth is not the fertile "mother" from whom all life is born, but the creature that at God's command becomes home to all plants, animals, and humans. The idea of "nature" as an autonomous sphere does not exist in the Old Testament. The creation faith leads to praise of God (Ps 8:1; 19:1-4) with joyful acceptance of the goodness of creation (Psalm 104; Sir 43:1-33). The idea that the created world is the scene of a battle between a good and an evil deity, as in *Enuma Elish*, is rejected.

Humans have a place of honor as the highest of all creatures, little less than God (Ps 8:5-8), and are to exercise sovereignty, but always within God's sovereignty, so that all earthly creatures may find their right relation to God. Although all creatures are to praise God, only humans can make their praise articulate, have an I–Thou relationship with the Creator, and communicate with God. This is probably the primary meaning of their being created in the image of God.

Creation and chaos

Earlier I noted that not only Genesis 1 and Genesis 2, but virtually all non-biblical creation stories, have creation from an initial chaos. This concept seems to be like an archetype in the Jungian sense, a primordial image in the collective human unconscious. God creates not by destroying chaos, but by ordering it, by pushing back chaos in three separations (Gen 1:2-10). This leads to the idea of a remaining element of chaos in the world, to which I return in more detail in chapter 6.3.

In some native religions, the existence of a remaining element of chaos in the world is reflected in the distinction between the sacred and the profane.[13] The sacred is the world of reality, so a village is laid out in a manner that imitates a divine model, and thus it participates in sacred reality. The space outside the village, the jungle, is considered profane, because it is not ordered according to the divine model; it is an expression of "remaining chaos." The sacred can serve as a principle of order because it possesses the power to order. The continued ordering of the sacred space of the village is necessary in order to prevent it from being overwhelmed by the surrounding jungle, the chaos of the profane.

3.6 Creation in the New Testament

The New Testament continues the Old Testament's line on creation by affirming that God alone created the world by the divine Word (Heb 11:3) and set its purpose at the beginning. Jesus quotes Gen 1:27 for the creation of man and woman (Mark 10:6; Matt 19:4). He links the horrors of the last day to the original creation (Mark 13:19; Matt 24:21). Paul writes that the Gentiles could have known God through creation (Rom 1:19-20). References to creation are also implied in the use of the expressions "from the foundation of the world" (Matt 25:34; Luke 11:50; Eph 1:4) and "from the beginning of creation" (2 Peter 3:4). The goodness of everything created by God is affirmed (1 Tim 4:4), and God is praised for having created all things (Rev 4:11).

Christ and Creation

In the New Testament, Christ comes to be seen as having a key role in creation. Through the resurrection experience, the disciples recognize Jesus as the Messiah promised in the Old Testament, the fulfillment of Israel's history and expectations, and the inaugurator of the new covenant. From this, Paul and John conclude that Christ is a chief actor in creation through the *Logos*, the creative Word of God. This amazing new insight was written down in John's gospel and Paul's letters between 50 and 65 CE, if we accept John Robinson's dating.[14]

John's gospel opens with the magnificent words "In the beginning was the Word, and the Word was with God, and the Word was God. He was in the beginning with God. All things came into being through him, and without him not one thing came into being" (John 1:1-3). Then, "And the Word became flesh and lived among us, and we have seen his glory, the glory as of a father's only son, full of grace and truth" (John 1:14). These words link Christ with the Genesis 1 account of creation by the Word of God.

Paul makes a similar statement: "For us there is one God, the Father, from whom are all things and for whom we exist, and one Lord, Jesus Christ, through whom are all things and through whom we exist" (1 Cor 8:6). The words *from the Father* and *through Christ* imply John's more explicit statement. And elsewhere Paul says, "In him [Christ] all things in heaven and on earth were created, things visible and invisible, whether thrones or dominions or rulers or powers—all things have been created through him and for him. He himself is before all things, and in him all things hold together" (Col 1:16-17). Everything, Paul seems to say, has its center in Christ, through whom God creates, upholds, and redeems the world.

However, it seems to me that a distinction must be made between the *Logos* before and after the incarnation. Only after the incarnation of the *Logos* in the human Jesus of Nazareth can we speak about the Christ. I find it difficult to conceive of a preexistent Christ, because in that case, Jesus of Nazareth would not have been fully human and could not be the redeemer of humanity. So for me, the non-incarnate *Logos* brings the world into being and makes it develop through cosmic and biological evolution, and then Christ, the incarnate *Logos*, brings it to completion in his decisive redemptive act, sealed in the resurrection and to be manifested on the last day. I shall return to this point in chapter 9 (sections 9.2 and 9.3).

The new creation in Christ

The role of Christ in creation is integrated with the New Testament message about his central role in human salvation and the coming kingdom. The title applied by Second Isaiah to God (Isa 44:6; 48:12) is given to Christ: "I am the Alpha and the Omega, the first and the last, the beginning and the end" (Rev 22:13). Here the link is made with the Old Testament expectations about a new creation. The heart of the New Testament message is that, in Christ, God has introduced the new creation, which the Old Testament prophets had been expecting. This new creation assures us that, at the end of time, there will be a new heaven and a new earth, without evil and death (Rev 21:1-4). This is the paradox of C. H. Dodd's idea of "realized eschatology": Christ's resurrection is the decisive victory, which in God's good time will bring the final liberation of creation.

The New Testament authors recognize that we live in a fallen world ruled by an evil power (John 12:31; 16:11; 1 Cor 1:21; Gal 4:9). Paul says bluntly, "The whole creation has been groaning in labor pains until now; and not only the creation, but we ourselves" (Rom 8:22-23). But, he says, "if anyone is in Christ, there is a new creation: everything old has passed away; see, everything has become new!" (2 Cor 5:17). In the human Jesus, God has restored humanity as intended in our original creation. He is the New Man, the likeness of God (2 Cor 4:4), the firstborn of all creation (Col 1:15). Through Christ we may put on this new nature and live in a new relation to God and to our fellow humans.

3.7 Continuing creation

Several texts suggest that creation is not instantaneous but is a continuing process. This is already implied in the six days with a day of rest of Genesis

1. As mentioned before, the Hebrew word *tov* in the repeated phrase "God saw that it was good" does not mean that the initial creation is perfect, but that it is on the way to perfection.

This idea is confirmed in several sayings in the Old Testament:

- "When you send forth your spirit, they are created" (Ps 104:30).
- "The Holy One of Israel has created it," referring to the placing of trees in the desert (Isa 41:20).
- "He who created you, O Jacob" (Isa 43:1)—not merely the first couple is created.
- "Everyone who is called by my name, whom I created for my glory, whom I formed and made" (Isa 43:7).
- "They are created now, not long ago" (Isa 48:7).
- "It is I who have created the smith who blows the fire of coals" (Isa 54:16).
- "But be glad and rejoice forever in what I am creating" (Isa 65:18). This statement is coupled with the creation of new heavens and a new earth in verse 17.
- "For the Lord has created a new thing on the earth" (Jer 31:22).
- "In the place where you were created, in the land of your origin" (Ezek 21:30).
- The Lord said to Ezekiel: "On the day that you were created" (Ezek 28:13) and "from the day that you were created" (Ezek 28:15).
- "Has not one God created us?" (Mal 2:10).

The idea of a continuing creation is also affirmed in several places in the New Testament:

- "For in those days there will be suffering, such as has not been from the beginning of the creation that God created until now" (Mark 13:19). Jesus is speaking to Peter, James, John, and Andrew about the future destruction of the temple.
- "For we are what he has made us, created in Christ Jesus for good works" (Eph 2:10).
- "To clothe yourselves with the new self, created according to the likeness of God" (Eph 4:24).
- "[You] have clothed yourselves with the new self, which is being renewed in knowledge according to the image of its creator" (Col 3:10).
- "Foods, which God created to be received with thanksgiving" (1 Tim 4:3).

- "All things continue as they were from the beginning of creation" (2 Peter 3:4).
- "The origin [or beginning] of God's creation" (Rev 3:14).

Thus, the concept of a continuing creation (*creatio continua*) in the period between the initial creation and the last day is firmly rooted in the Bible. It finds a parallel in modern scientific insight, which tells us that stars and galaxies are still being formed and that the evolution of living beings is continuing. I suggest that in the initial creation, God set the stage in the big bang and the institution of the physical laws and fundamental constants. Then follows the continuing creation, as a process of development (now already lasting 13.7 billion years), in which we see God creatively involved, until the fulfillment of creation on the last day. However, initial and continuing creation should be seen as one continual process of creation.[15]

In contrast, there is the idea of "preservation" (*conservatio*): creation is initially complete and perfect but is subsequently damaged by the fall in Genesis 3 and is then "preserved" by God until its redemption on the last day. I have three arguments against this idea: (1) It rests on a misinterpretation of the word *tov* in Genesis 1 as good in actuality, rather than good for the purpose. (2) The belief that Adam's sin could lead to the corruption of a perfect creation overrates the damage that human sinfulness can do to God's creation and underrates purpose and power of the Creator. (3) It neglects our modern scientific insights about cosmic and biological evolution. The awareness of the utter dependence of creation and all creatures on God's benevolence implied in the idea of preservation is better expressed by the concept of "contingency," which I shall consider in more detail in chapter 9.

3.8 Summary

This chapter presents the theological worldview, derived from nonbiblical and biblical creation stories. Where the scientific worldview considers only "origins" and "beginnings," creation stories assume a supernatural agent, a god or gods, as responsible for bringing forth the world in a purposeful act.

The common theme in the nonbiblical creation stories, from different continents and times, is the imposition of order on an initial chaos by a divine agent. Only the *Rig Veda* and the two cited Chinese stories have no clear divine creative agent. The Australian aborigines seem to think that their ancestors created themselves, but in saying that they were "sung to life," they imply a supernatural agent. The *Popol Vuh, Edda,* and *Enuma Elish* stories have a theogony, a creation of the gods.

The Bible has two creation accounts, the older one in Genesis 2 and the later one in Genesis 1. These have some elements in common. Both accounts begin with God ("In the day that the Lord God made the heavens and the earth" Gen 2:4b; "In the beginning when God created the heavens and the earth" Gen 1:1). There are no other gods; there is no theogony. There is one Creator who stands apart from the created world, who is transcendent. Both accounts have an initial chaos, from which God creates a lifeless desert (in Genesis 2) or a formless void (the Hebrew *tohu wabohu,* in Gen 1:2). In both stories, God is said to create by turning uncreated chaos into created order.

The accounts differ in terms of the sequence of events. The older story (Genesis 2) speaks first about the forming of the man from the dust of the ground, and only then about the creation of plants, animals, and finally the woman for companionship. God provides the man with a garden, an oasis in the desert, to be cared for and to provide food. In the later story (Genesis 1), God is said to create from the initial chaos by three acts of separation (light and darkness; water and heaven; earth and sea), followed by five acts of ordering (filling earth with plants; firmament with stars, sun, and moon; sea with animals and air with birds; earth with animals; human creation). This sequence reflects a prescientific intuition of what we now call the cosmic and biological evolution.

The words *in (the) beginning* (Gen 1:1) indicate that God creates time. The phrase *God saw that it was good* does not indicate completeness and perfection of the initial creation, since the Hebrew word *tov* means good for the purpose, rather than good in actuality. "Six days" with a day of rest and many other biblical texts imply a continuing creation process that moves through time toward its goal. The words *let there be* indicate that God creates with the divine Word, the *Logos.* In the New Testament, John claims that through the incarnation of the *Logos,* the human Jesus of Nazareth becomes the Christ, the Son of God, who will bring creation to perfection.

4

Creation out of Nothing: Origin and Problems

4.1 The chaos archetype

The preceding chapter (section 3.2) reviewed sixteen stories of origin from all over the world. Those stories are remarkable for their descriptions of the initial state:

1. *Rig Veda* (India): There was neither nonexistence nor existence; darkness was hidden by darkness; all this was water.
2. *Upanishad* (India): In the beginning the cosmos was self alone, in the shape of a person. This self (*atman*) split in two, husband and wife.
3. Pangu story (China): In the beginning only dark chaos prevailed in the universe.
4. Taoist story (China): There was confusion: primal simplicity, commencement, beginnings, material. Things were not yet separated.
5. Australian aborigines: The ancestors created themselves from clay.
6. New Zealand Maoris: The universe was in darkness; water was everywhere; there was no light.
7. Hawaiian story: There was deep darkness; gods came out of the night.
8. Mayan story *Popol Vuh*: The universe was resting, motionless and silent; the heavenly expanse was empty. There was only the resting water, the silent sea.
9. North American Indian story: The initial being awoke, wondered what to do, and finally began to cry. His tears formed the waters.
10. Rwandan story: In the beginning, the Creator created two lands: the land above clouds, sun, and stars, and the land below without beauty and happiness. Before this double creation, there was nothing; only the Creator existed.

11. Greek Hesiod poem: At the beginning of everything was chaos, out of which came amid much violence earth, gods, and humans.
12. Icelandic *Edda* story: There was an initial chaos, the great void, from which various gods arose.
13. Finnish *Kalevala* epic: There was nothing but the foaming sea and clouds above it.
14. Egyptian creation story: A primeval hill emerged from the primeval flood *Nu*.
15. Memphite creation story: The god Ptah conceived the elements of the universe with his mind and brought them into being by his commanding word.
16. Babylonian creation story *Enuma Elish*: There was a chaos without heaven and earth; only water existed, from which the gods arose.

All but one of these stories describe some form of an initial chaos, and in half of the cases, this is a watery chaos. The only story that speaks about "nothing" at the beginning is the Rwandan story, which was recorded in the nineteenth century by a Roman Catholic priest.[1] His use of the word *nothing* may well have been the result of his commitment to the doctrine of *creatio ex nihilo*.

The two biblical creation stories also have an initial chaos—a lifeless desert in Genesis 2 and a watery void in Genesis 1. Thus, we see that creation stories born from animistic, polytheistic, and Jewish monotheistic religions have virtually without exception an initial chaos. The New Testament adheres to the Genesis creation account except for the revolutionary innovation of seeing Jesus Christ as the incarnation of God's creative Word. The nearly universal idea of creation from an (unexplained) initial chaos suggests to me that this represents a Jungian archetype, a belief embedded in the universal human subconsciousness, resulting from prehistoric divine revelation.

How then could the church in the late second century exchange this nearly universally held belief for the doctrine of creation out of nothing (*creatio ex nihilo*) and retain this without much further discussion for the past 1,800 years? To answer this question, we must consider the influence of Platonism on the thinking of the early church, as well as the phenomenon of Gnosticism.

4.2 Influence of Platonism

Plato's "Ideas" and Middle Platonism

Plato (428–348 BCE), one of the founding fathers of Greek philosophy, believed that above and beyond the world as we perceive it with our senses, there exists a divine, unchangeable world. He considered the human soul to be a fallen deity, captive in an earthly body. Only the purifying effect of rational thinking can help us reach our initial divine state. All things present in our world are to us only shadows of the eternal realities, Ideas, existing in the divine world, like the Table behind all tables, the Human behind all humans, the Light behind every light that has ever shone or still shines. Plato used the image of being in a dark cave to explain that in our fallen state, we can merely see glimpses of these Ideas, like flickering shadows on the wall of a cave. The highest Idea was to him that of the Good. The eternal Ideas are the rational version of the mythical gods. Plato believed in an eternal "matter" beside God, a receiving principle from which everything can develop. The cosmos is an eternal, divine emanation of the timeless and impassive Upper Being, without beginning or end.

In the first century, educated pagans, dissatisfied with the mythical gods of Greek religion, turned to Plato's teaching. This led to its further development in what is called "Middle Platonism." This philosophy emphasizes a dualism of matter and mind. It recognizes a hierarchy of divine principles with emphasis on the transcendence of the supreme Principle, the Upper Being. The Ideas are placed in the divine mind, becoming the thoughts of God. Middle Platonism is preoccupied with the problem of evil, attributed to an evil world soul or to matter. This leads to an otherworldly attitude demanding a "flight from the body," an ascent of the mind to the divine and eternal.

Philo of Alexandria and Jewish Platonism

The main purpose of Greek-speaking philosopher Philo of Alexandria (c. 10 BCE–50 CE) was to reconcile Jewish scripture and tradition with Platonist philosophy. He thus became the founder of Hellenistic Judaism, and even to some extent a forerunner of Christian theology.[2] His education in a Greek school made him thoroughly familiar with Greek philosophy, although he was an observant Jew. He used Platonism in the exposition and defense of Judaism and attempted to show that the revelation given to Moses accorded with the views of Middle Platonism. He interpreted the Old Testament in an allegorical way without losing sight of the literal meaning of the texts.

Philo considered the world to be created from preexisting formless matter, the origin of which he did not explain. In one place he described matter as bad and as one of the causes of evil, but elsewhere he wrote about its passivity, its lack of quality or form unless it is filled with divine power. He recognized the existence of a host of beings between God and the world, the hierarchy of divine principles of Middle Platonism, but to him God is the essential Being of the world. Together, the powers of God form the *Logos* or divine Reason, which created and rules the world. Through the *Logos*, God is revealed to us. Since the human soul is part of God, the soul can come to know the *Logos* through mystical contemplation. If we could liberate ourselves from the stain of matter and senses, we might through ascetic exercise and contemplation become for one moment pure spirit and see God. Philo anticipated later Christian doctrine by calling the *Logos* the first-begotten Son of God.

One may ask how Philo could at once embrace a philosophy that holds the idea of eternal matter, the involvement of a hierarchy of divine persons or principles in creation, the idea of an immortal soul and its reincarnation, and the doctrine of Ideas, which so flagrantly contradict the creation stories in Genesis. As one reviewer writes, "Philo's works are rambling, repetitious, artificially rhetorical, his style is involved, allusive, strongly tinged with mysticism, and often obscure, possibly a deliberate attempt to discourage the uninitiated."[3]

Christian Platonists

Platonism, and Philo's use of it in interpreting Jewish teaching, had a considerable influence on early Christianity, which at that time had not yet developed a comprehensive theology. Thus, the early Christian thinkers accepted the essentials of Platonic religious philosophy, being confident of its harmony with Christian teaching. They regarded Platonism, the dominant philosophy in the Mediterranean area in that time, as the best means for understanding and defending the teachings of Scripture and church tradition. They assumed (in their unhistorical approach and allegorical exegesis of texts) that all that is rationally certain in Platonism would accord with the Christian revelation. They stressed the transcendence of God but also God's deepest immanence in the world. They took a dualistic view of soul and body, although accepting bodily resurrection, and emphasized the primacy of the spiritual while insisting on the goodness of God's material creation.

Prominent early Christian Platonists were Justin Martyr (c. 100–165), Clement of Alexandria (c. 150–215), and Origen (c. 185–254). Origen produced a synthesis of Christianity and Middle Platonism that influenced both sides at the councils of Nicea (325) and Constantinople (381). Later Christian Platonists were Augustine (354–430), Anselm (1033–1109), John Duns Scotus (1264–1308), Thomas Aquinas (1225–74), G. W. F. Hegel (1770–1831), and the originator of process theology, A. N. Whitehead (1861–1947).

4.3 The threat of Gnosticism

The second century was a time of turmoil for the early church. From a Jewish sect, it had become a rapidly growing movement with Jewish as well as pagan members. Politically the church fell under Roman imperial rule and was subject to persecution by Roman authorities for its refusal to offer sacrifices to the emperor. Culturally it was influenced by the dominant Greek philosophy, which was attractive to intellectuals of the time, including, as we have seen, the early Christian thinkers. The Old Testament and New Testament writings were only beginning to be studied in some depth. At the same time there was religious confusion in the Mediterranean area. Greek and Roman polytheisms were no longer attractive to the educated people. Eastern cults spread through the area: Egyptian worship of Isis and Osiris, Syrian worship of Baal, Persian worship of Mithras, the Greek mysteries, and Babylonian astrology. Common to all of them was the idea that the material world was only transitory but that there was another world beyond it. Through asceticism and magic initiation, the soul could find unity with the divine principle and thus overcome mortality.

The strongest challenge to the church during the second century was presented by Gnosticism.[4] Its origins lie in the dualism of Persian religion, the allegorical idealism of Middle Platonism, and the apocalypticism of Jewish mystics. It is only with the rise of Christianity that gnostic syncretism comes to full expression. The second-century Christian Gnostics use the allegorical method to support their ideas from the Hebrew and Christian scriptures. Although most of the gnostic literature has been lost (except for some apocryphal gospels, a harmony of the four Gospels called *Diatessaron*, and the Coptic *Nag Hammadi* manuscripts), we know that the key point of gnostic teaching is that redemption is obtained through esoteric knowledge (*gnosis*), acquired by divine revelation to the initiated, rather than by rational philosophy or empirical observation.

Gnosticism acquired its dualism after expanding into the Hellenistic world, where it borrowed from Platonism and Persian religion the doctrine that a lower demiurge is responsible for the creation of the world. The teaching of Valentinus (Egypt, Rome), Basilides (Antioch, Alexandria), and Marcion (Rome) incorporates this popular teaching in Hellenized and Christianized form. Hellenistic Judaism could accept creation from eternal matter without seeing this as diminishing God's omnipotence; for example, Justin Martyr reads Gen 1:1-2 as a description of this eternal matter.

In the Platonic-gnostic view, particularly that of Marcion, there is no fundamental distinction between creator and creature. The unconscious self of humans is consubstantial with the Godhead, but through a tragic fall, it is thrown into a world that is completely alien to its real being. Through revelation from above (*gnosis*), humans become conscious of their origin, essence, and destiny. Gnostic revelation differs from philosophical enlightenment as it cannot be acquired by force of reason, and from Christian revelation as it is not transmitted by Scripture. Rather, it is the intuition of the mystery of the self. Aware of the evil in the world, Gnostics believe in creation by an evil demiurge from evil matter. The created world is dominated by the demiurge, who Marcion and some other Gnostics believe to be Yahweh, the God of the Old Testament. This world is to be redeemed by the good God, the Father of Jesus Christ.

Although no single creedal statement of Christian gnostic belief exists, its main points can be summarized as follows:

- An evil demiurge, often identified with Yahweh, the God of the Old Testament, created the world from evil eternal matter.
- Salvation is obtained by *gnosis*, esoteric knowledge revealed by the good God, the Father of Jesus Christ.
- Humanity is divided into three categories: (1) a spiritual elite able to achieve salvation; (2) "psychics" capable of a modified form of salvation; and (3) "material" people cut off from salvation.

The gnostic movement nearly absorbed Christianity in the second century. The confrontation forced the church to clarify its thinking on vital issues like creation theology. The Apologists played a role in this process by defending the church against intellectuals such as Galen and Celsus, and by refuting Gnosticism. The main Apologists were Justin Martyr (100–165), Clement of Alexandria (150–215), Theophilus of Antioch (c. 185), Irenaeus (c. 130–200), and Tertullian (c. 160–220). Clement drew on Greek philosophy to clarify Christian teaching and wrote in Philo's allegorizing way against the Gnostics. His reasoning is dominated by the idea of the *Logos*, who created the universe and manifests for him the Father in Old Testament Law, Greek philosophy, and the Incarnation. Irenaeus criticized the Gnostics even more systematically, as in his attack on Valentinus's dualism of good spirit against evil matter. He founded the Catechetical School of Alexandria as a meeting place of Hellenism, Judaism, Gnosticism, and Middle Platonism. In the next section, I shall say more about Theophilus. In passing, it is interesting to note that Gnosticism has persisted in religious thinking through the ages: the Cathars, Rosicrucians, Swedenborgians, theosophy, anthroposophy, and currently in New Age religion.

4.4 Origin of *creatio ex nihilo*

The biblical thought of creation from an initial chaos, as related in the Genesis accounts, seems to have been retained until the end of the second century. This appears from the writings of Justin Martyr and Clement of Alexandria. The latter points to a passage in the Wisdom of Solomon: "For your all-powerful hand, which created the world out of formless matter" (Wis 11:17). However, elsewhere Clement challenges the Greek philosophical tradition of eternally existing matter and asserts that the will of God is the sole ground of creation.[5] It can be said that *creatio ex nihilo* is not found in Old Testament, apocryphal, and New Testament writings, and neither is it in the work of early Christian writers until Theophilus of Antioch and Irenaeus.[6]

Theophilus of Antioch (c. 185) appears to have been the first to introduce explicitly and unambiguously the concept of creation out of nothing, *creatio ex nihilo*. In the oldest-known commentary on Genesis, he states, "God has created everything out of nothing into being." Theophilus seems to have been a rather confused and rash theologian, as he considered *Logos* and Spirit to be identical, calling them the Wisdom of God.[7] Neither did he see that his doctrine made God responsible for the presence of evil in creation.

Nevertheless, Irenaeus (bishop of Lyons, c. 190) quickly embraced the doctrine, apparently after reading Theophilus's lost treatise against Hermogenes. Irenaeus does not go beyond the fundamental proposition that creation was out of nothing, God using divine will and power as matter. Against the gnostic belief in a demiurge and other divine beings, Irenaeus upholds the one true God of the Bible. Thereafter, Tertullian (c. 200) and Hippolytus (c. 220) accept the idea that God created the world out of absolutely nothing.[8] Origen (c. 230) writes that he cannot understand that so many eminent men had believed that matter was eternal and not created by God.

The doctrine was subsequently adopted by Augustine (c. 300), and from there on, it was almost universally accepted in the church. It was dogmatically formulated at the Fourth Lateran Council (1215), adopted by Martin Luther and John Calvin, and reaffirmed by the first Vatican Council (1870). As David Fergusson says, what is most surprising is that the doctrine of creation out of nothing came so quickly and with so little controversy to be the accepted teaching of the church.[9] No doubt, its major attraction was that it at once disposed of the eternal evil matter and of the evil demiurge-creator of the Gnostics, thereby upholding Jewish-Christian monotheism.

However, our experience with the doctrinal statements adopted during the sixteenth-century Reformation conflict shows that doctrine formulated in the heat of religious battle and confusion, as certainly existed in the second century, bears some further study under more settled conditions. It should be noted that *creatio ex nihilo* is not included in the early creeds (Apostles' Creed, Nicene Creed, and Athanasian Creed). Nor does it seem to have been a subject of discussion at the four great councils from Nicea (325) to Chalcedon (451), since it is not mentioned in the texts of these councils published in the Denzinger collection of doctrinal statements of the church.[10] *Creatio ex nihilo* plays little or no role in other major Christian doctrines, including eschatology, the doctrine of the perfection of the creation, and the resurrection of the dead on the last day. Logically, a solid creation theology should lead to a belief in the fulfillment of the creation.

4.5 Problems with *creatio ex nihilo*

From my reading and thinking, I have come to the conclusion that *creatio ex nihilo* presents five serious problems. These are (1) the conceptual problem, (2) the biblical problem, (3) the scientific problem, (4) the theological problem, and (5) the problem of evil.

(1) Conceptual problem

None of us can picture absolute nothingness. This has led several theologians to assume an "existing" nothing (*nihil ontologicum*) instead of a true nothing (*nihil negativum*). Augustine equates the "nothing" from which God creates with "formless matter, entirely without feature."[11] Thomas states that everything depends on God, so saying that the world was created by God implies that it was made "out of nothing." The true meaning is "not out of anything"; it is wrong to think that creation changes *nihil* into a creature.[12] Both Karl Barth and Emil Brunner hold to an existing nothing.[13]

However, these various forms of an existing nothing are not really different from an initial chaos. The same is true if one says, with John Polkinghorne, that *creatio ex nihilo* is merely a "metaphysical" statement.[14] Therefore, I shall adhere to a strict interpretation of *nihil* as the complete absence of matter, energy, physical laws, information, structure, and order. Theophilus must surely have had such a strict *nihil* in mind in his attempt to refute the gnostic belief in an eternal evil matter.

(2) Biblical problem

Creatio ex nihilo cannot be read into either of the creation accounts in Genesis. In his authoritative commentary on Genesis, Claus Westermann states, "Such an abstract way of thinking was not part of the thought pattern of P (author of Gen 1); . . . it is clear here that there can be no question of a *creatio ex nihilo*."[15] W. H. Bennett writes in his commentary on Genesis about the word *bara* (to create; see chapter 3.4): "*Bara* . . . does not in itself necessarily express creation out of nothing. According to the more probable view of this passage, the Creation started, not from nothing, but from the primeval chaos; the author did not trouble himself as to the origin of this chaos."[16]

Four texts are usually quoted in support of creation out of nothing:

1. Job 26:7—"He stretches out Zaphon [or 'the north'] over the void, and hangs the earth upon nothing."
2. Rom 4:17—"God . . . who . . . calls into existence the things that do not exist."
3. Heb 11:3—"The worlds were prepared by the word of God, so that what is seen was made from things that are not visible."
4. 2 Macc 7:28—"God did not make them out of things that existed."

These texts can hardly be seen as evidence for creation from nothing, as they fit equally well with creation from initial chaos. The same conclusion is reached by David Fergusson and, for 2 Macc 7:28, by Gerhard May.[17]

Gerhard May concludes, "Nowhere in the [New Testament] is the doctrine of *creatio ex nihilo* explicitly developed as a cosmological theory."[18] Westermann comments that the Hebrew term *tohu wabohu* denotes a state of utter disorder, a threatening chaos, but the various wording used in Gen 1:2, Isa 34:11, and Jer 4:23 indicates that in their prescientific age the authors were unable to conceive of utter chaos without reference to matter. Yet, he says, it cannot be equated with the preexisting, evil matter of the Gnostics, which abstract concept is foreign to the thinking of the authors of Genesis 1 and 2.[19] Georg Singe concurs:

> The first verses of Genesis 1 do not speak about a *creatio ex nihilo*, as posed in later Christian dogmatics (but which was foreign to semitic thinking), but about a creation from some Ur-Etwas, a "primordial something." . . . This chaos stretches into and influences the present world (*creatio continua*) but cannot limit the freedom and sovereignty of the Creator.[20]

(3) Scientific problem

Physical science, whether classical, quantum-mechanical, or relativistic, is unable to explain the origin of the universe from a *nihil*, defined as the absence of matter, energy, physical laws, information, structure, and order. This is the conclusion drawn by the Lutheran theologian Mark Worthing from an extensive study.[21]

The most widely accepted theory for cosmic beginnings, the big bang theory, assumes an initial "explosion" at $t = 0$, as described in chapter 2.2. But this theory cannot say anything about the conditions before and during the explosion, only about the events after the initial fraction of a second. An initial explosion requires some form of preexisting energy, physical laws, information, or a combination of these, which is not a *nihil*. Some physicists describe the cosmic origin as a "quantum fluctuation in a vacuum,"[22] but this does not constitute an initial *nihil*. As John Polkinghorne says, "A quantum vacuum is a hive of activity, full of fluctuations, of random comings-to-be and fadings-away, certainly not something which without great abuse of language could be called 'nothing.'"[23] Arthur Peacocke appears to agree when he says, "It was not just 'nothing at all' even if it was 'no thing.'"[24] The ironic fact is that if science could explain a beginning of the world from nothing, then there would be no need for a Creator. Mark Worthing ends his survey with the conclusion: "Any theory explaining how something has come from nothing must assume some preexisting laws or energy or quantum activity in order to have a credible theory. Nothing comes out of nothing."[25]

(4) Theological problem

Explaining a cosmic origin from a true *nihil* causes as much of a problem for theologians as it does for scientists. Augustine, Karl Barth, and Emil Brunner gave up on true *nihil* and substituted for it some existing nothing, which is not essentially different from an initial chaos. Paul Tillich realizes this and writes, "The *nihil* out of which God creates is . . . the undialectical negation of being."[26] Mark Worthing, who concludes that creation out of absolute nothingness is an impossibility, also rejects a creation out of God's own "substance" as leading to a pantheistic deification of the physical world, but he seems to come close to this in his final conclusion: "*Creatio ex nihilo,* therefore, signifies the theological recognition that God created a universe distinct from the divine being, not out of any preexisting matter or principle, but out of nothing other than the fullness of God's own being."[27] Oxford theologian Keith Ward rightly distinguishes between "origin" in the cosmological sense and "creation" in the theological sense, and he argues the case for a created universe but does not discuss, much less explain, *creatio ex nihilo,* even though this section in his book is titled "Creation out of Nothing."[28]

Jürgen Moltmann has made a serious attempt to offer a theological explanation for a true *creatio ex nihilo.*[29] The first problem to be solved, he says, is where to locate an initial "nothingness." Initially, "it" must be inside God, so as not to limit God's omnipresence, but for creation, "it" must be externalized to avoid pantheistic deification of the created world. Therefore, Moltmann invokes two ideas from the Jewish Kabbalah (mysticism): *zimsum* (God's concentration and contraction, a withdrawing of God into God's self) and *shekinah* (contraction of the infinite God's presence so that God can dwell in the temple). Moltmann combines these concepts, stating, "Where God withdraws himself from himself to himself, he can call something forth which is not divine essence or divine being." This something he calls a *nihil,* a God-forsaken space, hell, absolute death, annihilating nothingness, in which God establishes the creation. Next, Moltmann applies Paul's idea of *kenosis*, God's self-emptying in the incarnation of Christ (Phil 2:5-8), and the idea of God's self-humiliation in Christ's death on the cross. This leads him to four statements: (1) God withdraws *into* himself in order to go *out of* himself in creation. (2) If God is creatively active in the "nothing" that he has ceded and conceded, then the resulting creation still remains in God who has yielded up the initial "nothing" in himself. (3) The initial self-limitation of God, which permits creation, then assumes the glorious, unrestricted boundlessness in which the whole creation is transfigured. (4) In relating initial creation to eschatological creation, Christ's death overcomes the "annihilating nothingness, which persists in sin and death."

David Fergusson calls this argumentation "ultimately unconvincing," and Alan Torrance also offers severe criticism.[30] I, too, have several objections against Moltmann's rather obscure reasoning. First, the attraction of a strict *creatio ex nihilo*, as emphasizing God's absolute creative power, is largely negated by the need to invoke *zimsum, shekinah, kenosis,* and God's self-humiliation. Second, the latter two concepts apply to incarnation and crucifixion of Christ, rather than to creation. Third, an "annihilating nothingness, which persists in sin and death" is no less mysterious than an unexplained initial chaos; moreover, sin and death are not falling into *nihil*, but rather into chaos. Finally, a nothingness that annihilates can hardly be considered as a true *nihil*.

(5) Problem of evil

Creation out of nothing would imply that God is responsible for the evil in this world, both physical evil in natural disasters and disease, and moral evil that we humans commit. This monstrous thought has never been resolved in 1,800 years of *creatio ex nihilo*. In recent years, the problem has been honestly faced by several theologians.[31] However, no one can solve the problem—not with Origen's doctrine of original sin, nor with the Augustinian idea of *privatio boni* (evil is the absence of the good), nor with the Irenaean idea of evil as falling within God's good purpose. Brian Hebblethwaite closes his perceptive book with the plaintive words "But even if these things are so [happiness bestowed by God in the end], there still remains the problem of the cost of human suffering and wickedness here on earth. It is very hard to reach a balanced view on this problem."[32] Even Pope John Paul II seemed to admit the intractability of the problem of evil in his encyclical *Fides et Ratio* (Faith and Reason).[33] Even more emphatic is John Sanford, who concludes his book with the words, "the problem of evil is unresolved in Christian theology."[34] The Gnostics with their evil demiurge and preexistent evil matter at least had an explanation, while the doctrine of *creatio ex nihilo* stumbles against the problem of evil.[35] Moltmann's attempt to attribute evil to *nihil* in his "annihilating nothingness" is unsatisfactory. In chapter 8, I discuss the question of the origin of evil in detail.

Recently, Paul Copan and William L. Craig published an extensive defense of *creatio ex nihilo*.[36] However, in their argumentation they miss most of the problems I have set forth here. The problem of evil is relegated to a footnote on page 162. On the biblical evidence for the doctrine, they do not quote Claus Westermann and David Fergusson for their negative conclusions.

4.6 Ineffectiveness of *creatio ex nihilo*

In addition to the problems discussed so far, there is also the point that the doctrine of *creatio ex nihilo* does not seem to have played a significant role in the formulation of any major Christian doctrine. There is no evidence that it featured in the development of the key doctrine of Christology at the four great councils (section 4.4). Ideally, it seems to me, creation theology should be the foundation of all major topics of Christian theology: the doctrines of God, Christ, incarnation, salvation, and eschatology. However, these doctrines seem to have been directly developed from Scripture without much regard to a doctrine of creation.

Not only has the doctrine of *creatio ex nihilo* not satisfied the demand that may be made of an effective creation theology, it has also led to the unsatisfactory doctrine of original sin as an ad hoc solution for the problem of the origin of evil, which problem arose from the doctrine of creation out of nothing. The doctrine of original sin is bound up with the equally unsatisfactory and unbiblical idea of an initially perfect creation, which is later spoiled by human sinfulness. In turn, this has led to the mistaken view that Christ's reconciling work applies only to human salvation. Thus, the cosmic dimension of Christ's work (see chapter 10) is lost, and the Christian faith tends to turn into an anthropocentric, individualistic belief. Claus Westermann writes, "Once theology has . . . become detached from Creator-creation, . . . it must become an anthropology and begin to disintegrate from within, and collapse around us."[37] S. Wesley Ariarajah, who is engaged in interreligious dialogue, writes that a theology of religions "can emerge only when it begins its theology where it all began—'Creation'—rather than with the 'Fall.'"[38]

Awareness of the serious problems and shortcomings of the doctrine of *creatio ex nihilo* has led me to return to the biblical idea of creation out of chaos and to develop from this a revised creation theology, which I call "chaos theology." I will explain chaos theology in chapter 6, following chapter 5's critical survey of current thinking about creation theology.

4.7 Summary

A brief review of the findings in chapter 3 shows a nearly universal belief in creation from a primordial chaos in the biblical and nonbiblical creation stories. This belief came under attack from Platonism and Gnosticism in the second century. Platonism was then the prominent philosophy in the Mediterranean area. Plato proposed that all earthly objects have a transcendent, eternal image and form behind them (for instance, the Table behind all tables). This led him to consider matter as being unreal. The dualism between matter and mind is emphasized in first-century Middle Platonism, which attributes evil to an evil demiurge and preexistent evil matter.

Philo attempted to reconcile Jewish scripture with Platonism, leading to Hellenistic Judaism. He accepted creation from preexisting formless matter, and the existence of a host of heavenly beings, the hierarchy of divine principles of Middle Platonism. Together these constitute the *Logos* or divine reason, through which God creates. Platonism and Philo's Hellenistic Judaism had a considerable influence on early Christian theologians (Clement of Alexandria and Origen) and even many later ones (Augustine and the Scholastics).

In the first two centuries, there was an upsurge of Gnosticism, which combined Persian dualism, Middle Platonism, and Jewish mysticism with an allegorical reading of the biblical writings. Creation is thought to be from evil matter by an evil demiurge, for many the God of the Old Testament. Salvation is obtained by the initiated through *gnosis*, esoteric knowledge imparted by the good God, the Father of Jesus Christ.

In his battle against Gnosticism, Theophilus of Antioch introduced around 185 a new creation theology, creation from nothing (*creatio ex nihilo*). It was quickly accepted by Irenaeus, Tertullian, Hippolytus, and Origen, and later by Augustine. Since then, it has become without much discussion the accepted teaching of nearly all churches. Nevertheless, it was not included in the ancient creeds and does not seem to have played a significant role in the development of the major Christian doctrines.

Creatio ex nihilo presents five serious difficulties. (1) The conceptual difficulty is that no one can picture absolute nothingness, leading many theologians to assume an "existing" nothing, which does not really differ from an initial chaos. Others have called it merely a metaphysical or philosophical statement or say that it only means creation from "no thing." (2) The biblical problem is that *creatio ex nihilo* cannot be reconciled with the initial chaos, *tohu wabohu*, in the Genesis stories, while the four texts usually quoted as supporting the doctrine (Job 26:7; Rom 4:17; Heb 11:3; 2 Macc 7:28) fit equally well with creation from chaos. (3) The scientific difficulty is that no physical theory can deal with absolute nothing (absence of matter, energy, physical laws, structure, and order). (4) A theological problem is that no satisfactory theological formulation of creation from nothing has been provided. (5) With regard to the origin of evil, creation from nothing would make God responsible for the existence of physical and moral evil in the world, a problem that has not been solved in the 1,800-year history of the doctrine.

These serious problems of *creatio ex nihilo* have led me to develop a revised creation theology, which I call chaos theology. Before explaining this in chapter 6, I will present a critical survey of current thinking about creation theology in the next chapter.

5

Contemporary Creation Theologies

Given the problems with the traditional doctrine of *creatio ex nihilo*, as described in the preceding chapter, it is appropriate to review how prominent contemporary theologians are coping with the doctrine of creation. All too briefly, I shall characterize their positions on *creatio ex nihilo*, continuing creation, the problem of evil, and the modern scientific view of an evolutionary world.

5.1 Continental European theologians

Karl Barth

Karl Barth (1886–1968) deemed science to be irrelevant to theology, because in his view the two disciplines operate in two fundamentally distinct spheres, the realms of the transcendent and the empirical. Thus, dogmatics has no business to broaden out into cosmology. In the more than two hundred pages in his *Church Dogmatics* devoted to the concept of time in creation, there is not a single reference to Einstein and his relativity theory. Neither does he mention evolution.

Over against his adamant position on science stands his mitigated view on *nihil*. He believes that the biblical account of creation provides "incontestible" evidence for a "material used by God in the act of creation." He reconciles this with *creatio ex nihilo* by assuming a *nihil privativum*, a material or principle that already exists. He writes, "It is not nothing, but something at the edge of nothing. The nothing is that which God as creator did not choose, did not want, that which he passed by as creator, which he according to Gen 1:2 left behind as chaos without giving it being and existence."[1] He thus elevates "nothingness" (*das Nichtige*) to the status of a preexisting principle out of which God calls forth being.

Barth sees creation as the expression of the covenant between God and humanity, an external ground of the covenant in Genesis 1 and an inner ground in Genesis 2. He clearly takes an anthropocentric view of creation. He also holds to providence rather than believing in continuing creation. Evil is for him an aspect of *das Nichtige*, the chaos from which God creates and the counterforce to God in this world.

The main element of Barth's eschatology seems to consist of "justification" in a juridical sense, a justification resting only on God's grace and our faith, with good works being to no avail.

Emil Brunner

Emil Brunner (1889–1966) holds to a very mitigated form of *nihil*: "There never was a 'nothing' alongside of God. What we know as creation is never *creatio ex nihilo*, it is always the shaping of some given material."[2]

Based on our knowledge of evolution, Brunner is willing to accept the idea of continuing creation (*creatio continua*).[3] This idea is not alien to the Bible, Brunner says; we are both the product of our ancestors and a new creation of God. Hence he sees no difficulty in reconciling creation and evolution.[4] However, he warns, one can never prove creation from evolution. He does not seem to realize that the problem is the opposite: to prove that evolution does not exclude creation. Brunner maintains that the created world has a beginning in time, since a world without beginning, an eternal world, leads to deification of the world and thus to pantheism.

Brunner accepts the idea of God's providence in the sense that God intervenes in the course of history, working miracles, while upholding the laws of nature.[5] On evil, Brunner finds all theories for a theodicy wanting and seeks the solution in the cross as "God's sovereign act of redemption." He writes, "Here, at the cross, it becomes evident that . . . God has such power over this evil, which he does not will, that he is able to make it an instrument of his saving work."[6] However, this does not explain the *origin* of evil.

On eschatology Brunner is brief, centering it on the realized eschatology of the presence of the kingdom in Jesus.[7]

Wolfhart Pannenberg

In contrast to Barth, Pannenberg (b. 1928) maintains that theology cannot ignore the scientific description of the world. In his *Systematic Theology*,[8] he develops the idea of creation through the Spirit operating as a divine field of force according to the physical field theory developed by Michael Faraday for the explanation of the long-distance effects of electric and magnetic forces. In this way, God works immanently in the material universe and is present in space and time. Pannenberg also applies this field theory to embryonic development and even to angels.

Pannenberg's field theory has been criticized by several authors. Colin Gunton says that describing the Holy Spirit as a divine field of force depersonalizes the third person of the Trinity.[9] Mark Worthing points out that physicists now recognize that the fields and lines of force of Faraday's field theory are not a physical reality, but merely a metaphor.[10] In identifying the work of the Spirit with Faraday's field theory, Pannenberg erroneously suggests that all forces in the cosmos can be reduced to a single field of force that determines all changes in the cosmos. It is an example of the confusion that can arise from the injudicious use of metaphors (see chapter 1.3).

On *creatio ex nihilo*, Pannenberg states that, rather than speaking about presence or absence of matter at $t = 0$, the doctrine emphasizes God's absolute freedom and rejects gnostic dualism. Although he assigns a primary role in creation to the Spirit, he emphasizes the role of the Son in initiating creation in his self-distinction from the Father but fails to distinguish between the non-incarnate and the incarnate *Logos*.

Continuing creation he sees merely as God's preserving activity through the angels. He does not pay much attention to the evolutionary development of cosmos and life. He ascribes evil to the activity of evil angels, who strive against the will of God.

On eschatology, he finds it difficult to reconcile the biblical eschatological vision and the scientific extrapolations of the future degradation of the universe. Apparently, he does not see that these extrapolations are based on the assumption of a closed universe—one without any external influence, divine or otherwise (see chapter 14.2). He strangely embraces Frank Tipler's Omega Point theory for the resurrection of the dead (see chapter 14.4).[11]

Jürgen Moltmann

To my knowledge, Jürgen Moltmann (b. 1926) is the only theologian who has made a serious attempt to offer a theological explanation of *creatio ex nihilo*.[12] I have described this in chapter 4.5 and explained why it is unsatisfactory. Although Moltmann holds to a strict *nihil*, he ends up with "an annihilating nothingness that persists in sin and death," which can hardly be considered as a true *nihil*. He embraces panentheism in the sense that he believes that God dwells in the created world and that the world exists in God.

Moltmann feels that science can help us understand the immanence of God in nature. He offers a theological approach to the ecological crisis and pays brief attention to the trinitarian aspect of creation, but is silent on the problem of evil. He accepts an idea of continuing creation in which evolution theory has a place: "Creation is not yet finished, and has not as yet reached its end."[13] But later he reduces this idea to God's sustaining and preserving the created world and preparing it for the final perfection.[14] Although he devotes an entire chapter to "the evolution of nature," he does not succeed in integrating this into his creation theology.

Moltmann deals with eschatology in a section titled "The eschatological glorification of human beings"[15] and in a concluding chapter titled "The Sabbath: the feast of creation."[16] As these titles indicate, his emphasis is on the joyful and glorious aspects of the perfection of creation, but he neglects crisis and judgment inherent in eschatology.

Hendrik Berkhof

Dutch theologian Hendrik Berkhof (1914–95) devotes a large part of his dogmatics to creation.[17] He deplores the narrowing (reduction) of creation theology in the last two centuries as a result of the work of Friedrich Schleiermacher, Albrecht Ritschl, Rudolf Bultmann, and Karl Barth. He also criticizes the anthropocentric thought that everything was created for humans' sake. He rejects attempts to derive creation theology from salvation theology, as Barth does, and claims, "Creation is the overture to and is aimed at salvation."

Creatio ex nihilo means for Berkhof our dependency on God's initiative and on nothing else; there are no other deities and powers to be feared. It does not mean that we are created out of "the Nothing" as from a dark and chaotic power that threatens our life.

Berkhof accepts continuing creation, reminding us that the Hebrew word *tov* in Genesis 1 does not mean perfect, but fit for the purpose, which means that the created world is imperfect reality, to be fulfilled in time. His claim that continuing creation ends and conservation begins with the fall seems to incorrectly link a transition in time to a nonhistorical event.

Berkhof states that we must express creation theology in today's evolutionary worldview. He mentions Anglican theologians and Teilhard de Chardin as the pioneers in this. However, he rightly criticizes Teilhard for not doing justice to the realities of sin and reconciliation and for turning Christ into a cosmic principle. He says evolution provides good parallels with creation theology but does not further elaborate on this thought.

Berkhof does not discuss the problem of evil, but only that of sin. He rejects dualistic solutions and the idea that sin is simply the mark of an imperfect creation. The freedom given to humans is the best answer for him, but there is also a mysterious element of tragedy. He considers the doctrine of original sin untenable.

Berkhof sees eschatology as extrapolation, as completion and perfection of creation. He hesitantly admits the possibility of an interim existence between death and the last day. However, he does not take this into account in his thinking about judgment and hell.

5.2 Anglo-Saxon theologians

John Macquarrie

In his *Principles of Christian Theology*, John Macquarrie (b. 1919) neglects the scientific worldview.[18] He accepts *creatio ex nihilo* without much explanation, as if it were an axiom in geometry. He merely says that it was presumably framed to differentiate creation from Plato's idea of creation out of preexistent matter, and that it stresses the utter difference between an act of creation and the act of "making" one thing from another. But he admits, "This distinction is not very clear. A matter (*hulé*) that is formless and completely without any determinate characteristics would be indistinguishable from 'nothing', and so too would be pure undifferentiated being."[19] This comes very close to accepting creation from chaos, and in many of his further statements, "chaos" can be substituted for "nothing" without changing their meaning. Actually, he frequently speaks about "slipping into nothing" (for example, as a consequence of sin), where science and our own experience tell us that this is impossible and that "reverting to chaos" would be a more adequate saying. He accepts Augustine's claim that time was created with the world, but later says that creation is not tied to a moment of time at the beginning.[20]

Macquarrie offers an interesting trinitarian formulation of creation: The Father is the creator. The Son is the active agent in creation, from the beginning as *Logos*, Word of God, and from the incarnation to the fulfillment as Christ, the incarnate *Logos*. The Spirit unifies the creation and lifts it to God.[21]

Continuing creation is for Macquarrie the divine providential activity, which implies a direction in events.

Evil is for him a reversal of the positive, affirmative tendency in creation. It is not simply to be identified with "nothing," which is neutral, neither good nor evil. Yet, in the next sentence Macquarrie claims with Athanasius that evil is "slipping back into nothing."[22] He attributes natural evil to the "risk" of creation, the risk God takes with the "nothing," the tragic element in the creative process. He then makes the strange claim that there is a "cosmic fall" in creation and that some kind of natural evil is necessary but is neither fate nor divine punishment. Is it due to God's fumbling, then? Moral evil, which he calls sin, denotes disorder and imbalance, alienation from God. The basic sin is idolatry, perverted faith, misplaced commitment.

After accepting the doctrine of original sin (but rejecting the doctrine of total depravity), he concludes his discussion of moral evil with the following statement:

> Just as natural evil is the dissolution of beings into "nothing", so sin is the still more terrible dissolution of the highest earthly creature into nothing, through his own wrong decisions. Whether the sin of man aggravates disorder in the rest of creation and heightens what we called the "cosmic fall" is an open question, and very possibly it does. But natural evil and human sin are alike unavoidable possibilities in a creation the end of which is good.[23]

Macquarrie's discussion of eschatology lacks from the neglect of our current scientific ideas about the future of the universe.[24] He finds the traditional eschatology unsatisfactory, but his suggestion to replace it with Dodd's "realized eschatology" offers no solution, because this still implies a final eschatology on the last day. He accepts resurrection and eternal life but defines final judgment as "the hope that what is now ambiguous will resolve itself, and the good will prevail over evil," a rather vague idea. On heaven, he says God will never cease from the quest for universal reconciliation.

Colin Gunton

Colin Gunton (1941–2003) edited and contributed to a collection of eight critical essays on the doctrine of creation.[25] Gunton seems to regret the "laicisation" of the doctrine and the intrusion of science in the discussion. This may explain why the essays are written for an erudite theological audience. Continuing creation is accepted in the last essay, but more as preservation than as a continuous process of creation as suggested by cosmic and biological evolution. The problem of evil is not discussed. *Creatio ex nihilo* is a given for all contributors.

Gunton's later, much more readable monograph, *The Triune Creator*, shows in a valuable historical overview that the doctrine of *creatio ex nihilo* rests on rather primitive and confused arguments with a substantial dose of Platonism, from Theophilus to Thomas Aquinas. After its formulation and confirmation by the Fourth Lateran Council (1215), Gunton says, it had a marginal existence, and with the rise of science it became essentially a function of science. Gunton seems to prefer providence and preservation over continuing creation. About the problem of evil, he feels that the created order suffered a primal catastrophe due to human sin, which is to be overcome on the last day. On eschatology he remains rather vague, speaking about an "openness to change" of the creation. In spite of the title of his book, Gunton does not offer a clear trinitarian formulation of creation. Surprisingly, he sees the Spirit, rather than the Word (*Logos*), as "the energy of the Godhead" that drives creation.

David Fergusson

David Fergusson reviews the history of *creatio ex nihilo*, finds it not supported in Scripture, considers Moltmann's theological explanation of the doctrine "ultimately unconvincing," rejects process theology, and concludes that creation out of nothing simply means that God created "not out of something."[26] He discusses the relevance of the big bang theory, but without mentioning the fact that science cannot deal with a *nihil*.[27] He accepts continuing creation as complementary to *creatio ex nihilo*. He discusses the problem of evil, admitting that the doctrine of original sin is unsatisfactory and untenable, but in the end he is unable to offer a better explanation than that "It is a risk due to God's letting-be of creation."[28]

On eschatology, Fergusson considers the gloomy scientific predictions of the long-term future and the "solutions" proposed by Freeman

Dyson (adaptation) and Frank Tipler (conversion of humans to computers). He agrees with Polkinghorne, who says, "I regard physical eschatology as presenting us with the ultimate reductio ad absurdum of a merely evolutionary optimism."[29] Fergusson doesn't seem to realize that the scientific predictions assume a thermodynamically closed universe. He then turns to the more hopeful biblical eschatology and embraces this with the proviso that the continuity from the present to the new world implies that we cannot shrug off the ecological consequences of our exploitation of our earthly environment.

Arthur Peacocke

With Arthur Peacocke (b. 1924), I come to the first of three scientist-theologians who have seriously considered scientific insights in their formulation of creation theology. In his *Creation and the World of Science*, Peacocke admits that there is "a consensus that the principal emphasis in Israel's understanding of creation was that Yahweh created order, a cosmos, out of chaos."[30] Nevertheless, he affirms *creatio ex nihilo* in the rather minimal sense of "an analogical word representing God's relation to the cosmos now, a relation of absolute dependence of the cosmos on God's will for its very being."[31] Elsewhere he says, "It was not just 'nothing at all' even if it was 'no thing'!"[32] Peacocke accepts the idea that space and time were created at the beginning of the creative process. He also accepts continuing creation in the full sense of "the world still being made." He regrets the excessive anthropocentric outlook on creation of medieval and "Newtonian" theologians.

In his later book, *Theology for a Scientific Age*, Peacocke compares three models of creation: making, emanation, and artistic creation.[33] Making (the English equivalent of the Hebrew word *bara*, used for creating in the Old Testament) is the analogy of a potter making a pot, something that did not exist before in that form. This model points to the dependence of what is created on the creator for both its form and its existence. It also points to the intention and purpose in the mind of the creator and to the relatively independent existence of what is created. Making stresses the transcendence of God and that the act of creation entirely stems from the free, divine initiative. However, says Peacocke, the model is defective in implying that the "matter" used for creating was already in existence, so it does not express the idea of *creatio ex nihilo*, which is so essential to the doctrine of God as creator, as the one source of being of all-that-is.

Emanation is less biblical (stemming from Gnosticism) but supplements and corrects the first model. It is compared with the sun's emission of rays that stimulate warmth and life on Earth. This model emphasizes the immanence of God in the created order (for which Peacocke uses the term *panentheism*, to be distinguished from *pantheism*, where God's presence in the created world is identified with that world). Emanation pictures creation as a continuous process, not an on–off event. It is defective in suggesting that emanative creating is inevitable, such that there can be no free act of will and love on God's part.

Therefore, Peacocke proposes a third model, artistic creation. The artist brings into existence that which existed up till then only as an idea in the mind of the maker. The artist's transcendence over the work of art is quite clear, and his immanence shows in the energy that must enter into his creatures. The artwork also attains a certain independence of its maker. So we have continuing creation, with both transcendence and immanence of the Creator, a certain autonomy of the creature, and a feedback of the creatures to their Creator.

As expansive as Peacocke is on these models of creation, he is very brief on the problem of evil. He limits himself to natural evil, saying that death, pain, and suffering are intimately connected with the possibilities of new life. Natural evil is a necessary prerequisite for the emergence of free, self-conscious beings, the result of random effects of "chance."[34] He connects this with the anthropomorphic idea of a suffering God, which I find an unsuitable image of God, particularly defective for understanding natural evil.

On eschatology, Peacocke notes an analogy between our present insight about the end of life on earth (in some 5 billion years due to the sun turning into a red giant) and the apocalyptic predictions in the Bible. He then says:

> The basis of hope is therefore our trust that God will continue this relation [with his human creatures] and bring his purposes to fruition beyond even the disappearance of that part of the material cosmos, the Earth, in which he has been at work to achieve his ends. ... On this view, our destiny is in God's hands but our lives here and now are ours to direct, in his way, if we so choose.[35]

John Polkinghorne

Like Peacocke, John Polkinghorne (b. 1930) accepts *creatio ex nihilo* in a minimal sense, as saying that the material world sprang into being and is maintained in being by God's command alone.[36] In a later book, he says that *creatio ex nihilo* is merely a "metaphysical" statement, expressing the universe's inherent contingency. Nothing else existed to prompt or constrain the divine creative act. It certainly does not mean, he says, that God started things off by manipulating a curious kind of stuff called "nothing."[37] He rejects the idea of a quantum fluctuation in a vacuum as creation out of nothing, but on physical rather than on theological grounds. He notes that with the emergence of the world came space and time, for they are linked with matter in a way that was articulated scientifically by Einstein in his general theory of relativity. He also quotes Augustine: "There is no time before the world began. There is no space beyond this world, because without motion and change there is no time."[38]

Polkinghorne accepts continuing creation in the full sense of affirming a continuing creative interaction of God with the world the Creator holds in being. It is the immanent pole of divine creativity, while *creatio ex nihilo* is the transcendent pole.[39]

With respect to the problem of evil, he follows Irenaeus, saying, "The world's suffering is not gratuitous but a necessary contribution to some greater good which could only be realized in this mysterious way."[40] God does not will evil but allows it.[41] For moral evil, Polkinghorne chooses the "free-will defense," saying that a world of freely choosing beings is better than a world of perfectly programmed automata. For physical evil, he adopts a parallel "free-process defense": God permits the whole universe to be itself and is not the puppet master of either humans or matter. Saying that he stays with a relation between free-will and free-process defenses, he remarks, "It is the most perplexing of all the difficulties that confront the religious believer."[42]

On eschatology, Polkinghorne takes for a fact the gloomy prediction of science that the cosmos is condemned to eventual futility.[43] It makes an evolutionary optimism absurd. He does not seem to recognize that the gloomy scientific scenario is based on the assumption of a closed universe in which God has no influence. He says that the "matter" of the dying universe will be transformed into the new world, transmuted by God in the faithful action of cosmic resurrection. But wouldn't this come down to a second creation with the implication that the first creation would have been a failure? The new world, says Polkinghorne, will have new properties, consistent with the end of transience, death, and suffering, fully integrated with the divine life through the universal reconciliation brought about by the cosmic Christ. However, can we speak of "reconciliation" after the present universe has gone to complete degradation? Polkinghorne then claims that the new universe will become sacramental, infused with the divine life. I would suggest that the present world, as the visible sign of God's creative work, is sacramental, but that this cannot apply to the new world with the visible presence of God in it.

Mark Worthing

The science–theology dialogue is a main element in Mark Worthing's book on creation theology.[44] After a rather feeble defense of the scriptural basis of *creatio ex nihilo*,[45] he shows that a *nihil* is incompatible with physical theory.[46] Yet he retains the doctrine on the meager grounds that it is "an inescapable conclusion," because "a matter existing with God from all eternity is ruled out as constituting a radical spirit-matter dualism that Jewish and Christian theology has always rejected on biblical as well as philosophical grounds." He overlooks the fact that chaos is not matter, but a condition. He further claims that only a God who creates out of nothing can be considered to be transcendent, as if the God of Genesis 1 and 2 would lack transcendence. He feels that "the admission of 'matter' as existing independently of the divine activity would destroy the feeling of absolute dependence," as if falling back into chaos would not constitute absolute contingency. He cites process theology (see section 5.4) as an example of what we come to when rejecting *creatio ex nihilo*. Interestingly, he seems to turn the argument around when he argues for a divine creation from nothing because physics cannot explain an origin from *nihil*.[47]

Worthing accepts the idea of continuing creation, but as a form of divine sustenance, conservation, and providence, not as ongoing *creatio ex nihilo*.[48] Here appears another difficulty with *creatio ex nihilo*: since we do not see any evidence for creation from nothing in our present world, this is automatically seen as a nonrepeatable, initial event. Hence, many theologians do not wish to accept the idea of continuing creation, or they limit it to mere conservation of the once-created universe. This idea clashes with the evolutionary worldview described in chapter 2. Worthing realizes this problem when he says, "It is precisely in this non-static process that God sustains the universe." He reviews various physical theories and finds them unsuitable for explaining conservation. He also finds that classical and quantum physics offer no explanation of the concept of God's providence (general and special) beyond providing some metaphors. He mentions chaos theory (see chapter 7) but does not elaborate on it.

Worthing reviews past attempts to explain the problem of evil in the *ex nihilo* context[49] and rejects the idea that ours is "the best possible of all worlds" with evil as a necessary part of it. He recognizes a "striking and significant correspondence" (though not an identity) between evil and entropy, the physical concept of disorder. He quotes Philip Hefner: "Chaos provides the possibilities without which there can be no actuality; it is the womb of creativity and actuality ... Creation and chaos belong together by nature."[50] This comes very close to the concept of evil in my chaos theology (chapter 6.5).

Finally, Worthing studies the question of eschatology, confronting the somber scenarios for the demise of the universe and the hopeful message of theology.[51] He rejects the escape models of Freeman Dyson and Frank Tipler. But, like Polkinghorne, he does not seem to recognize that the scientific scenario is based on a closed universe without any external influence.

5.3 Teilhard de Chardin and process theology

The reason for bringing Teilhard de Chardin and process theology together in one section is that both offer a strongly evolutionary creation theology.

Teilhard de Chardin

The French Jesuit priest and geologist Pierre Teilhard de Chardin (1881–1955) proceeds from two essential principles: (1) Evolution is a process of union; and (2) Evolution becomes meaningful in humans.[52] On the first principle, he says the union of protons, neutrons, and electrons leads to atoms, first hydrogen, then helium, and eventually all ninety-two elements. Atoms unite in molecules, which provide a multitude of novel possibilities. Small molecules unite in large biomolecules (for instance, amino acids in proteins), which combine to form a living cell. Everything coming out of the process of evolution emerges as a higher level of being but then in turn becomes an element of some higher stage of union. For Teilhard, union comprises all sorts of links, from energetic links in the atom to personal links between humans. Every higher-level being is more than the sum of its lower-level components. Thus, a carbon atom in a brain cell is not only a carbon atom, but also participates in human thinking. God moves this process from matter to spirit, from Alpha to Omega, culminating in the cosmic Christ, the Omega, and making the universe a sacrament of his presence.

On the second principle, Teilhard says it is insufficient to explain evolution as a process of random mutations followed by natural selection. Although humans have evolved through the process of evolution, they alone have developed the capacity to think. In them, the real unifying force appears as consciousness, mind, soul. Teilhard feels that during evolution, matter loses its principal place to mind. He sees matter as having "spiritual potency," so it is more interesting to understand how the mind evolved than to understand the evolution of the bodily structures.

From this it will be clear that Teilhard supports a continuing creation in the fullest sense. He also seems to retain a *creatio ex nihilo* when elsewhere he speaks about a "creatable nothingness."[53] About evil he says that because his only purpose is to show how all things can help us to unite ourselves with God, there is no need to concern ourselves with evil deeds.[54] Our efforts, he writes, must be aimed at divinization of our activities. If we purify our intentions, then all our activities will be filled with God, and we shall attain mystical union.[55] He speaks about human passivity rather than sinfulness, which means that what is not done by us must be undergone.[56] But with God as our ally, we are always certain of saving our souls.[57] Imperfection, sin, and evil are to him mainly aspects of a retrograde step, which ceases to exist the further we penetrate into God.[58] The terms *reconciliation* and *redemption* do not appear in his writings.

Teilhard's optimistic evolutionary view also appears in his eschatology. He says that in the final stage, evil on earth will be reduced to a minimum; disease and starvation will be conquered by science; and hatred and internecine struggles will have disappeared in the ever-warmer radiation of Omega.[59] He concludes *The Phenomenon of Man* with an appendix on evil in a world in evolution.[60] In this appendix, he wonders whether there might perhaps be, in addition to the normal effect of evolution, an extraordinary effect of some catastrophe or primordial deviation. He considers original sin as the reaction of the finite to the creative act, as an expression in a single act of the perennial and universal law of imperfection operating in humankind in its development, and as the inevitable by-product of the unification process. In conclusion, I would say that Teilhard's ideas represent an overly optimistic, evolutionary mysticism that does justice neither to the biblical message about the cost of reconciliation nor to our experience of the reality of evil in the development of the world and humankind.

Process theology

Process theology is a creation theology based on the philosophy of A. N. Whitehead (1861–1947). It has four main tenets:

1. Life is found in the choice of novelty and in the quest for aesthetic enrichment.
2. God acts in this process as a localized "lure" opposing the move toward increasing entropy.
3. Change is not by chance but is an expression of a subjective aim at an unconscious level.
4. God is limited by allowing self-determination to the evolving universe. God is seen as developing within time, as realized through the evolution of the creation.[61]

Serious criticism can be leveled at this approach, particularly the proposed image of God. John Polkinghorne says, "The God of the Bible is involved in the world, but not tied to it to the extent that the process theologians suppose."[62] Keith Ward writes, "Whitehead has changed the 'cosmic tyrant', against whom he so strongly protests, into a 'cosmic sponge'."[63] A god who develops with and in his creation, and who only "lures" his creatures into evolving, is not the biblical God of the universe.

Alister McGrath asks, "What of natural evil? What of earthquakes, famines, and other natural disasters?"[64] To this question, the process theologians reply that God cannot force nature to obey the divine will or purpose; rather, God can only attempt to influence the process from within, by persuasion and attraction. They also claim that individual components of the world are likewise free to ignore divine attempts to influence or persuade them; these components are not bound to respond to God. Thus, God is absolved of responsibility for both moral and natural evil. To this, McGrath responds that God's transcendence is abandoned. God has become an entity in the process, God only outlives and surpasses other entities. Process theology also leaves unanswered two questions: How does the "lure" work, particularly at the lower levels, where physical patterns predominate over mental ones, and physical laws over freedom? And how can what is said about the becoming of a human person apply to a nucleotide? Hence, process theology does not seem to offer a valid evolutionary creation theology.

On evil, the process theologians state that God suffers with us in our suffering. But this can hardly be considered an explanation for the origin of evil, and it presents a picture of the rather powerless god of process theology. With regard to eschatology, it can be noted that Whitehead's eschatology is based on two premises: (1) the future is fully and radically open; and (2) progress occurs as a gradual improvement of human society by human efforts.[65] Thus, a change of our self-identity is required to allow our body to extend to all human beings and all creatures. In contrast to Teilhard's idea of movement toward the Omega Point, there is no assurance that the human species will move forward. Human life is more than a succession of events between birth and death. God aims at personal life as the condition of intensities of experience, God saves what can be saved, and death and perpetual perishing are not the last word. But there remains a profound mystery that even Whitehead's intuition could not penetrate.

5.4 Summary

In this chapter I consider how thirteen contemporary creation theologies are coping with the *creatio ex nihilo* doctrine and how they deal with the related topics of continuing creation, evil, and eschatology. Table 5.1 summarizes their positions. Of course, such a schematic presentation cannot do justice to the full scope of these theologies and the underlying arguments. Yet the inescapable conclusion is that there is a great divergence of views, whether or not the theology takes into account the modern scientific worldview.

With the exception of process theology, all the theologies accept the doctrine of *creatio ex nihilo*, although only Pannenberg and Moltmann hold to a strict *nihil*. The others employ some form of "mitigated" *nihil*, which in my opinion does not really differ from accepting an initial chaos. Moreover, it seems reasonable to assume that the Gnostics believed in true preexisting matter, so Theophilus and Irenaeus must have proposed a true *nihil*. Theologies that employ a mitigated *nihil* can thus be said to advance a revised form of *creatio ex nihilo*, coming close to creation from chaos.

Only Peacocke, Polkinghorne, Teilhard, and process theology accept the idea of "continuing creation" rather than "conservation" (*conservatio*). Those who deny continuing creation (Barth, Macquarrie, and Gunton) do not take note of cosmic and biological evolution. They assume, explicitly or implicitly, an initially complete and perfect creation, which was subsequently damaged by the human fall. Process theology emphasizes continuing creation but has hardly an "initial creation," because it has the Creator develop in and with the creation. Berkhof takes the strange position of

Table 5.1. Thirteen Creation Theologies

Author	Creatio ex nihilo	Continuing Creation	Conservatio	Evolution	Evil	Eschatology
Barth	+	-	+	-	*nihil*	justification
Brunner	(+)	+	+	(+)	cross	vague
Pannenberg	++	-	+	-	demons	biblical
Moltmann	+++	+	+	(+)	——	perfection
Berkhof	+	+ to fall	+ after fall	(+)	free will	biblical
Macquarrie	+	-	+	-	*nihil*, risk	vague
Gunton	++	-	+	-	fall	vague
Fergusson	+	+	-	(+)	vague	biblical
Peacocke	+	++	-	++	vague	vague
Polkinghorne	+	++	-	++	Irenaean	full decay
Worthing	++	(+)	+	(+)	entropy	full decay
Teilhard	++	++	-	++	passivity	Omega
Whitehead	0	++	-	++	freedom	vague

Key
+++ *full acceptance*
++ *limited acceptance*
+ *very limited acceptance*
(+) *questionable position*
– *nonacceptance*
0 *rejection*

limiting "continuing creation" to the period before the fall with "conservation" operating after this mythical event.

The wide diversity of positions on the subject of evil supports my claim that "evil" forms one of the major problems for the *creatio ex nihilo* doctrine (see chapter 4.5). Barth attributes evil to the *nihil*, seeing it as the counterforce to God. Brunner appeals to the cross. Pannenberg invokes demons acting through his "field of force." Berkhof ascribes moral evil to human freedom of will and to a "mysterious element of tragedy." Macquarrie describes evil as the "slipping back into nothing," due to the "risk" of creation and a "cosmic fall." Gunton considers the fall to be the cause of the evil in the world. Fergusson rejects the doctrine of original sin but can only describe evil as a "risk" of the freedom given by God to the creation. Peacocke speaks rather vaguely about natural evil being "a necessary prerequisite for the emergence of free, self-conscious beings," "random effects of chance," and "a suffering God." Polkinghorne takes the Irenaean approach that good must come from evil and uses a "free-will defence" for moral evil and a parallel "free-process defence" for natural evil. Worthing finds a "striking and significant correspondence" (though not an identity) between evil and entropy, the physical concept of disorder. Teilhard minimizes the problem of evil, using the term *passivity* for human sinfulness, and considers that evil will disappear in the "ever-warmer radiation of Omega." Process theology attributes evil to the freedom that a God who is merely "luring" creatures to fulfillment must leave to his creation.

On the topic of eschatology, there is also a wide diversity. For Barth, it all turns around "justification," indicating his anthropocentric view of creation. Moltmann focuses on "a final perfection" and "the eschatological glorification of human beings." Teilhard has his Omega Point to which God draws the evolving creation. Brunner, Pannenberg, Berkhof, and Fergusson stay rather close to the biblical view. Polkinghorne and Worthing believe in the full decay of the universe but neglect that the scientific prediction is based on the assumption of a closed universe to which God has no access. Macquarrie, Gunton, Peacocke, and process theology remain rather vague on eschatology.

It seems clear that contemporary creation theology is in a state of turmoil. In my opinion, this primarily results from the inadequacy of the *creatio ex nihilo* doctrine and, in many cases, from insufficient attention to the scientific worldview or its incorrect application. Against this background, I shall in the next chapter present a revised creation theology, which I call chaos theology.

6

Chaos Theology:
An Alternative Creation Theology

6.1 Why revise creation theology?

As I summarized in chapter 3, the stories in Genesis 1 and 2 and virtually all nonbiblical creation stories feature some kind of initial chaos. Furthermore, as I argued in chapter 4, the *creatio ex nihilo* doctrine, a late-second-century ad hoc refutation of the gnostic idea of creation from eternal evil matter by an evil demiurge, poses five serious problems: conceptual, biblical, scientific, theological, and related to the origin of evil. A review of thirteen contemporary creation theologies (in chapter 5) showed that all but one (process theology) retain *creatio ex nihilo*, but they do so to varying degrees, some of them seeming to pay only lip service to the doctrine. And there is great divergence on the related matters of continuing creation, evil, and eschatology. A major shortcoming is that *creatio ex nihilo* does not provide a solution to the problem of the origin of evil—it may even be said to have caused the problem. In addition, *creatio ex nihilo* doesn't appear to have been very fruitful in the subsequent development of Christian doctrine. Neither is it very helpful in the science–theology dialogue, since science cannot deal with "nothing." Process theology, the only one to reject the doctrine, does so without satisfactory arguments and with a dubious image of God.

These issues have led me to develop a revised creation theology, "chaos theology," in which I propose a return to the biblical idea of creation from an initial chaos.[1] In this chapter, I shall set forth this theology, which can be summarized in the following four points:

1. The initial creation was from a primeval chaos.
2. There is continuing creation with a remaining element of chaos.
3. The remaining chaos will be abolished and creation perfected on the last day.
4. Evil arises from remaining chaos.

The first three points are biblically supported, the fourth point is in my opinion a reasonable conclusion from them. In the next sections I present each point with the arguments for it. The chapter is then concluded with a discussion of some critical questions that have been raised about chaos theology.

6.2 Initial creation from primeval chaos

As I mentioned in chapter 3 (sections 3.3 and 3.4), both biblical accounts of creation—the earlier one in Gen 2:4b-25 and the later one in Gen. 1:1—2:4a—have God initiate creation from an unexplained primeval chaos, the Hebrew *tohu wabohu* in Genesis 1.[2] Chaos is thought to have existed before creation began, as concluded by Robert H. Pfeiffer, Theodor C. Vriezen, Claus Westermann, and others.[3] The very different descriptions of this primeval chaos (Gen 1:1-3 calls it "a formless void and darkness covered the face of the deep, while a mighty wind swept over the face of the waters"; Gen 2:4-6 a lifeless desert) indicate that the biblical authors are at a loss to define the initial chaos. Yet, for them it was neither the gnostic preexisting evil matter nor a *nihil* as in the second-century doctrine of *creatio ex nihilo*.[4] The idea of creation from a watery void also sounds in Ps 24:2: "for he has founded it [the earth] on the seas."

"In the beginning" (Gen 1:1) suggests that time begins when God with the commanding and powerful Word calls forth light on the first day. This idea was strongly expressed by Augustine: "There is no time before the world began. There is no space beyond this world, because without motion and change there is no time."[5] Big bang cosmology also assumes that time and space separated and commenced immediately after the initial explosion (chapter 2.2). "In the beginning" also suggests that God stands outside time. We as creatures are within time, as we are within the space of the universe, captives of both time and space. This means that we cannot meaningfully speak about what was before time and what is outside the universe in which we live. We can only say that at $t = 0$ there is chaos—a matterless chaos, according to cosmology—from which God creates the world.

Creation is initiated by God's commanding word: "Then God said, 'Let there be light'; and there was light" (Gen 1:3). This word was not spoken to anyone, because there were not yet any creatures.[6] It is a creative command, which cannot be executed by anyone except by God. It is not a magic word, like the word by which Marduk in *Enuma Elish* destroys and then creates again a garment by magic. It is more like the Egyptian theology of Memphis, which ascribes the creation of the world to the word of a god. It is God's powerful Word (Hebrew *dabar*, Greek *Logos*), echoed in John 1:1-4, which in terms of current cosmology would provide the energy required for the initial explosion and the rapid inflation of the early universe (see chapter 2.1). The light is not the warm light of the sun, which appears later (Gen 1:16-18), but the equivalent of the extremely energetic gamma radiation emerging from the big bang, from which the first particles are later produced and of which we see a weak remnant in the cosmic background radiation.

It is the first of three separations: light from darkness, heaven from waters, and land from sea (Gen 1:3-10). These find a parallel in current cosmology (chapter 2.2), which also has three separations at the beginning: time and space, the four fundamental forces (gravity, strong and weak nuclear forces, and electromagnetic force), and the elementary particles (electrons, quarks, and gluons). In both views, these separations set the stage for a process of ordering, leading to the appearance of the heavenly bodies, galaxies, stars, and planets, and on planet Earth, plants, animals, and humans. I use the term "initial creation" for the separation phase and the term "continuing creation" for the ordering phase (Gen 1:11-31).

6.3 Continuing creation and remaining chaos

In the biblical view, creation is seen as a continuing process, starting with the initial creation and continuing until its perfection on the last day (see chapter 3.7). The early church fathers Clement of Alexandria, Origen, Tertullian, Chrysostom, Gregory of Nyssa, and Augustine affirmed the idea of continuing creation.[7] Continuing creation implies that the present universe is not yet perfect. While the idea of *creatio ex nihilo* seems to lead many theologians to the assumption that *nihil* is exhausted by God in the initial creation, this is not necessarily the case for the primeval chaos in creation from chaos. The separations in the initial creation in Genesis 1 do not suggest that chaos was abolished, but rather that God pushed back chaos. The ordering in continuing creation implies a decrease but not necessarily a complete abolition of chaos.

Science can provide further insight into this. Continuing creation is paralleled by the scientific account of cosmic and biological evolution, which has been proceeding for 13.7 billion years since $t = 0$. Science employs the concept of entropy as the physical measure of disorder or chaos. Using the Boltzmann-Schrödinger equation for entropy, information theorist Tom Stonier has derived a new equation that relates the information content of the developing cosmos to its entropy.[8] According to Stonier's equation, there is an inverse relation between information content and entropy, such that at $t = 0$, the information content of the universe is zero, while the entropy (disorder) is infinite. Thereafter, during cosmic evolution, the information content increases, and the entropy decreases, indicating increasing order. This agrees with the insight obtained by cosmologists from quantum-gravity theory, which poses that at $t = 0$, there could be no information in the beginning universe.[9] Thus, science suggests that chaos was maximal at the beginning of the universe and has been steadily decreasing ever since but is not abolished until the end of time.

In theological terms, the primordial chaos is diminished but not abolished during the process of creation. Hence, there is remaining chaos in our world. The Old Testament offers ample evidence that the Jewish people recognized this as a threat. They symbolize remaining chaos as the "sea" (in some places, as Leviathan, the mythical sea monster)[10] because the sea was frightening for them as a desert people. They see God as battling this remaining chaos, as shown by the following Old Testament texts:

- "Am I the Sea, or the Dragon, that you set a guard over me?" (Job 7:12).
- "[God] alone stretched out the heavens and trampled the waves of the Sea" (Job 9:8).
- "By his power he stilled the Sea" (Job 26:12).
- "Who shut in the sea with doors when it burst out from the womb?" (Job 38:8).
- "Can you draw out Leviathan with a fishhook, or press down its tongue with a cord?" (Job 41:1).
- "Then the channels of the sea were seen, and the foundations of the world were laid bare at your rebuke, O LORD" (Ps 18:15).
- "You divided the sea by your might; you broke the heads of the dragons in the waters" (Ps 74:13).
- "You crushed the heads of Leviathan; you gave him as food for the creatures of the wilderness" (Ps 74:14).
- "When the waters saw you, O God, when the waters saw you, they were afraid; the very deep trembled" (Ps 77:16).
- "You rule the raging of the sea; when its waves rise, you still them" (Ps 89:9).
- "For he commanded and raised the stormy wind, which lifted up the waves of the sea" (Ps 107:25).
- "He made the storm be still, and the waves of the sea were hushed" (Ps 107:29).

- "The sea looked and fled; Jordan turned back" (Ps 114:3).
- "Why is it, O sea, that you flee? O Jordan, that you turn back?" (Ps 114:5).
- "When he assigned to the sea its limit, so that the waters might not transgress his command" (Prov 8:29).
- "The oracle concerning the wilderness of the sea. As whirlwinds in the Negeb sweep on, it comes from the desert, from a terrible land" (Isa 21:1). Chaos is here applied to the capture of Babylon either by Merodach-Baladin in 722 BCE or by Cyrus in 538 BCE.
- "On that day the LORD . . . will punish Leviathan . . . , and he will kill the dragon that is in the sea" (Isa 27:1)—an apocalyptic-eschatological vision.
- "By my rebuke I dry up the sea" (Isa 50:2).
- "I placed the sand as a boundary for the sea, a perpetual barrier that it cannot pass" (Jer 5:22).
- "Therefore thus says the LORD: I am going to defend your cause . . . . I will dry up her sea and make her fountain dry" (Jer 51:36).
- "And four great beasts came up out of the sea, different from one another" (Dan 7:3)—an apocalyptic vision in which evil is seen to arise from the sea.
- "He rebukes the sea and makes it dry" (Nahum 1:4).

In the New Testament, it is said of Jesus that he rebukes and calms the sea, that the sea obeys him, and that he walks on the sea, suggesting that the Son opposes and controls remaining chaos:

- "He said to them, 'Why are you afraid, you of little faith?' Then he got up and rebuked the winds and the sea; and there was a dead calm" (Matt 8:26).
- "He woke up and rebuked the wind, and said to the sea, 'Peace! Be still!' Then the wind ceased, and there was a dead calm" (Mark 4:39).
- "And they were filled with great awe and said to one another, 'Who then is this, that even the wind and the sea obey him?'" (Mark 4:41).
- "When he saw that they were straining at the oars against an adverse wind, he came towards them early in the morning, walking on the sea" (Mark 6:48).
- "When they had rowed about three or four miles, they saw Jesus walking on the sea . . . , and they were terrified" (John 6:19).

Twice the sea appears in an apocalyptic setting, in the latter text as the source of evil, as suggested in Dan 7:3:

- "There will be signs in the sun, the moon, and the stars, and on the earth distress among nations confused by the roaring of the sea" (Luke 21:25).
- "And I saw a beast rising out of the sea, having ten horns and seven heads; and on its horns were ten diadems, and on its heads were blasphemous names" (Rev 13:1).

These texts provide ample evidence that in both Old and New Testaments, the sea stands as a symbol for the remaining chaos in the world, and that in several places the Father and also the Son are portrayed as battling, subduing, and overcoming this chaos. In Luke 21:25 and Rev 13:1, it is indicated that this "battle" will last till the end of times.

This concludes the arguments for the second tenet of my chaos theology: continuing creation with a remaining element of chaos. However, two final remarks are in order:

1. In distinguishing between initial and continuing creation, I do not want to suggest that there are two separate types of creation. There is one uninterrupted process of creation ordained and guided by God, but with our present knowledge of cosmology, we might say that in the initial phase, God started the process and laid down the physical laws and fundamental constants guiding its further development. During the ensuing cosmic and biological evolution (continuing creation), God allowed a great degree of freedom while retaining the possibility of intervening where and when needed (chapter 7).
2. The idea of an initially perfect creation, damaged by a human fall and then preserved by God until "repairing" it on the last day, is both theologically and scientifically untenable. Theologically, because the Genesis 3 story is not a historical account, but a mythical explanation for the fact that all humans are prone to sin, to grasping for equality with God. The idea that human sinfulness could damage God's creation seriously overrates human capacity and underrates God's power. Scientifically, because in cosmic and biological evolution, we see clear progress to greater complexity with decreasing entropy. Only in the last few centuries does damage occur in the earthly ecosphere through human neglect and greed. However serious this may be for the future of humankind (see chapter 14), this has a negligible effect on the universe. Where the term *preservation* is used to express the dependency of creation on God, I prefer to use the term *contingency* (chapter 9, sections 9.4 and 9.5).

6.4 Remaining chaos abolished on the last day

In Rev 21:1 we read, "I saw a new heaven and a new earth . . . and the sea was no more." This is a vision of the perfection of the creation on the last day. The only explanation of the brief phrase *and the sea was no more* can be that at this point, the remaining chaos, symbolized as "sea," has definitively been abolished by the Creator who thus completes the creative process.[11] Then there will be no more death, mourning, crying, and pain (Rev 21:4). This is the third tenet of my chaos theology: remaining chaos will be abolished and creation will be perfected on the last day.

This idea is paralleled by the prediction from Stonier's equation described in the preceding section. However, it clashes with the prediction obtained by extrapolating big bang cosmology to the distant future (some 24 billion years from now).[12] This prediction presents the bleak picture of a full decay of the universe, the so-called big rip: All stars burn out and turn into neutron stars or black holes. These "evaporate" to a cloud of neutrons, which turn into quarks and gluons. Finally, these dematerialize into a cloud of photons. This outcome is a far cry from the "new earth" and "new heaven" of Rev 21:1. How can the biblical expectation and the cosmological prediction contrast so sharply? The answer is that the cosmological scenario is based on the assumption of a thermodynamically closed universe, meaning one without any outside influence. Under that assumption, the second law of thermodynamics prescribes an inexorable move toward ever higher entropy, toward ever greater disorder. Chaos wins! However, in the biblical scenario, the universe is thought to be open to the outside influence of God, who through the Son and the Spirit completes and perfects his creation (chapter 9.3). God wins!

Surprisingly, John Polkinghorne in *The God of Hope and the End of the World* seems to assume that the universe will go to full decay before God will bring about the new world.[13] This assumption is surprising because it calls into question the significance of God's present creation. How can one believe that God will allow the work of God's own hands to go to futility? Even when Polkinghorne says the "matter" of the dying universe (but a cloud of photons is not really "matter") will be transformed into the new world, transmuted by God in the faithful action of cosmic resurrection, wouldn't this amount to a second creation with the implication that the first creation had been a failure? I shall return to these eschatological issues in more detail in chapter 14. Here I confine myself to the claim that we live in an open universe, because God continues the creative work until, on the last day, the Creator will completely abolish remaining chaos and perfect the universe without letting it go to complete decay.

6.5 Evil arising from remaining chaos

The first three tenets of my chaos theology are fully supported by biblical evidence. There is less biblical support (except perhaps in Dan 7:3 and Rev 13:1) for the fourth tenet: evil in the world, both physical (natural disasters and disease) and moral (human evil), arises from remaining chaos in creation.

In chapter 4.5, I claimed that the problem of the origin of evil has remained insolvable in the context of *creatio ex nihilo*. As David Fergusson says, "The greatest difficulty facing any theology of creation is to provide an account of evil."[14] In chapter 8 I will survey the many attempts that have been made to provide a solution to this problem. The simple reason for this failure is that in creation out of nothing, the Creator inescapably becomes responsible for all that exists in the universe, including evil. The Gnostics at least had their evil demiurge and preexistent evil matter as an explanation, but an evil demiurge is unacceptable in Christian monotheism, and the assumption of uncreated matter is felt to violate God's omnipotence.

Can remaining chaos be the source of evil? In one and the same chapter of Revelation, it is proclaimed that in the new kingdom, remaining chaos ("the sea") will be no more (Rev 21:1) and that there will be no more death, mourning, crying, and pain (Rev 21:4). That the latter is the consequence of the former is strongly suggested by the phrase "the former things have passed away" at the end of verse 4.[15] How then does evil arise from remaining chaos? First, I consider both initial and remaining chaos as morally neutral. Chaos can give rise to creativity and freedom as well as to physical and moral evil.

In the case of physical evil—natural disasters and illness—it is not difficult to see that it can arise from chaos. Chaotic behavior of Earth's interior leads to earthquakes, volcanic eruptions, and tsunamis. Chaotic behavior of Earth's atmosphere leads to tornadoes, floods, and droughts. All of these cause immeasurable human suffering. In chapter 12 I argue that diseases like cancer and mental illness can be seen as an expression of remaining chaos in our body cells. In the case of moral evil, consider the words of Paul: "I do not understand my own actions. For I do not do what I want, but I do the very thing I hate" (Rom 7:15). This suggests to me that "chaotic thinking" or temptation leads us to evil behavior. I return to these matters in chapter 8.6 in more detail.

6.6 Usefulness of chaos theology for the science–theology dialogue

Chaos theology can advance the dialogue between the two worldviews of science and theology. While the Bible is certainly not meant to be a science textbook, it can be said, in the words of Old Testament scholar T. C. Vriezen, that "Gen. 1 shows marks of profound reflection in the field of religion as well as that of natural science."[16] To those who maintain that the Genesis 1 account is merely meant to proclaim that the universe was created by a sovereign God, I say that the author could then have limited himself to a single sentence. To me, it seems obvious that he was not only interested in the *why* question, but also in the *how* question, which nowadays is the province of science. It is therefore legitimate and useful to consider in the light of the Genesis 1 story the extent to which the description of the reality of our world by each worldview can be reconciled. In the preceding sections, I have already in several places used scientific insights to clarify biblical concepts, but here I consider some fundamental aspects.

Initial mystery

Both science and theology are confronted with initial mystery. The *tohu wabohu* in Gen 1:2 remains a mystery, as we are not informed about conditions and origin of this initial chaos. The same is the case for the "big bang" at $t = 0$ in cosmology. In the big bang theory, the entire course of 13.7 billion years of cosmic evolution can be calculated backward from the present state of the universe until 10^{-43} second after $t = 0$ (where 10^{-43} means 1 divided by 10^{43}). This time of 10^{-43} second is called Planck time. Although Planck time is a very small fraction of a second, nevertheless, it is a decisive gap. Extrapolation to $t = 0$ only leads to a "singular" point with an infinitely small, infinitely dense, and infinitely hot "mysterium." Some theorists describe the situation at and before $t = 0$ as a quantum vacuum with zero-point energy and fluctuations, in which pairs of particles and antiparticles arise and then annihilate each other (see chapter 2.2). Such a state would certainly qualify as a primordial chaos (but definitely not as a *nihil*). At $t = 0$, an extremely energetic fluctuation would then have caused the big bang from which creation started.

Separation and ordering

I have already mentioned (section 6.2) the parallel between the three separations in Gen 1:3-10 (light and darkness, water and heaven, earth and sea) and those of the big bang theory (time and space, the four fundamental forces, and the elementary particles). In both accounts, these separations set the stage for a process of ordering, which leads to galaxies, stars, and planets, and on planet Earth, plants, animals, and humans. In Genesis 1, it is God's creative Word that turns primordial chaos into created order (Gen 1:11-31). In chapter 9, I shall argue for a role of the Spirit in providing the information needed to guide the process. The sequence of the ordering process bears a striking resemblance to that assumed in cosmic and biological evolution, except that author P of Genesis 1 has the plants appear before the sun: P was apparently oblivious to the process of photosynthesis!

The element of physical and moral evil in our world is introduced by P in Gen 6:9-22 with the story of the flood, and by author J of the older creation account (Genesis 2) in the story of the fall (Genesis 3). As I previously explained, I attribute the presence of evil to the remaining chaos in creation.

Some other analogies can be mentioned.[17] The conclusion that time (our time) began with the big bang finds an analogy in Augustine's statement that the universe was created "with" rather than "in" time. The cosmological insight that the universe has no center has a counterpart in the theological insight that God is everywhere and not limited to one location. The fact that the entire cosmos was required to enable the emergence of humans on planet Earth is reflected in the unique place assigned to humans in Genesis 1.

Chaos and entropy

In section 6.3, I mentioned the parallel between the biblical idea of chaos and the physical concept of entropy, the measure of disorder or chaos. Primeval chaos compares to the entropy at $t = 0$, which Stonier's equation sets at infinity in agreement with cosmological theory. During the further development of the universe, the entropy declines, which parallels the ordering process in Genesis 1. The remaining chaos, symbolized as "sea," is paralleled by the fact that in Stonier's equation, the entropy does not reach zero during cosmic development. Only at the end of time does the entropy reach zero, which agrees with the remark in Rev 21:1 ("the sea is no more") that on the last day, remaining chaos is abolished.

Chaos and eschatology

The apparent clash between the scientific prediction of a universe going to full decay and the biblical expectation of the new kingdom after the removal of remaining chaos can be ascribed to the difference between an open and a closed universe. According to the second law of thermodynamics, the entropy of a closed system goes to maximal values, but this is not so when external energy and/or information enter the system, as we may expect from the Creator who makes his creation develop and eventually transforms it into the new creation. This explains why we don't have to accept Polkinghorne's idea of a full decay of the present universe before God will bring forth the new creation, an idea that poses serious difficulties for the doctrine of redemption by Jesus Christ.

Contingency of creation

Both theology and science recognize that the universe is "contingent," which means dependent, endangered, and accidental. Here I confine myself to a brief comment, but in chapter 9, I shall go into more detail. Theologians have always been aware of the contingency of the creation, which is implied in the biblical account of creation as coming about by the creative Word of God. If God would withdraw this Word, the universe would revert to . . . what? To "non-being" or "nothing," says Paul Tillich, who holds to *creatio ex nihilo*.[18] However, this idea clashes with the law of conservation of mass/energy. Once you have a universe made up of mass and energy and governed by physical laws, it cannot disappear into nothingness. So here we encounter another problem for *creatio ex nihilo*. Chaos theology can simply substitute "chaos" for "nothing" and speak about "falling back into chaos," in which case there is no violation of the law of conservation of mass/energy.

Science has become aware of the contingency of the cosmos much more recently (chapter 9.4). We now know that only the exquisite fine-tuning of some twenty-five fundamental physical constants (for example, strengths of the fundamental forces; mass and charge of the elementary particles) has permitted the development of the universe and the formation of planet Earth on which life could arise and evolve. We know that life on Earth is threatened by the ecological crisis and by asteroid impacts. This means that we live in a universe that is extremely "accidental" and also threatened—a contingent universe.

Progressiveness and purpose in evolution

Both believing and nonbelieving scientists must admit that science by its nature cannot deal with the concepts of progressiveness and purpose in the evolutionary process, for which in recent years the term "intelligent design" is unfortunately often used (chapter 9.7).[19] When I see in this process the purposeful action of a loving Creator, I make a theological rather than a scientific statement. The same is true when I explain the "improbability" of our universe as the result of purposeful design by the Creator. A scientist should, however, always look for a scientific explanation before invoking a theological interpretation. And it must be admitted, science can bring us very far nowadays in understanding the evolution of our universe and its creatures.

The late evolutionary biologist Stephen Gould vehemently argued against recognizing any form of progressiveness in biological evolution. He wrote, "Three billion years of unicellularity, followed by 5 million years of intense creativity and then capped by more than 500 million years of variation on set anatomical themes can scarcely be read as a predictable, inexorable or continuous trend toward progress or increasing complexity."[20] He is speaking here about the so-called Cambrian explosion in evolution. If he had merely said that as a biologist he cannot use the concept of progress, because it is a value judgment, then he would have been in his right. However, in denying a trend toward increasing complexity in evolution, he is plain wrong, as everyone must admit that mammals are more complex than bacteria.

Dale Russell notes that in recent decades, evolutionary biologists have come to the conclusion that there is a progressive pattern present in evolution.[21] Simon Conway Morris argues that—in contrast to Gould's claim— if evolution were to be repeated, it would have the same outcome.[22] He illustrates this with examples of "evolutionary convergence," such as the same body form and swimming behavior of the dolphin, descending from an ancestor of the dog, and the ichthyosaur, descending from a lizard. Such convergence is due to the physical constraints operating in evolution.

6.7 Some critical questions considered

In many discussions I have had about chaos theology, six critical questions have been raised that deserve to be answered:

1. *Can one abandon the doctrine of* creatio ex nihilo, *which has been nearly universally held for 1,800 years?* As an Anglican, I hold to the *tripos* of Bible, Tradition (as expressed in the ancient creeds), and Reason (with which to consider the first two). I have shown that *creatio ex nihilo* is not biblical and is not contained in the ancient creeds. It is thus part of the ongoing tradition of the church, which is not unchangeable.

2. *Does creation from initial chaos reintroduce gnostic dualism?* I do not think so. First, I do not invoke a demiurge but maintain with Genesis 1 the absolute sovereignty of the one God who creates by the authoritative Word. Second, initial chaos is entirely different from the gnostic eternal matter; it is an immaterial condition rather than a matter (sections 6.2 and 6.3). Other types of dualism, including those between order and chaos, good and evil, belief and unbelief, light and dark, particle and wave, are simply characteristics of our universe.

3. *Who created initial chaos, if not God?* This is the type of question we cannot meaningfully ask, because here we encounter initial mystery. Augustine supposedly replied to someone who asked him what God did before creating, "Then he created hell for people who pry into mysteries."[23] Some, in order to force *creatio ex nihilo* into Gen 1:1-2, read into this text that God first created "chaos" from nothing, and then from this chaos, the universe.[24] However, this reading, already unlikely on the basis of textual study, places God's creative ability in doubt.

4. *Is there any difference between an immaterial initial chaos and* nihil? Yes, there is. Not so much in the initial state, which remains a mystery for both science and theology. But important differences are that *nihil* is not biblical, that it saddles us with the problem of evil, and that it hinders the science–theology dialogue, because science knows no *nihil*. Furthermore, *creatio ex nihilo* has not contributed to further doctrinal development (Christology, eschatology).

5. *Am I embracing process theology in my chaos theology?* True, the process theologians also reject *creatio ex nihilo*[25] and accept continuing creation, but they base themselves on Whitehead's philosophy rather

than on biblical evidence. Although they describe continuing creation as "a continuing struggle between order and chaos," they do not use this insight to understand the origin of evil as I do, but offer the unsatisfactory notion of "God suffering with us in our suffering."[26] In particular, I emphatically reject their notion of an evolving creator, who is merely acting as a goad to novelty and whose knowledge is dependent on the decisions made by the worldly actualities.[27]

6. *Does the idea of God battling remaining chaos diminish God's power?* I feel that a God who is battling remaining chaos till the final victory on the last day (a thoroughly biblical belief, as shown in section 6.3) is more powerful than a Creator who allows the initial creation to be spoiled by wayward humans, as assumed by those who believe in "preservation." "Battling" is the way the Old Testament authors speak about God's handling of the "sea" and is merely our anthropomorphic way of expressing God's action in the world.

It can be said that chaos theology does not suffer from the problems that I found for *creatio ex nihilo* in chapter 4.5. It rests on a solid biblical basis. It presents no great conceptual difficulties, particularly when taking into account the insights from cosmology. It is in harmony with our scientific insights into cosmic and biological evolution. Its theological formulation does not present great problems. It offers an explanation for the origin of both physical and moral evil that does not make God responsible or require the introduction of a Satan or demiurge. And it offers new insights into the doctrines of God, Christ, Spirit, salvation, and eschatology (see chapters 9, 10, and 14).

6.8 Summary

This chapter presents the four basic tenets of chaos theology with supporting evidence. The first is initial creation from primordial chaos. God creates with the powerful Word from an unexplained primordial chaos, which is neither gnostic evil matter nor a *nihil.* Time begins at this moment, as is also assumed in cosmology, which means that we are captives of time. Initial creation consists of three separations, which find a parallel in cosmology.

The second tenet is continuing creation with remaining chaos. A continuing creation process is supported in the Old and New Testaments and finds a parallel in cosmic and biological evolution. Arguments against the alternative view of preservation are presented. There is also ample biblical evidence for the idea of remaining chaos, symbolized as sea (or the sea monster Leviathan) and for seeing God as battling it. Parallels can be seen in cosmology and information theory, which both suggest a very high entropy (physical measure of disorder) at $t = 0$, decreasing during cosmic development but never reaching zero until the end of time.

The tenet that remaining chaos is abolished and creation perfected on the last day is supported by Rev 21:1 ("I saw a new heaven and a new earth . . . and the sea was no more") and Rev 21:4 (no more death, mourning, crying, and pain). This is in sharp conflict with the cosmological prediction that, in the end, the universe will go to complete decay. However, this is based on the assumption of a closed universe, while biblical eschatology assumes God's influence—in other words, an open universe.

The final tenet, that evil arises from remaining chaos, is suggested by the apocalyptic texts of Dan 7:3 and Rev 13:1, as well as by the combination of Rev 21:1 and 4. Physical evil from earthquakes and volcanic eruptions is due to chaotic behavior of Earth's interior; that from tornadoes, floods, and droughts to chaotic behavior of Earth's atmosphere; and that from disease to chaotic processes in our body cells. Moral evil can be seen as arising from chaotic thinking as expressed in Paul's words in Rom 7:15 and reflected in temptation.

The usefulness of chaos theology for the science–theology dialogue is illustrated for the topics of initial mystery, separation and ordering, chaos and entropy, chaos and eschatology, and contingency of creation. The last section of the chapter answers some critical questions.

7

Chaos Theory and Chaos Events

7.1 How does God act in continuing creation?

The theological argument for a continuing creation, scientifically observed in cosmic and biological evolution (chapter 6.3), raises the question of how God is interacting with the evolving creation. Much of this process can increasingly be explained scientifically as a natural process, based on energy, information, and the physical laws laid down in the initial creation, unfolding seemingly without the need for further divine intervention. However, there is also the awareness, in theology and in science, of the "contingency" of creation, that is, its being dependent, endangered, and accidental, as I will discuss later (chapter 9.4).

Biblical authors describe God's action in the world either in an anthropomorphic way, as a human influencing his environment, or in a mythical way, through angels, demons, and beasts. What can science say about God's action in the world? It seems reasonable to assume that God's intervention in the evolving creation must involve physical processes, about which science should be able to provide insight. Classical Newtonian physics left little room for divine intervention after initial creation: once the universe had been set in motion, it would develop in predetermined fashion according to the physical laws. This view has changed greatly with the advent of quantum theory and chaos theory in the twentieth century.

In the science–theology dialogue, quantum events, self-organization, and chaos events have all been invoked as means whereby God might influence the evolving creation. After considering the three propositions (sections 7.2–7.7), I cast my lot with chaos events. Finally, I consider the concept of determinism, which is widely used in discussions of God's action in the world but often leads to confusion (section 7.8).

7.2 Does quantum theory offer an answer?

Essence of quantum theory

When we come down to the microlevel of atoms, deviations from Newtonian law appear. This was first discovered by Max Planck in 1900 for heat radiation. He found that the observed spectral energy distribution of this radiation could not be explained in terms of classical physics. In order to fit the experimental data, he had to assume that heat is radiated in small packages, called quanta. The energy of a quantum (ΔE) is equal to the product of the frequency of the radiation (ν) and a constant, now called Planck's constant (h):

$$\Delta E = h \times \nu$$

The Planck constant is very small (6.62×10^{-34} joule-second), so the quanta are also very small. At the higher energy levels we meet in daily life, we do not notice the quantization of energy, and classical physics applies.

Next came the discovery by Niels Bohr in 1913 that the spectral lines emitted by heated atoms cannot be calculated in terms of classical physics. He chose hydrogen, because it is the simplest atom, made up of one proton with one orbiting electron. In order to calculate its spectral lines, Bohr had to assume that the electron could orbit only at certain discrete distances from the proton nucleus. Absorption of a quantum of energy makes the electron jump to the next-higher orbit. When the electron falls back into the lower orbit, a photon with the same energy is emitted, producing one line in the hydrogen spectrum. This means that electron orbits are quantized (the energy difference between the orbits representing quanta of energy) and that light can behave as a stream of particles, called photons. In other phenomena, such as diffraction and interference, light behaves like a wave. It is now recognized that light propagates as a wave but interacts with matter as a particle stream. Conversely, when particles such as electrons are moving at high speed, they behave as a wave, as shown by the electron beam in an electron microscope. However, particle and wave behavior cannot be observed simultaneously. This particle–wave duality is called the "complementarity principle."

When Erwin Schrödinger in 1925 developed an equation for the wavelike character of particles, he obtained a probability, rather than an exact site for the particle. In other words, an electron orbiting an atomic nucleus appears to be spread out over space in a probability curve, with the highest probability of its location being the actual orbit. Nevertheless, his equation can accurately predict the energy levels of the hydrogen atom, and thus its spectral lines.

Another aspect of quantum behavior is presented by the "uncertainty principle," formulated in 1927 by Werner Heisenberg. This principle states that the uncertainties in the position (Δp) and in the velocity (ΔV) of a particle cannot both be reduced at will, at the same time, even in theory:

$$\Delta p \times \Delta V = h$$

(where h is the Planck constant). When the position is measured more exactly, Δp goes down, but then ΔV will go up; that is, the velocity becomes less exact. To illustrate this, let us say we want to determine both position and velocity of a moving electron with maximal accuracy. We would then use a microscope to determine its position. Since the resolution of a microscope is limited by the wavelength of the light used for observation, we employ an electron microscope, which uses a beam of high-speed electrons instead of light. This can easily provide a hundredfold higher resolution. However, the collision of electrons of the beam with the targeted electron will change the latter's speed, and even its direction.

The uncertainty principle also applies to energy (ΔE) and lifetime (Δt) of an excited state (for instance, an orbiting electron lifted to a higher orbit by the energy of an absorbed photon):

$$\Delta E \times \Delta t = h$$

This equation will reappear later in this chapter when I discuss chaos theory and chaos events (section 7.4).

The phenomenon of probability spreading of particles and the uncertainty principles, in combination with relativity theory, have led to the development of quantum field theories in which an electron is considered as a local ripple in a single cosmic electromagnetic field. This may help to explain the mysterious phenomenon of "entanglement" (the mutual influence between two distant particles through quantum information), which is currently being used in the development of a quantum computer and quantum network.[1]

Thus, it can be said that Newtonian exactness and unambiguity at human scales change to the probability and uncertainty of quantum behavior at atomic and subatomic levels. This has led some authors to speak of two different worlds: the world of classic behavior and the world of quantum behavior. However, recent experiments indicate that a transition between the two types of behavior can be elicited when relatively large systems are used. In one experiment, a stream of buckyballs (hollow spheres of seventy carbon atoms) was aimed at a grating.[2] The temperature of the buckyballs was controlled by means of a laser beam. At 1,000°K (equal to 727°C), the stream of buckyballs showed interference, indicating wave behavior, thus quantum behavior. When the temperature was raised to 3,000°K, the interference disappeared, indicating transition to classic behavior. A transition in the opposite direction, from classic to quantum behavior, has nearly been reached in experiments with a vibrating microfiber (0.2 micrometer in diameter, 8 micrometers long, kept at 0.06°K).[3] The authors of this study expect to reach quantum behavior by using a still smaller fiber or by further decreasing the temperature. An experimentally induced, smooth transition from particle-like to wavelike behavior of light also has been achieved.[4]

Does God act through quantum events?

In the volume *Quantum Cosmology and the Laws of Nature: Scientific Perspectives on Divine Action*, several contributors consider the possibility of God acting through quantum events, but unfortunately none of them explains how this would operate.[5] William P. Alston claims, "Because of quantum indeterminism God can act without violating physical laws, and . . . such acts, beginning at the subatomic level, can 'snowball' so as to make a difference at the macroscopic level" (pp. 185–206), without saying how they could "snowball." George Ellis sees quantum indeterminacy as providing a basis for divine inspiration (pp. 363–99) but again does not explain how. John Polkinghorne first describes chaos theory and then states that quantum physics provides similar insights, but he warns that we ought not to confuse randomness with freedom (pp. 429–40).

In the sequel volume, *Chaos and Complexity: Scientific Perspectives on Divine Action*,[6] Nancey Murphy states, "If God is to be active in all events, then God must be involved in the most basic of natural events, the level of quantum phenomena." She asserts, "At the quantum level it is impossible to know exactly when particles will act" (p. 340). She gives the example of a billiard ball, suggesting, "All atoms in the ball might go on a spree, moving it without outside force," so God can act by the intentional orchestration of many micro-events (pp. 344–45). Murphy bases her assertion on "the currently accepted supposition of indeterminacy at the quantum level" (p. 354). Thomas Tracy says he "finds quantum theory more help-ful than chaos theory," but, like Murphy, he bases this view only on the "indeterminacy" of quantum events (pp. 289–324). Finally, George Ellis cautiously agrees with Murphy, saying, "Quantum uncertainty; we do not know what it is; but it is linked with free will and morality" (p. 371). Also, "the nexus of interaction is quantum events" (p. 389), and "the necessity of microscopic uncertainty in physical laws virtually becomes a prediction of the understanding attained" (p. 395). In this questionable statement, he speaks about the "uncertainty" of quantum events rather than "inde-terminacy," the term used by Murphy and Tracy, but he provides no more explanation than they do.

The problem we face here is that there is no evidence that quan-tum events at the microlevel can have an effect on the human or cosmic macrolevels. We don't see a billiard ball suddenly move across the green cloth without application of any external force. Not so much because God doesn't play billiards, but because the quantum movements of the particles in the ball cancel each other. Compare this with the Brownian movements of small particles suspended in a fluid, which we can observe under the microscope. They go randomly in every direction but never in a concerted way in one direction. So they cancel each other and don't make the fluid move out of the vessel. We don't know any mechanism by which quantum effects on the microlevel could be magnified to be effec-tive at the macrolevel. This is the reason why Arthur Peacocke[7] and John Polkinghorne[8] reject the idea that God might interact with the creation through quantum events. Ian Stewart comments, "Quantum 'indetermi-nacy' is not a sign of anything irreducibly probabilistic about the universe, but a sign of the inescapable ignorance of the observer."[9]

Another consideration is that the fundamental equation in quantum theory, the Schrödinger equation, is linear. Therefore, it will not lead to cha-otic behavior, as the nonlinear equations of chaos theory do (section 7.4).

7.3 Self-organization

A recently much used and, I am afraid, abused concept in the science–theology dialogue is that of self-organization.[10] The first problem one meets when reading articles and books on the topic is the lack of a clear definition and good examples. Self-organization is, therefore, easily con-nected with very divergent topics, including design theory (pro and con), chaos theory, evolution, human behavior, earthquakes, and more. Peter Kirschenmann distinguishes between self-organization, where systems are organized out of preestablished elements, and autopoiesis, which would occur in "self-productive systems, whose components are themselves created in organized superstructures."[11] As an example of autopoiesis, he mentions "the special arrangements of molecules that make up the membrane of a cell." This is an unfortunate choice, because it falls under his definition of self-organization, rather than autopoiesis. The phospholipid bilayer making up the cell membrane is formed spontaneously without any cells present when one shakes a small amount of phospholipids in salt solution in a test tube: myriads of vesicles composed of a phospholipid bilayer membrane are formed within a minute! As I mentioned in chapter 2.4, this phenomenon may have played an important role in the origin of life.

Biochemists recognize three important cases of self-organization, all dealing with spontaneous formation of a specific spatial structure: the double helix of DNA, specific conformations of protein molecules, and the phospholipid bilayer. Each one depends on weak interactions (hydrogen bonds) between components or between components and water, which ultimately rests on the atomic structures of the biologically important elements and electromagnetic forces. The specific spatial structures arise spontaneously in cells as well as in the test tube because they are favored energetically. Other forms of self-organization in the cell occur in the formation of ribosomes (site of protein synthesis) and the cytoskeleton of protein filaments. All these forms of self-organization are of crucial importance for life, because these biomolecules and structures can carry out their assigned function only when they are in their specific conformation and configuration. Misfolding of proteins, for instance, can lead to a variety of diseases, including Alzheimer's disease.[12]

Limiting myself to these well-defined types of molecular self-organization (the only ones I know of), I can draw some conclusions about their theological significance:

- Self-organization is a spontaneous process that doesn't require any external stimulus.
- It has been operating ever since DNA, proteins, and phospholipids were first formed during prebiotic evolution.
- Since then, it has existed in all living and extinct species, which means that it cannot have favored one animal or plant species over another and thus has not played a major role in evolution, contrary to what Stuart Kauffman claims.[13]

- Self-organization has probably played a role in the competition between new molecules arising in the prebiotic stage.
- It has nothing to do with "anthropic principles" (chapter 9.5) and does not provide an argument for or against the Intelligent Design hypothesis (see chapter 1.4).
- It doesn't support process theology, as Palmyra Oomen claims in her "second order design" idea,[14] and it is even less likely to be involved in human behavior.[15]
- Gregersen's idea that self-organization plays a role in the eschatological process[16] cannot stand, since it may merely help to produce and maintain life in the present world but cannot be expected to bring about a new world with resurrected life.

My theological assessment of molecular self-organization is that it is a consequence of the marvelously successful initial conditions: the physical laws and the precise set of fundamental constants that God laid down at the very beginning of creation, conditions that have made possible the entire process of continuing creation. However, self-organization doesn't provide a locus for God's action in continuing creation.

7.4 Chaos theory and chaos events

In contrast to so-called quantum events and self-organization, which do not seem to provide feasible mechanisms for the action of God in the world, I think chaos theory and the so-called chaos events provide a much likelier mechanism.[17] First, I must caution that the meaning of the word *chaos* used here is entirely different from that in chaos theology: chaos refers to "disorder" in chaos theology but to "unpredictability" in chaos events. However, it appears that the two types of chaos may be linked (section 7.7).

Chaos theory is a physical theory that has developed only since the 1970s, when computers began to be widely used. This theory recognizes that many physical, chemical, and biological systems are governed by nonlinear dynamic equations for their development in time. The following equation is a typical example of such a nonlinear equation:

$$x_{n+1} = k \times x_n(1 - x_n)$$

This equation can be explained by using the example of the propagation of a moth colony.[18] In that case, n and $n + 1$ indicate successive generations of moths, and x represents the number of moths in a given generation. The proportionality factor k may represent the fertility level of the moths, which remains unchanged for several generations. The number of moths (x_{n+1}) is understandably proportional to the size of the preceding generation (x_n). But it can also be adversely affected by the size of the colony when an oversized population suffers shortages of food and spread of disease. This effect is expressed by the factor $(1 - x_n)$. The factor k may gradually change in time as the fertility level is affected by a gradual altering of the environment. For a given number of moths in generation n, the number of moths in future generations may be calculated for changing values of k. This practically necessitates the use of a computer.

From these calculations, we find a curve as shown in Figure 7.1. For values of k from 1.0 to 3.0, we have a single curved line. At $k = 3.0$, the line bifurcates, and at $k = 3.45$, both legs of the fork bifurcate again, and so on. At $k = 3.57$, there is an infinite number of bifurcations; the system has become fully chaotic. The computer plot shows that at a bifurcation, the population size may go up or down, but it does not tell us which leg of the fork will actually be followed, the one toward higher values of x or the one toward lower values. The system has become unpredictable for us.

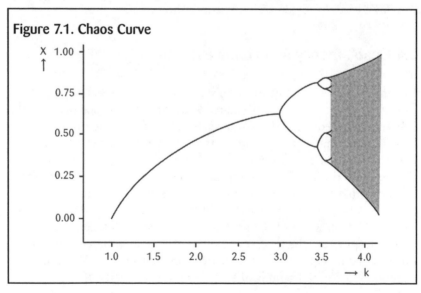

Figure 7.1. Chaos Curve

As there is no energy difference between the two legs, they have equal probability. This condition is like that of a bead at the top of a perfectly smooth wire in the shape of an inverted U. There is an equal probability of the bead sliding down either leg. To the human observer, the system has become fully unpredictable, not through lack of information on the observer's part, but by being inherently unpredictable.[19] The curve with all its bifurcations is fully "deterministic" in the sense of observing natural law, but the moth colony can take only one of the two paths at each fork. We cannot predict which leg it will take, since there is no energy difference between them. So the natural system becomes unpredictable (though not violating natural law) at each bifurcation point. A chaos event occurs.

7.5 Examples of chaos events

Do chaos events really happen in the natural world? First of all, we have to bear in mind that a plot like that in Figure 7.1 represents a model that approximates reality but cannot take into account all factors that may influence a natural system. Furthermore, testing the model once the system has become chaotic is impossible: the computer plot describes all courses that the system may follow, while a natural system like our moth colony can obviously follow only one course at a given time. Within these limitations, confirmation of the occurrence of chaotic behavior has been obtained in a number of cases.

Celestial systems with more than two objects are subject to nonlinear dynamics. For our solar system, this has been worked out by means of a computer simulation.[20] The current distance between the sun and Earth has been determined to be 150 million kilometers with an uncertainty of only 1 kilometer. The computer simulation shows that this uncertainty of 1 kilometer will increase in the astronomically short time of 95 million years to 150 million kilometers. This is not due to a change in orbital radius, but to variation in eccentricity of an elliptical orbit.[21] Therefore, at this moment, we cannot predict whether 95 million years from now, Earth will collide with the sun, be twice as far away from it as at present, or be somewhere in between. Neither extreme may ever come about, but the point is that we cannot predict the distance between the sun and Earth after 95 million years from now.

Another example is the weather: With all our advances in observation and computation, we are still unable to predict the weather for more than about a week ahead. After that, it becomes unpredictable through chaos events. As John Stanford says, "[The forecast] is extremely sensitive to the starting conditions, so much so that it may not even prove possible to predict weather accurately beyond a week or two, due to the fundamental complexities of chaotic dynamics."[22] Therefore, chaos theory is now commonly used to improve medium- and long-term weather fore-casts and is used in hurricane modeling for forecasting and, hopefully, finding ways to divert hurricanes from population centers.[23]

Chaos events may also be operating in cases of so-called chance events in evolution. An example is the Cambrian evolutionary explosion, when, after 3 billion years of evolution of unicellular life, there arose 540 million years ago in a mere 5 million years the ancestors of all currently existing life-forms.[24] Peter Smith acknowledges that random mutation in evolution may involve chaos events: "If similar environmental trig-gers always produced the same mutation, then evolution would be even slower than it is."[25]

Smith also suggests that our brains may well be among the chaotic systems to be found in the world: "The mathematical analysis of signal propagation in neural nets together with some suggestive experimen-tal work indicates that certain states of the brain may well evolve with a non-linear, chaos-prone, dynamics."[26] From experiments involving the balancing of a stick on a finger, scientists have concluded that the rapid, involuntary movements of the stick (faster than a conscious reflex reac-tion) result from electric noise in the nervous system, which has a chaotic component.[27]

In two cases, human control of chaotic behavior has been found possible. The first case involves turbulent flow. When helium is cooled to 0.001°K (above the absolute zero of −273°C), there is no friction, and rotating the vessel in which the helium is contained will not make the fluid rotate.[28] But when the temperature is lowered to between 0.0008°K and 0.0004°K, turbulence occurs, indicating chaotic behavior. This condi-tion may also describe the behavior of the rotating neutron "fluid" inside neutron stars.

The other case involves the movement of electrons through a semi-conductor device by means of an applied voltage.[29] At certain discrete voltages, the diffusion of the electrons becomes chaotic, as indicated by a large increase in the current flow. The chaotic diffusion can be switched on and off abruptly by manipulating the voltage. The extreme sensitivity of the phenomenon may provide a new switching method for electronic and photonic devices, permitting the development of novel devices.

These examples lend support to the idea that chaos events are real and have a wide occurrence on a cosmic scale, on our scale, and possibly even on a quantum scale.[30] They make the universe unpredictable and at the same time flexible and open to novelty. The last two examples show that chaos events are open to human control once the right parameter has been found and is set to the right values (such as temperature in the helium experiment and voltage in the electron diffusion experiment).

7.6 Can God act through chaos events?

The crucial point is that there is no energy difference between the legs of a bifurcation. Therefore, a minute influence, such as the infusion of a small amount of information, may "nudge" the system to follow one leg of the fork rather than the other. I suggest that in these events God can act, if God chooses to do so, through information input by the Holy Spirit without violating any physical law. This conclusion has previously been stated in *Chaos and Complexity*, with different degrees of caution, by Arthur Peacocke and John Polkinghorne.[31]

Yet, in the same volume, Willem Drees argues that it is physically impossible.[32] First, he says that if God were to act without input of energy, the action would be infinitely slow according to the Heisenberg uncertainty relation for energy (ΔE) and lifetime (Δt) of an excited state, mentioned in section 7.2:

$$\Delta E \times \Delta t = h$$

(where h is the Planck constant). For $\Delta E = 0$, the time Δt would become infinite, and an infinitely slow action will be ineffective, as energetic disturbances will have changed the situation by then. Second, Drees points out that information input always requires some energy expenditure:

$$\Delta E = \Delta I \times k_B \times T \times \ln 2$$

(where ΔI is the information input, k_B is the Boltzmann constant, and T is the absolute temperature in degrees Kelvin).

However, Drees does not calculate these equations. I have done so, and I come to a different conclusion. The minimum information input required to influence a chaos event (+1 or –1) is $\Delta I = 1$, the Boltzmann constant k_B is 1.38×10^{-16} erg per degrees Kelvin, T may be set at 300°K (equal to 27°C), and the natural logarithm of 2 is $\ln 2 = 0.6932$. Using these values, the energy required is as follows:

$$\Delta E = 3.3 \times 10^{-14}\,\text{erg} = 0.69 \times 10^{-21}\,\text{gram-calorie}$$

Substituting the calculated value of ΔE in the Heisenberg equation (where the Planck constant $h = 6.62 \times 10^{-27}$ erg-second), we solve for the time elapsed:

$$\Delta t = 2.0 \times 10^{-13}\,\text{second}$$

This tiny fraction of a second represents a speed that is 10 to 100 times faster than the fastest chemical reaction.

The very small amount of energy required for the insertion of one bit of information (0.69×10^{-21} gram-calorie, which is less than 1 percent of the energy of a quantum of visible light) could be withdrawn as heat from the immediate environment. Assuming that the rate of heat conduction is limited to the speed of light (3×10^{10} centimeters per second), a sphere of only 1.4×10^{-8} cubic centimeter would be accessible for heat extraction within this time. The temperature decrease within this sphere would then be about 10^{-14} °C, an undetectable effect with our present instrumentation.[33]

In personal correspondence, Drees agrees that my calculations are correct. But, he says, this occurrence would violate the law of conservation of energy. I do not see how this could be the case. Any time I insert a bit of information in my computer, the energy required for this is extracted from the electric current running in the computer, presumably without any violation of the law of conservation.

I conclude from these calculations that it is physically possible for God to influence a chaos event without violating any physical law. However, it is unlikely that we shall ever be able to "catch" God influencing a chaos event. Apart from the very small energies and times involved, we simply don't know the various parameters of the affected system with sufficient accuracy to be able to detect such intervention. Only in hindsight can we surmise that perhaps God has been at work in this way. Take the earlier case of the distance between sun and Earth (section 7.4). For the 4.5 billion years that the solar system has existed, this distance has not changed appreciably. As it is a nonlinear system, subject to the occurrence of a chaos event, it seems that God must on numerous occasions have influenced the system so as to keep the Earth at a safe, constant distance from the sun to allow the development and maintenance of life.

The reasons that so few as yet recognize the importance of chaos events for God's action in the world seem to me to be that chaos theory is of relatively recent date, it is rather complex, and the widespread occurrence of chaos events is only beginning to be understood. As Ian Stewart says, "Chaos teaches us that anybody, God or cat, can play dice deterministically [meaning in accordance with physical law], while the naïve onlooker imagines that something random is going on."[34] He adds later, "Maybe there's no such thing as a genuinely random event. All is determined, but we're too stupid to see the pattern."[35] John Barrow explains how chaos and order can coexist.[36] Furthermore, information is not a purely abstract mathematical concept but has physical embodiment and requires some energy to insert it into a system. It exists everywhere in the universe. This goes along with the theological idea that the Spirit, the Communicator, transmits information from God to us everywhere in the world and from us to God.

7.7 Are the two types of chaos linked?

Earlier in this chapter, I warned that we must make a clear distinction between chaos in the sense of disorder, as in chaos theology (chapter 6), and chaos in the sense of unpredictability, as in chaos events. Now it appears that a link may exist between the two types of chaos. This is derived from a reconsideration of the classical Boltzmann equation for entropy, the physical measure of disorder in a system:

$$S = k_B \times \ln W$$

where S is the entropy, k_B is the Boltzmann constant, $\ln W$ is the natural logarithm of W, the total number of all possible configurations that all molecules in the system can assume (a very large number). However, this equation applies only for a system in a state of thermal equilibrium.

The Brazilian mathematician T. Tsallis has proposed a modification of the equation for systems that are far removed from thermal equilibrium and verge on a state of chaos, represented by the term q:[37]

$$S = k_B \times \ln \left[(W^{1-q} - 1) / (1 - q) \right]$$

The term q can vary between 0 (at thermal equilibrium, no chaos) and 1 (far from equilibrium, a state of chaos). It is clear that when q approaches 0,[38] the logarithmic term becomes equal to W (W is very much larger than 1), and the original Boltzmann formula returns. Experimental support for this equation has been obtained by the English theoretical physicist C. Beck. From published data for the turbulent flow of water (a typical example of chaotic behavior) he was able to calculate a value of q, which fits with the Tsallis equation.

This suggests that there may be a link between the two types of chaos, chaos as disorder (entropy, S) and chaos as unpredictability (q). It leads me to the conclusion that we may see here a convergence of the physical notion of "chaos events" and the theological notion of the "chaos element" in creation. Perhaps we may see this as an example of the holism of the universe.

7.8 Problems with "determinism"

Determinism can have different meanings, which may lead to confusion when an author doesn't define the term as used by him or her. For some it means "according to Newtonian law," fully fixed and predictable; quantum theory and chaos theory are then considered "indeterministic." For others it means "according to all physical laws," in which case both quantum theory and chaos theory are deterministic. For still others, deterministic phenomena are those that God cannot touch because they are set by "law."

The first question raised here is the meaning of physical laws. In the volume *Quantum Cosmology and the Laws of Nature: Scientific Perspectives on Divine Action*, William Stoeger quite rightly points out that natural laws, while revealing fundamental regularities in nature, are not the *source* of these regularities, and he strongly affirms that God acts in the world through the laws of nature.[39] The natural laws are human constructs derived from our observation of the regularities in nature. God bestowed these regularities (and the fundamental constants) on the emerging creation in the very beginning as a crucial part of the divine plan for it. God makes full use of them in the continuing creation, which is why we come to see them as "laws." As humans, we tend to think that God cannot violate these "laws," but theologically I would say that God, as their author, is not bound by them. But God knows that the creative plan is good (the Hebrew *tov* in Genesis 1) and so would not arbitrarily deviate from these "laws." Having given the creation great freedom, God does on occasion need to correct its course where it seems to go astray.

Therefore, we seek "loopholes" for God. Some find this in what they call the indeterminacy of quantum events. However, I have shown that quantum mechanics is a refinement of the Newtonian laws of motion at the (sub)atomic level and that there is a transition between Newtonian and quantum behavior, where Newtonian certainty changes to quantum probability for the human observer (section 7.2). So quantum events are not indeterministic in the sense of not obeying physical laws. Further, I have noted that there is no known mechanism by which quantum events can be amplified to the human or cosmic level. Thus, quantum mechanics does not seem to offer a "loophole" for God. And if one wishes to use the label "deterministic" for Newtonian behavior, then it is also applicable to quantum behavior and chaos events.

Another so-called loophole—one that I believe in—is the influencing of chaos events (sections 7.4–7.7). In *Chaos and Complexity*, Wesley Wildman and Robert Russell claim, "God would still have to intervene in nature by breaking or suspending its natural causal sequences," and a little further, they add that they have shown there is no justification for the idea that chaos theory makes room for divine acts: "Chaos theory actually strengthens the hypothesis of metaphysical determinism. For him [the theologian] the strengthening of the deterministic hypothesis by chaos theory will be bad news."[40] The error they make is that they use the term *deterministic* to mean "according to physical law," and then they assume that this implies that chaos events are out of bounds for God. The same mistake is made by Taede Smedes, who claims that not only the two legs of a fork are "deterministic," but also the choice of which leg to follow. (Smedes also uncritically accepts the argument of Willem Drees, which in section 7.6 I have shown to be invalid.)[41] These authors do not realize that although every fork and its legs in Figure 7.1 conform to the physical law of chaos theory, the *choice* of the leg is not determined because there is no energy difference between the two routes. Thus, when God or a human (see the last two examples in section 7.5) influences the route, this does not constitute breaking or suspending physical law, just as the deflection of the straight course of a light ray by means of a mirror does not break or suspend optical law. John Polkinghorne basically comes to the same conclusion as I do—namely, that chaotic systems, though governed by deterministic equations, allow for divine action.[42]

However, whereas the scientist can only prove that it is physically *possible* for God to influence chaos events without violating physical law, the theologian must consider whether God might indeed use this avenue to keep creation on track to the intended goal. And this is what I have tried to do in this chapter. Thus, I feel that the use of the concept of determinism is confusing and unhelpful. It prevents those who use it from actually studying the scientific evidence for chaos events and the influencing of them. Smedes even claims, "Recently there has been some doubting whether there is 'pure' chaos in the real world,"[43] but without substantiation (see section 7.5 for contrary evidence).

7.9 Summary

How might God act in the continuing creation? Some believe that quantum theory provides an answer. Quantum theory applies to the microlevel of atomic and subatomic particles and is characterized by quantization of energy, particle–wave complementarity, probability spreading of particles, and inherent uncertainty in measuring position and velocity of moving particles. Newtonian exactness and unambiguity at macrolevels changes to quantum probability and uncertainty at microlevels. In relatively large microsystems, a transition between these two states can be observed. There is no evidence for the amplification of quantum events to the human and cosmic macrolevels, because they tend to cancel each other. Hence, quantum theory does not seem to provide a locus for God's action in the world.

The concept of self-organization, in its molecular manifestation (the only concrete examples known to me), is part of the marvelously successful initial conditions—including physical laws and a precise set of fundamental constants—that God laid down at the very beginning of the creative process. Again, this phenomenon does not seem to provide a locus for God's action in the world.

Chaos theory applies to all systems obeying nonlinear dynamic equations, of which there are many (including all living beings, celestial systems, the weather, and turbulent flow). The example of the reproduction of a moth colony illustrates that under certain conditions, a bifurcation in the growth curve occurs. Since there is no energy difference between the two legs of the bifurcation, a very minute external influence, for example, information input, can "nudge" the system along one leg rather than the other. Calculation shows that it seems to be physically possible in this way for God to keep the evolving creation on track to its final destination, without violating any physical law. It now appears that the chaos in the unpredictability of chaos events is linked to the chaos as disorder in the remaining chaos of chaos theology.

Multiple interpretations of the determinism concept are the cause of confusion and neglect of scientific evidence, leading to wrong conclusions about the locus of God's action in the world. In conclusion, neither quantum events nor self-organization can, in my opinion, be seen as this locus. The influencing of chaos events appears to be the most likely locus of God's action in the world.

8

The Problem of Evil

This and the next six chapters present applications of chaos theology, beginning here with the problem of evil. In chapter 4.5, I included the presence of evil in a creation by a good and just God among the five problems I find with the *creatio ex nihilo* doctrine. In chapter 6.5, the four tenets of my chaos theology include, as the final tenet, the idea that remaining chaos is the source of evil. In this chapter, I shall discuss this subject in more detail, since it is a prominent topic of discussion in our present secularized Western world.

8.1 Reality of the problem

Our belief to be the vanguard of civilization has been rudely shaken by the Holocaust during World War II, the "ethnic cleansing" in the Balkan and some African countries, and now the atrocities of international terrorism. A rash of nontheological books on the subject with titles like *Radical Evil*, *Le Mal* (Evil), *Modernität und Barbarei* (Modernism and Barbarism), and *Das Böse* (Evil) have appeared in recent years. Even persons who have distanced themselves from a belief in a personal God are still attributing the responsibility for the existence of evil to "God." It seems to be their final thought about the God who is disappearing from their view, or it is the reason they give for abandoning the Christian faith.

This is exemplified by the prominent Dutch novelists Karel van 't Reve and Maarten 't Hart. The former writes, "God is more wicked than the most wicked human."[1] He bases this conclusion on some tragic cases of illness and on the story of Abraham being ordered by God to sacrifice his son Isaac (Gen 22:1-14). Maarten 't Hart recounts that as a boy he threw two Calvinist elders out of the family home because they troubled his desperately ill mother with talk about the fatherly hand that could also be a punishing hand (based on Sunday 10 in the Heidelberg Catechism: "Health and sickness, prosperity and poverty—all things, in fact, come to us not by chance but from his fatherly hand").[2] Suddenly he knew very surely "that somewhere far away in the universe god is now laughing satanically at my sorrow, the god of Sunday 10, who has with fatherly hand dealt my mother a deadly illness, a foretaste of suffering in hell."[3] A columnist in a prominent secular Dutch newspaper[4] paraphrases the questions first asked by the Greek philosopher Epicurus in 300 BCE:

> If god has created the world, why is there then so much misery? And if he cannot do anything about this, why is he then called almighty? And if he is almighty, but does not intervene, then he surely is not good? Isn't it time to realize that the god of the bible is an impossible construction? That whoever believes in this is fooling himself?[5]

In this context, a satisfactory solution of the problem of evil would be of immense value to millions of people, whether they are still adhering to the Christian faith or have already quietly abandoned it. In awareness of this, several theologians have published books on this problem during the past twenty-five years.[6]

8.2 Defining the problem

To make an attempt at resolving the problem of evil, it is first of all necessary to define evil and the problem it poses. But even defining evil presents difficulties. Dictionaries often call it "the opposite of good," or they simply give synonyms of the word *evil*. In Rahner's *Encyclopedia of Theology*, Klaus Hemmerle writes:

> Evil counts as one of the most distressing questions in theology. It cannot be thought of in itself; it is evil solely as opposed to the good. Being holy, God is also good, and is so of himself, not through participation in a good outside or prior to himself or greater than he. He is the principle and pure source of good, good absolutely as such. Consequently it is impossible for him to be the author of evil; he cannot will evil, and

no shadow of evil falls on him. But in that case, how can anything be or happen which is opposed to God and his goodness?[7]

There we have the problem in full, but without any attempt at solving it.

Three preliminary remarks need to be made. First, we must distinguish between physical evil (natural disasters and disease) and moral evil (evil committed by humans). Some authors omit physical evil from their consideration of evil; others claim that earthquakes and volcanic eruptions are simply natural phenomena and thus not evil. However, in the decade of 1994–2003, these natural phenomena claimed 478,000 dead and 2.5 billion injured and homeless. The Lisbon earthquake in 1755 killed 15,000 people, and the Indian Ocean tsunami of December 26, 2004, killed more than 225,000 people. Millions of people suffer debilitating chronic illness or die prematurely through fatal diseases. Where natural disasters and disease lead to death and suffering, this represents evil.

Second, the term *suffering* should not be used as an equivalent of evil, because it is instead a consequence of both physical and moral evil. Certainly, suffering should not be employed as an equivalent to physical evil, as Brian Hebblethwaite does.[8]

Third, considering the natural death of living beings and the extinction of animal species during biological evolution as evil is questionable. I shall return to this point in section 8.5.

The problem of evil can be succinctly defined by rephrasing the questions of Epicurus as three propositions that must be affirmed together, at least by Christians:

1. Evil exists.
2. God is all-powerful.
3. God is completely benevolent.

To these propositions, I would add as a fourth the basic Judeo-Christian tenet:

4. God is the one and only God.

Together, these propositions constitute the age-old problem of the theodicy, the defense of the goodness and omnipotence of God in the face of the existence of evil in the world. The word was coined by the German philosopher Gottfried W. Leibniz (1646–1716), whose attempt at a solution will be mentioned in the next section.

8.3 Attempts at solving the problem through denials

Various attempts have been made to resolve the problem by denying one or another of the four propositions just listed.

(1) Denying the existence of evil

The reality of evil was denied by the Stoics, who were indifferent to the material aspects of our existence. In Eastern religions, evil and good are transcended in the Absolute Spirit (*nirvana, brahman*) that is beyond good and evil. This resembles the solution of the book of Job, which "evokes such a sense of awe around the created universe that, discovering in this way a renewed sense of God's presence, one accepts both evil and good and contents himself verbally by acknowledging a final incomprehensibility."[9] In current New Age thinking, evil is claimed to be a "self-created illusion" to the point that an evil deed is considered "undesirable" rather than wrong.[10]

(2) Denying the omnipotence of God

God's omnipotence is abrogated by Gottfried Leibniz (1646–1716), who stated that God is limited by what is logically possible, meaning that the world we live in is the best possible that God could create.[11] American pragmatist philosopher William James (1842–1910) regarded God as having great but limited power. Modern theologians who in answer to the desperate question "Why does God allow this?" say that God is "suffering with us" (for example, Harold Kushner and Dorothee Sölle)[12] also are diminishing God's power. True, God is compassionate and loving, but this does not mean that God is helpless in the face of evil. The gnostic belief in creation by an evil demiurge also tends to deny God's omnipotence.

(3) Denying the benevolence of God

The goodness of God is only denied by persons who have rejected the Christian faith, including the Dutch novelists mentioned in the first section. Some Jewish thinkers, in relating the wrathful God of the Old Testament to Satan, seem to come close to negating the proposition that God is benevolent.

(4) Denying the unity of God

The unity of God was negated by the second-century Gnostics. They assumed an evil demiurge (often equated with the God of the Old Testament), who created the world from an eternal, preexisting evil matter. The good God (the God of the New Testament, the Father of Jesus Christ) is perfecting this world, and we may participate in this perfect world through knowledge (*gnosis*). This element is also present in the New Age ideas about a host of "intermediate beings."[13] A similar approach is to invoke a Satan who is responsible for the evil in the world. When this Satan is considered as an autonomous agent, God is absolved, but Judeo-Christian monotheism is abandoned. When Satan is thought to be under the control of God, as in the book of Job, then God is ultimately responsible for evil. Elaine Pagels, in *The Origin of Satan*, concludes, "Satan is often just a container that we fashion to hold our own poisons. We have met the old enemy: he is us."[14] Right, but she neglects physical evil.

It seems reasonable to conclude that rejecting one or more of these propositions does not provide a satisfactory solution for the problem of the theodicy within the context of the Christian faith. In the next section, I shall briefly review the many attempts that have been made to solve the problem while upholding all of these propositions.

8.4 Attempts at solving the problem in *creatio ex nihilo* context

An extensive survey of the attempts to solve the problem of the theodicy in traditional *creatio ex nihilo* context has been provided by John Hick.[15] He groups these efforts under two models: the Augustinian model and the Irenaean model.

Augustinian model

The Augustinian model involves several key points:

1. Evil is the absence of good (*privatio boni*). However, this does insufficient justice to the reality of evil and its consequences. Evil is the absolute opposite and negation of what God is and wants human creatures to be in the exercise of the free will God gave them. Thomas

agrees with the idea that evil is the privation of the good, as "blindness is the privation of sight."[16] On physical evil, he says God did not will it, yet God willed it for the sake of the perfection of the universe. On moral evil, he says God did not will it, but permitted it.

2. The created world is wholly good, so evil does not come from God. However, this point rests on a wrong translation of the Hebrew word *tov* in the phrase "God saw that it was good" in Genesis 1. The Hebrew word does not mean good in actuality, but good for the purpose, that is, God's ultimate purpose for the ongoing creation.[17]

3. Evil originates from our misuse of freedom. However, this point does not really explain the origin of evil, and it neglects physical evil. This so-called free-will defense, recently restated by Patricia Williams,[18] may *describe* the occurrence of many instances of moral evil, but it does not *explain* what makes God's image bearers abuse their freedom. Moreover, by embracing the idea of predestination, Augustine still makes God responsible for evil.

4. Physical evil is supposed to have arisen because Adam's sin corrupted nature. However, this point overlooks the fact that physical evil preceded the appearance of humans by millions of years. Dinosaurs already suffered from arthritis and cancer, as their fossils tell us. Only in the last two centuries have humans, through population increase and industrialization, been affecting the earthly ecology. Moreover, considering life's trials as punishment for the sin of Adam contradicts God's justice and our individual responsibility. Finally, it is wrong to literalize the mythical story of Genesis 3 and to reverse its direction: the author conceived it as an explanation of human sinfulness by posing a mythical human protopair. In the doctrine of original sin, the protopair is taken literally and as conferring sinfulness on all successive generations, as if it were a hereditary disease.

Irenaean model

The Irenaean model is less harsh and impersonal in maintaining that evil exists ultimately within God's good purpose. It is said that God could have created differently but knew that early humans were too immature to receive, contain, and retain perfection. The doctrine of original sin does not occur in this model. However, while the model tries to uphold God's goodness, it seems to compromise God's omnipotence. A proponent of the Irenaean model is Schleiermacher, but he caricaturizes it when he writes, "Sin has been ordained by God; for otherwise redemption itself could not have been ordained."[19] This amounts to causing a shipwreck in order to allow the staging of a rescue operation, which I find theologically unacceptable. Paul also vigorously rejects this idea: "Why not say (as some people slander us by saying that we say), 'Let us do evil so that good may come'? Their condemnation is deserved!" (Rom 3:8).

Another form of the Irenaean model, often called "soul making," suggests that suffering from evil is God's way of making us grow spiritually. However, this compromises God's goodness. True, we often see that people suffering from evil—for example, in the form of serious illness—grow spiritually. But it is horrible to think that God would inflict such evil in order to make this happen.

Wolfhart Pannenberg softens this when he writes, "Wickedness and evil . . . entered creation with God's knowledge and permission, but they are not objects of his will."[20] In the end he falls back on the free-will defense, concluding, "We are to seek the root of evil . . . in revolt against the limit of finitude, in the refusal to accept one's own finitude, and in the related illusion of being like God."[21] Here applies the objection I made in comment 3 about the Augustinian model, namely, that abuse of free will may describe the occurrence of moral evil, but it does not explain why God's image bearers abuse their God-given freedom; in other words, it is not the root of evil.

Edward Schillebeeckx states that it is right to claim that everything there is comes from God. Acknowledging the existence of evil in the world, he says, "The good comes from God and is deeper than evil and precedes it. God is in no way 'the first cause' of any evil, but the possibility of physical and moral evil is inherent to the finitude of this world, although by creating finite beings, God is indirectly involved in evil to some extent."[22] David Fergusson reviews all these explanations of evil in *creatio ex nihilo* context and concludes, "Theodicy attempts to justify the unjustifiable."[23]

8.5 Evil in evolutionary context

Neither the Augustinian nor the Irenaean model takes into account the evolutionary nature of creation. Since death and extinction are typical aspects of biological evolution, it is logical to consider the problem of evil in an evolutionary context. Surprisingly, few modern theologians have done this. An exception is the Dutch theologian H. M. Kuitert, who applies evolution in his discussion of the theodicy but concludes, "Evolution is an unpredictable process: it has no purpose."[24] Thus, he does not integrate it in his further discussion of "the riddle of the good creation." Since he still interprets the Hebrew *tov* as good in actuality, he encounters more problems and rejects more traditional explanations than he offers solutions. His conclusions that "Evil is part of life and we have to put up with it" and that "God can turn to good what we had thought evil" can hardly be considered to constitute a satisfactory solution of the problem of the theodicy.

What does the eminent evolutionary thinker Pierre Teilhard de Chardin have to offer in this respect? John Haught has analyzed the views of Teilhard and Paul Tillich on evil and redemption in an evolutionary creation.[25] Teilhard rejects an initial perfection, and extends evil and redemption to the entire creation rather than to humans only. He considers sin, evil, suffering, and death as tragic inevitability and introduces in his Omega concept a God who as an "attractor" draws the world to perfection through the evolutionary process. It seems to me that Teilhard has not fully integrated evil into his thinking about evolution. He presents physical and moral evil as "external and internal passivity of diminishment," with passivity meaning "that which is not done by us, is by definition undergone."[26] Paul Tillich posits that the present state of the world ("estranged being") is separated from a primordial wholeness of being ("dreaming innocence"). Estranged being must move to "essential being," a state of perfection, a unity of all beings with God the "Ground" of all being. Christ as the "New Being" is to be the mover in this process. So Tillich, although accepting the idea that evil and redemption apply to the entire creation, still believes in an initially perfect creation, which somehow has "fallen." It seems to me that Tillich also has not fully integrated the evolutionary process of creation in his thinking about evil and redemption.

In a 1988 issue of *Zygon Journal of Religion and Science*, several authors have considered the problem in the context of sociobiology (Edmund Wilson) and the selfish-gene idea (Richard Dawkins). Biologist George Williams feels that the position of Thomas Huxley (1894)—that process and products of evolution are morally unacceptable—is supported by the ideas of sociobiology.[27] He considers natural selection to be a process for maximizing shortsighted selfishness. Anthropologist Sarah Hrdy disagrees, saying we cannot sensibly turn to nature for templates in moral matters.[28] We can merely say that what we "consider fine moral qualities, as well as those we deem despicable," are represented in nature. Philosopher Michael Ruse agrees with Williams that both questions and answers about our moral nature lie in our biological origin, but he feels that Williams fails to show that nature is morally evil.[29] To Ruse, the products of evolution are morally neutral, and morality is functional; it is an adaptation "intended" to make us social, and sociality makes us biologically more fit.

Theologian Ralph Burhoe strangely believes that our rapid rate of learning "greatly accelerates" our genetic evolution, giving us a "radically high rate of evolution."[30] Actually, the evolutionary rate declines in the sequence of rat → dog → monkey → human,[31] and evolution is probably ending through the effect of modern medicine and technology on natural selection. Burhoe feels that the selfishness of genes and memes (hypothetical replicators of culture) is not evil, but good and necessary. Only selfishness that leads to socially destructive behavior is evil. He proposes that the dual human natures of genotype and culture type are out of phase and incompletely adapted to each other, which leads to evil behavior. This seems to me a rather unsatisfactory explanation of evil, certainly of physical evil.

Process theologian John Cobb claims that the Christian doctrine of nature affirms the goodness of creation, especially of life, and that evolution is good.[32] But this leaves open the question of the moral goodness of creatures as they inflict suffering on others. Cobb rightly states that declaring nature our enemy does not help in solving the problem of evil. In his reply, Williams maintains his claim that evolution is not good.[33] Evolution, whether genetic or cultural, does not normally head in the right direction, which presumably, in his opinion, is a state of full morality. According to Williams, there is no corrective feedback in evolution that keeps it going in a morally preferable direction. He neglects the fact that nearly 4 billion years of evolution have led to *Homo sapiens*, believed to be the first creature that can contemplate moral questions.

Arthur Peacocke speaks about "the ubiquity of pain, predation, suffering, and death in the creative evolutionary process." However, he offers no solution beyond urging us to understand "the biological parameters discerned by science to be operating in evolution."[34]

More recently, Christopher Southgate has offered a fresh approach to the problem of evil in the evolutionary process.[35] After finding the solutions proposed by other authors wanting, he summarizes his position in five points: (1) He acknowledges the pain, suffering, death, and extinction in evolution. (2) He affirms God's co-suffering with every sentient being in creation. (3) He takes the cross as indicative of God's compassion and the inauguration of creation's transformation. (4) He considers divine fellowship with human creatures as implying that we are of particular concern to God. (5) He stresses the importance of the redemption of nonhuman creatures ("pelican heaven," that is, a heaven in which animals are also present).

All the authors quoted in this section are overlooking some obvious points. The first is that mortality is a necessity for the process of evolution to proceed. Second, extinction of species is not significantly different from the natural death of individual living beings; after all, natural selection leads to slightly decreased birthrates and/or slightly raised mortality. The idea of God's co-suffering with God's creatures seems to me to curtail God's omnipotence without answering the question of the origin of evil. God apparently chose biological evolution as the most effective way to allow primordial microbes to develop all complex life-forms and eventually humans with whom God can communicate. Also, we should clearly distinguish between extinction of species in the course of evolution, which is a "necessary" physical evil, and the extinction of species by human intervention during the past few centuries, which is a moral evil.

The question "Couldn't God have chosen another way?" is meaningless, since we as creatures cannot know the mind of the Creator. We can only trust that the omnipotent, omniscient, and benevolent God has chosen the right way. Finally, I suggest that evolution takes place in an as yet unfulfilled creation, where God battles remaining chaos.

It is interesting to note that the authors quoted here do not speak about creation theology, and particularly not about *creatio ex nihilo*. This confirms my earlier contention that the *creatio ex nihilo* doctrine has not proved to be a fruitful creation theology.

8.6 What can chaos theology tell us about the origin of evil?

The unavoidable conclusion from the preceding three sections seems to be that we have been unable to resolve the problem of the theodicy either in traditional or evolutionary context. Some authors dealing with the problem even admit this explicitly. John Sanford says at the end of his book on evil, "The problem of evil is unresolved in Christian theology."[36] Paul Ricoeur says we should recognize the aporetic (insoluble) character of the problem.[37] Even Pope John Paul II seems to admit that the problem has not yet been solved, when writing in his encyclical *Faith and Reason*: "The philosopher who learns humility will also find courage to tackle questions which are difficult to resolve if the data of Revelation are ignored—for example, the problem of evil and suffering."[38] How then shall we explain the existence of evil in God's creation without lapsing into dualism or limiting either God's goodness or God's omnipotence?

Any satisfactory solution of the problem of evil must rest on an adequate creation theology. Traditional theology has for the past 1,800 years held to the *creatio ex nihilo* doctrine. In chapter 4.5, I have argued that our inability to find a satisfactory theodicy is ultimately due to this doctrine, because it implies that God created everything, including evil.

This is one of the problems with *creatio ex nihilo* that have led me to propose a revised creation theology, which I call chaos theology (chapter 6).[39] In chaos theology, I return to the biblical idea (also common to nonbiblical creation stories; chapter 3.2) of an initial creation from an undefined and unexplained initial chaos (Gen 1:2; 2:5-6). God orders and pushes back this chaos in the continuing creation, observed by scientists as the cosmic and biological evolution. There remains an element of chaos, symbolized in many places in the Old Testament as the sea. In the continuing creation, God is battling remaining chaos until abolishing it on the last day: "I saw a new heaven and a new earth . . . and the sea was no more" (Rev 21:1), thus completing and perfecting God's creation. In chapter 6.7, I have answered critical questions about origin and nature of the initial chaos. Both modern cosmology[40] and information theory[41] suggest that at the moment of the big bang, the entropy (the physical measure of disorder or chaos) was maximal or even infinite.

I propose that remaining chaos is the source of evil, both physical and moral evil. Remaining chaos itself is morally neutral. It has a positive aspect in that it allows the Creator freedom and creativity, of which God grants some to human creatures, resulting in culture, science, and technology. It has a negative aspect in that evil emerges from remaining chaos. Evil is thus not created, either by God or by a demiurge.

How can evil come from remaining chaos? Physical evil is simply the consequence of the presence of remaining chaos in the created world, expressing itself in chaotic tectonic forces leading to earthquakes and volcanic eruptions, in chaotic behavior of the atmosphere leading to cyclones, and in random mutations leading to cancer and other diseases (chapter 12). Note that "chaotic" applies to the dynamic behavior of nonlinear systems, which makes them unpredictable for us but also opens a way for God to influence such events in the course of God's creative work (chapter 7). In section 8.2, I stated that where natural disasters and disease lead to death and suffering of humans, this represents evil. This does not negate the facts that tectonic forces have also played a beneficial role in making the earth habitable for God's creatures and that random mutations are essential for biological evolution. These facts reflect the positive aspect of remaining chaos in God's creative work.

Moral evil I ascribe to "chaotic thinking," as expressed in the words of Paul: "I do not understand my own actions. For I do not do what I want, but I do the very thing I hate" (Rom 7:15). This is what we call temptation. It is remaining chaos at work in our minds, I suggest. Yet, knowing the difference between good and evil and having been given freedom of will, we remain fully responsible for our actions. Jesus was also subject to temptation, as recorded in a story in all three Synoptic Gospels (Mark 1:12-13; Matt 4:1-11; Luke 4:1-13). The three temptations to which Jesus was subjected were satisfying his hunger after weeks of starvation (Matt 4:3-4), achieving power (Matt 4:5-7), and obtaining publicity for himself (Matt 4:8-10). Remaining chaos was at work in him, indicating his full humanity. Jesus withstood these temptations, which is in principle open to all of us, though rarely accomplished but always to be striven for. Experiencing temptation is not sinful, only submitting to it is (Heb 4:15). James writes, "Blessed is anyone who endures temptation," and adds, "God . . . himself tempts no one. But one is tempted by one's own desire" (James 1:12-15). Here I would replace *desire* with "chaotic thinking," which leads us to a wrong understanding of our desires and a wrong action upon them.

My calling the Holocaust an example of chaotic thinking led one critic to remark that this horrible crime was perfectly organized, so how can it be attributed to chaotic thinking? To this I say that Hitler was guilty of chaotic thinking in an extreme form in developing his Nazi ideology of the superior "Germanic race," leading him to order the wholesale destruction of those of "inferior race." This form of chaotic thinking was only compounded by his "rational" use of the technical means at his disposal. The same argument applies, in my opinion, to the present Islamic terrorists, who are guilty of the chaotic thought that Allah would be pleased by their killing as many "infidels" as possible by means of the use of cleverly organized, advanced techniques. "Rational thinking" leading to utterly immoral deeds is to me an extreme example of chaotic thinking. These forms of chaotic thinking may even have a neuronal substrate as there is some theoretical and experimental evidence that certain states of the brain may be subject to nonlinear, chaotic dynamics.[42]

This explanation of the problem of physical and moral evil offered by chaos theology seems to me more satisfactory than any of the other explanations described in sections 8.3–8.5. Evil no longer needs to be attributed to God or to the disobedience of the mythical protohuman

Adam. We do not have to diminish God's omnipotence and benevolence. The created world can be seen and enjoyed as wholly good, not in actuality, but in its God-intended goal of future perfection, in which we may ultimately hope to share.

8.7 Some further considerations

With Anton Houtepen,[43] I see in our incessant search for a theodicy an awareness of the "possible good," reflecting some innate intuition of what a divinely created world should be like, while it also implies an awareness of the imperfection and incompleteness of creation at the present stage.

My propositions about initial and remaining chaos and about evil arising from remaining chaos find some resonance in the thinking of others. Philip Hefner connects creation with chaos: "Chaos is the womb of creativity. . . . Creation and chaos belong together by nature."[44] This is what I call the positive aspect of remaining chaos. Mark Worthing connects evil with the concept of entropy, the physical measure of disorder or chaos.[45] Harold Kushner sees creation as God's ordering of initial chaos and recognizes a remaining element of chaos, symbolized for him in the sea monster Leviathan (Job 41).[46] However, he does not recognize the evolutionary course of creation as God's battle with remaining chaos. Therefore, to the question "Why does God not intervene?" he can only reply that God cannot do everything, that God is suffering with us. To this I say that God does intervene, not in instantly curing each of our ills, but in an ongoing battle with the Leviathan of remaining chaos and in occasionally influencing a chaos event.

To the question "Why does it take God so long to prevail over chaos?" I have two responses. (1) Science tells us that cosmic and biological evolution could not have brought forth human creatures in a much shorter time. (2) Creation is like a great work of art that also requires a large amount of time and effort for its completion. The impatience sounding in this question has led in the past to the idea of an immediately perfect creation, which was spoiled by Adam's sin, and which God must then hold together (*preservatio*) until finally "fixing" it on the last day. To which I say that this seriously overrates human capability and downgrades God's omnipotence.

Is God's omnipotence diminished in my claim that God "battles remaining chaos" until perfecting the creation on the last day? To this I say that assuming the initial creation was not yet perfect (remembering that the Hebrew word *tov* for good in Genesis 1 means "good for the purpose," rather than "good in actuality"), God is still at work in perfecting creation—a process I describe in the anthropomorphic terms of doing battle. In addition, I do not see this as a lack of control by God, but rather like the artist's wrestling with the materials in creating a work of art. Finally, God in infinite wisdom chose the way of cosmic and biological evolution to make creation ready for perfection on the last day.

I hope to have made here a reasonable case for a satisfactory theodicy, based on chaos theology. The key elements are initial creation from chaos and continuing creation with a remaining element of chaos, from which physical and moral evil arise. God battles remaining chaos until eliminating it on the last day through the cosmic Christ, who thereby redeems and perfects the entire creation. However, borrowing the motto of the Dutch tax service, "We cannot make it more pleasant, but we can make it easier," we can say that evil does remain just that, but chaos theology makes it more understandable. Such understanding is not only of theological importance, but also of great pastoral significance in responding to those who grievously suffer from physical or moral evil.

As a final note, I suggest that through the centuries, Christian theology has dwelled too much on evil and human redemption from it. We should rather recognize the marvelous gift God has bestowed on us in the creation of the cosmos and the gifts of human intelligence and free will that allow us to rejoice in God's creation and to contribute to God's work. God must have been fully aware that providing us with intelligence and free will would lead to our abuse of them, but through the resurrection of the cosmic Christ, God brings the creative work to completion and perfection, offering us a part in the new creation if we will just say yes to it.

8.8 Summary

In this chapter, I discuss the problem of evil, which nowadays receives so much attention. In this discussion, we must consider both physical evil (natural disasters and disease) and moral evil (evil committed by humans).

Some have attempted to resolve the problem by denying one of four propositions: The idea that evil exists has been denied by Stoics, Eastern religions, and New Age spirituality. The understanding of God as all-powerful has been denied in Leibniz's "best possible world" and in the notion that God is "suffering with us." The proposition that God is completely benevolent has been denied only by atheists. And the belief that God is the one and only God has been denied in Gnosticism, New Age religion, and belief in an autonomous Satan. Rejection of any of these propositions does not offer a satisfactory solution of the problem.

Attempts at solving the problem in traditional (*creatio ex nihilo*) context have upheld all four propositions. These attempts may be grouped under the Augustinian and Irenaean models. Key points of the Augustinian model are that evil is the absence of good (which doesn't do justice to the reality of evil); that the created world is wholly good, so evil does not come from God (a view stemming from a mistranslation of the Hebrew word *tov* in Genesis 1, which actually means not good in actuality, but good for the ultimate purpose); that evil originates from abuse of free will (which describes moral evil but doesn't explain its origin); and that physical evil results from Adam's sin (but it precedes human existence, an interpretation that wrongly literalizes and reverses the mythical story of the fall). The Irenaean model maintains that evil exists ultimately within God's good purpose. But in trying to uphold God's goodness, it compromises God's omnipotence. Neither model can solve the problem.

Those considering evil in evolutionary context overlook some obvious points. First, mortality is necessary for evolution to proceed. Second, extinction of species is not significantly different from natural death of individual living beings. Third, God apparently chose biological evolution as the most effective way to allow primordial microbes eventually to develop humans. Finally, extinction of species in the course of evolution is a "necessary" physical evil, to be distinguished from the moral evil of extinction through human intervention.

A solution has not been found in either traditional or evolutionary context, so I call on chaos theology with its claim that remaining chaos is the source of physical and moral evil. Physical evil is the result of remaining chaos, expressing itself in chaotic tectonic forces (earthquakes and volcanic eruptions), in chaotic atmospheric behavior (cyclones), and in random mutations (cancer and other diseases). Moral evil is due to "chaotic thinking" (Paul in Rom 7:15). Temptation is remaining chaos at work in our minds, encountered but resisted by Jesus (Matt 4:1-11) and unfortunately often not resisted by us. Knowing the difference between good and evil, we are fully responsible for the evil we commit when submitting to chaotic thinking.

To the question "Why does God not intervene?" I reply that God does intervene by battling against remaining chaos. To the question "Why does it take God so long?" I reply that cosmic and biological evolution could not have brought forth human creatures in a much shorter time. Saying that God battles remaining chaos is an anthropomorphic way of recognizing that God is bringing a still incomplete creation to fulfillment.

May this provide a satisfactory solution for the problem of evil, permitting us to rejoice in God's creation and gift of intelligence and free will that allow us to play our intended role as God's cocreators.

9

God's Action in the World

9.1 Transcendent and immanent action of God

How are we to describe God's interaction with the world?[1] In the Genesis 1 creation story, we are given a majestic account of God's action in the initial creation. There was no matter, no universe, only chaos: "Then God said, 'Let there be light'; and there was light" (Gen 1:3). The mighty Word of God is a creative command. Here we see God in full transcendent majesty. Then the universe evolves in the continuing creation according to the plan laid down in the initial creation and with great freedom and self-sufficiency. Yet God still has to intervene at critical moments, visible in the contingency of cosmic and biological evolution (sections 9.4 and 9.5). Intervening in the existing universe implies an immanent activity of God. But even in this immanence, God maintains transcendence; God does not become identical with the creation.

So we see God acting in two ways: one transcendent and predictable, the other immanent and unpredictable. Predictably, God works through the natural laws, which are the human formulation of the orderliness of natural events as ordained by God in the initial creation. In accordance with these laws, God creates and assures a reliable existence for all creatures. Here we see God outside and above creation, as transcendent. In the further development of the universe according to the natural laws laid down initially, God retains freedom in the form of a creative use of "chaos events" (chapter 7). Here we see God acting within the evolving creation, as immanent. God's immanent activity is unpredictable and invisible to us, except in hindsight in the course of evolution and in the course of our own life.

I suggest that this is not the picture of an "interventionist" God, who with brute force micromanipulates every aspect of the creation. God will intervene only gently and rarely by "nudging" a chaos event where necessary to safeguard the goal set for creation from the beginning. I like to compare this with a father teaching his child to ride a bicycle. At some point the father will have to let go of the bicycle in order to allow the child to learn how to keep balance. But he will run behind the bicycle with outstretched arm to grab the saddle when the child seems about to fall.

Other terms have been used for God's dual action. John Polkinghorne speaks about the God of "being" (in the timeless regularity of physical law) and "becoming" (in the evolving history of complex systems in chaos events).[2] I find *being* too passive a term for God's transcendent activity, while *becoming* sounds too much like the God of process theology.[3] Arthur Peacocke uses the term *panentheism* to express that the world is in God, yet God is ultimately other than the world.[4] I avoid this term because it is easily confused with *pantheism*, and it doesn't clearly express the two different modes of God's activity in the world. Peacocke also likes to describe God's immanent activity as holistic (influencing the entire cosmos) rather than localized. I do not see a real contradiction. I like to think that the action will be local, where it is needed, but through the coherence of the universe, it will also be holistic. So I prefer to stay with the time-honored terms *transcendence* and *immanence*. The immanence of God in creation means that God remains creatively active in this world in the continuing creation, in the struggle with the remaining chaos element until its definitive removal on the last day. This is supremely manifested in the earthly life and activities of Jesus Christ and in the overcoming of his execution by his resurrection (chapter 10).

Need for both types of action

A transcendent-only image has existed in the Western church, among the deists, but also in the doctrine of conservation. In the latter doctrine, creation is seen as immediately complete and perfect; there is only an initial creation and no continuing creation. The imperfection, noticed as the evil in our world, is attributed to the primordial sin of Adam and Eve. Thereafter God must "conserve" the damaged creation until "repairing" it in the end through Jesus Christ. My theological objection is that this overrates human power (in damaging a perfect creation by human sin) and underrates God's power by seeing him as a "repairman." The scientific objection is that physical evil in the form of natural disasters and disease was present long before humans came to the scene.

An immanent-only view of God's activity is noticeable in process theology, which sees God as developing in time, as realizing God's self in and through the evolution of the creation.[5] Whitehead came to this idea from his desire to integrate evolution theory in theology. This led him to the following four statements: (1) Life is found in the choice of novelty and in the quest for aesthetic enrichment. (2) God acts in this process as a localized "lure" opposing the move toward increasing entropy (disorder). (3) Change is not by chance, but is an expression of a subjective aim at an unconscious level. (4) God is limited by allowing self-determination to the evolving universe.

To this Keith Ward says:

> Whitehead has changed the 'cosmic tyrant', against whom he so strongly protests, into a 'cosmic sponge'. A god who develops with and in his creation, and who has to 'lure' his creatures into evolving is not the biblical God of the universe. The God of the Bible is involved in the world, but not tied to it to the extent that the process theologians suppose.[6]

Process theology also leaves unanswered several questions: How does the "lure" work, particularly at the lower levels, where physical laws operate rather than human free will? How can what is said about the becoming of a human person apply to a nucleotide? And where do human sin and its consequences enter? Process theology is a speculative philosophy rather than a biblically based creation theology. Its emphasis on God's immanence is so strong that God's transcendence and the distinction between God and creation are lost.

It seems clear to me that we must hold to the belief in a God who acts both transcendently in initiating and preserving creation and immanently in correcting its course where necessary.

Prayer and miracles

What I have said here about God's transcendent and immanent action also has implications for prayer. God's transcendent institution of physical laws implies that we cannot properly pray for a change of day and night, because God has fixed this in the laws governing Earth's rotation; their momentary suspension would have catastrophic effects. On the other hand, God's immanent activity in influencing chaos events means that the weather and our bodies can be a proper subject for prayer, as they are prone to chaos events. In these events, God may act through the Spirit as information transmitter without violating physical law. We may trust that God in complete knowledge of all parameters will know whether it is in the long-term interest of ourselves and all creatures to grant our petition. A miracle can be understood as a manifestation of God's immanent activity in influencing chaos events, rather than as a deviation from physical law. In theological terms, a miracle is a sign of God's immanent love and power.

9.2 God's creative agent(s)

These ideas give rise to a question: Who or what is God's creative agent? Although this question is rarely considered by modern theologians, the early fathers strongly felt that God's transcendence implies the use of a creative agent. Irenaeus (c. 190) stated, "The Son and the Spirit are the two hands of God by which he created all things."[7] In this section I consider three candidates: *Logos*, Spirit, and Wisdom. After considering those options, I bring science to bear on the question in section 9.3.

Logos

Can we consider the *Logos*, the Word of God, as God's creative agent? The Hebrew *dabar* (Greek *Logos*) means a powerful word that issues in action. In the Old Testament, *dabar* is used for the means by which God does four things: reveals himself (Gen 15:1; 1 Sam 3:21); makes his will known to the prophets ("The word of the Lord that came to . . ."; "Hear the word of the Lord"); achieves his purposes (Isa 55:10-11); and indeed, creates the heavens and the earth (Ps 33:6).[8] In Genesis 1 we read that God called all things into being by the Word: "God said . . ." (vv. 3, 6, 9, 11, 14, 20, 24, 26).

Logos as a specific aspect or activity of God first appeared in Jewish literature in the writings of Philo (20 BCE–50 CE).[9] Under the influence of Greek philosophy, which saw the *Logos* as the force that brings order in the universe, Philo made the *Logos* the intermediary between God and the created order and even calls him "God's first-born son." For Philo, God is absolutely transcendent and thus cannot interact with creation directly. Philo sees the *Logos* not as a person, but as the chief power of God, *energeia*, through which the world was made.[10]

In the New Testament, *Logos* as the Word of God is variously used for the law (Mark 7:13; Matt 15:6), as God's revealed will and purpose for humankind (Luke 11:28; Rom 9:6; Col 1:25-27), and as the word preached by Jesus (Luke 5:1). However, the most remarkable use is by John in the prologue to his gospel. Here *Logos* is the preexistent Word (John 1:1) through which all things came into being (John 1:3) and the world and humans were created (John 1:10). The Word then becomes incarnate in Jesus of Nazareth (John 1:14), making him the Christ.[11] John uses the *Logos* both in the Jewish sense of the Word of God "by which the heavens were made" and in the Greek sense of "the rational principle of which all natural laws are particular expressions," thus making himself understandable for both groups.[12] And in affirming the incarnation of the *Logos* in Jesus of Nazareth, John is in harmony with the New Testament Christology. "In the beginning" in John 1:1 resembles the term in Gen 1:1, but here it means "before all time," not just from the beginning of creation. As C. K. Barrett says, "The Word does not come to be with God; the Word is with God in the beginning."[13]

The early fathers made several attempts to develop a theology of the *Logos*.[14] Justin Martyr (d. 165) defined *Logos* as God's intermediary in creation, not a power or an effluence but a person, begotten and not created. The *Logos* featured prominently in the christological discussions at the Councils of Nicea (325) and Constantinople (381).[15] At Nicea the teaching of Arius (the *Logos* was created by God to be God's instrument in creation) was condemned, and it was affirmed that the *Logos* is God in the full sense. At Constantinople, in reaction to the teaching of Apollinarius, it was affirmed that the *Logos* is fully the divine Word of God, and is God's personal agent in creation as well as in the incarnation. Around 650 the Greek theologian Maximus the Confessor defined the *logoi* of creation as the energies of God, as distinct from the essence of God.[16]

I conclude that there is ample biblical and theological ground for considering the *Logos* as God's creative agent, not as a person (as Justin believed), not created (as Arius believed), but as the energy (Philo, Maximus) or the "expression" of God (Phillips). However, this still leaves the question of the "mechanism of action" of the *Logos* in creation, to which I shall return in section 9.3.

Spirit

Pneumatology, the doctrine of the Spirit, is a relatively underdeveloped area of theology. The Council of Constantinople (381) recognized the

Spirit as "the Lord and giver of life, who proceeds from the Father, and is worshipped and glorified with the Father and the Son." A specific role for the Spirit in creation was not claimed, except as "Life-giver" reflected in Gen 2:7, where God's breath of life (Hebrew *ruach*, with the triple meaning of wind, breath, spirit) made the first human come to life. Since life first arose on Earth some 10 billion years after the initial explosion, this can be seen as a role of the Spirit in continuing creation but not in the initial creation.

There is, however, the phrase in Gen 1:2b that traditionally was translated "the Spirit of God hovered over the face of the waters" and was then seen as indicating a creative action of the Spirit. However, the question is whether *ruach* stands here for spirit or for wind. After an extensive discussion, Claus Westermann reaches the following conclusions:[17]

- There is no reason to separate verse 2b from verse 2a.
- Taking verse 2b as the first work of creation clashes with the further narrative in Genesis 1 where each section begins with "and God said," indicating the *Logos* as the creative agent.
- The verb *merachefet* means to flutter, flap, or shake, which indicates that *ruach* here means wind, rather than spirit. In Hebrew, the verb determines the meaning of the noun.
- The phrase *ruach elohim* occurs nowhere else in the Old Testament either as "wind of God" or as "spirit of God," so *elohim* is presumably used as a superlative of *ruach*: "mighty wind."
- Comparison with Egyptian cosmogony reinforces the idea that verse 2b is part of the description of the primordial chaos.

The translation then becomes "a mighty wind swept over the face of the waters." Others concur in this translation,[18] and recent Bible versions use this translation or list it as an alternative to the traditional phrase. So in Gen 1:2b no creative role for the Spirit can be found.

I shall, however, argue for a distinct and essential function of the Spirit in the initial creation. The numerous scriptural references to the Spirit can be arranged under five headings: (1) Life-giver, (2) Unifier, (3) Revealer, (4) Sanctifier, and (5) Counselor. I suggest that these can be brought together by defining the Spirit as the divine Communicator, who transmits information from God to his creation. In section 9.3, I shall show that this insight leads to recognizing a role of the Spirit in initial creation.

Wisdom

In *Creation through Wisdom*, Celia Deane-Drummond argues that Wisdom is the agent of creation.[19] She bases her argument primarily on Prov 8:22-31 and Wis 7:18-22 and on the mystical writings of Russian Orthodox theologian Sergii Bulgakov. However, the common biblical meaning of "wisdom" is that of a quality, not a person. S. H. Blank defines wisdom as "a quality of the mind or the utterances of wise men" and calls the personification of wisdom in Prov 8:22-31 and Sir 24:9 a form of poetic exuberance.[20] W. O. E. Oesterley calls Wisdom a "quasi-personification,"[21] similar, I would say, to the use of a statue of Dame Justice in law courts.

In his extensive review on Wisdom in the *Encyclopedia of Theology*, Eugen Biser nowhere mentions the idea of Wisdom as creative agent.[22] Westermann mentions wisdom in several places in his commentary on Genesis 1–11, but never as the agent of creation.[23] Neither does Alan Richardson.[24] John Macquarrie mentions the personification of Wisdom in postbiblical literature but does not connect it with creation.[25]

I conclude that there is no good reason to see Wisdom as the creative agent, by itself or in combination with Spirit and/or *Logos*. It seems more reasonable to consider wisdom as a quality of God's creative work.

9.3 Creative agent and cosmology

When speaking about the creative activity of the *Logos*, we are in the realm of the universe, so we may use our scientific insight concerning the origin of the universe (chapter 2.2). The idea of an initial, non-incarnate *Logos* as God's *energeia* can then be linked to modern cosmological theory, which teaches us that the cosmos originated in a tremendous explosion, the big bang. Although the theory cannot tell us about the origin of this explosion, it is certain that it required a tremendous amount of energy (at least 10^{22} kilowatthours). This energy served partly as the kinetic energy for the expanding cosmos and partly for conversion into the primeval matter, quarks and gluons, from which arose the light elements, hydrogen, helium, and lithium.[26] In theological terms, it is reasonable to assume that this energy would have been provided by the powerful, energetic *Logos*.

However, information is needed to order the brute force of the explosion into a creative process. This information comes in the form of the laws of nature, the four physical forces, and the fundamental constants. Present evidence suggests that at the moment of the big bang, no information was present.[27] An equation relating information content to entropy (the physical measure for disorder) of the developing cosmos shows that at $t = 0$, the moment of the big bang, the information content was zero and the entropy infinite. Thereafter, information content increases and entropy decreases.[28]

Quantum-gravity theory poses that at the quantum level (which applies to the very early universe), the information content is limited to 1 byte per square Planck distance (10^{-35} meter).[29] Therefore, information can only have been brought in some time after the explosion, when the fireball had begun to expand. It must have happened just before the start of the "inflation," a very fast expansion, lasting only 10^{-30} second, increasing the diameter of the universe from 10^{-30} meter to about 10 centimeters, which determined the entire further course of the cosmos (chapter 2.2). Simple calculation shows that the cosmos immediately before the inflation, with a diameter of 10^{-30} meter, could contain at most ten gigabytes of information (less than what current computer hard disks can hold). This amount of information could certainly have contained the physical laws and fundamental constants, needed to initiate the inflation and to guide the further cosmic evolution. Theologically speaking, this information must have been brought in by the Spirit, who is God the Communicator. So here we find a crucial role for the Spirit as a creative agent in initial creation.

This provides us with a trinitarian definition of creation: The Father acts transcendently through the non-incarnate *Logos* in the energy transmission for the big bang (initial creation), the Spirit is immanently active in providing the information needed for cosmic evolution and as lifegiver during the past 3.5 billion years of biological evolution. The cosmic Christ (chapter 10.5), the incarnate *Logos*,[30] acts in deflecting the cosmos from its path toward complete degradation in the next 24 billion years,[31] leading God's creation to completion and redemption. In this process, we may expect the incarnate *Logos* to provide the energy while the Spirit will transmit the information needed. This definition recognizes an essential and distinctive role for each of the three members of the Trinity in the total creation process, without a need to invoke any personifications beyond what is taught by Bible and tradition, and without confusion of the role of the second and third persons of the Trinity.

This idea of God's creative agents comes pretty close to that of Irenaeus (quoted at the beginning of 9.2), "the Son and the Spirit are the two hands of God by which he created all things," if we read for the Son the non-incarnate *Logos* in the initial creation, and the incarnate *Logos* for the perfection on the last day.

9.4 Contingency in cosmic and biological evolution

In addition to the creative activity of God mediated by the creative agents, discussed in the preceding two sections, we must also consider God's action in maintaining the evolving creation. This aspect of God's activity, long recognized in theology under the term *conservatio*, has now become strikingly evident in modern science as the contingency of the universe— its being dependent, endangered, and unpredictable. In this section I present examples of contingency in cosmic and biological evolution.

Contingency in cosmic evolution

It is now realized that cosmic evolution, which eventually led to the appearance of Earth and its inhabitants, has moved within very narrow tolerances. John Gribbin and Martin Rees speak of two cosmic coincidences: the fine-tuning of the fundamental constants and the "flat" universe.[32]

The fundamental constants appear to have just the right magnitude for cosmic evolution to have led to an environment suitable for the development of life and eventually humankind.[33] And as far as we can tell, they have been constant throughout cosmic evolution.[34] For example, with a slightly weaker gravitational force, Earth would not have formed, and with a slightly stronger force, the universe would have collapsed long before life could have arisen. Likewise, if the strong nuclear force were 0.3 percent larger, no hydrogen could exist, and the atoms essential for life would be unstable; if it were 2 percent smaller, no elements heavier than hydrogen would exist, and thus no life. If the weak nuclear force were slightly larger, too much helium would have been formed in the big bang, and no heavy elements could have been ejected from stars. If it were smaller, too little helium would have been formed, leading also to a lack of heavy elements. Another astounding but inescapable fact is that the formation of this unbelievably large universe with its 30 billion galaxies and 3×10^{21} stars was needed to produce advanced life on at least one planet; a much smaller universe would have collapsed before advanced life could have arisen.

The second cosmic coincidence is that the Einsteinian space-time surface of the expanding universe appears to be "flat," implying that the universe is at the knife edge between expanding forever and eventually collapsing in a fiery crash ("big crunch"). This requires an extremely precise balance between the expanding force of the explosion and the gravitational force of better than 1 in 10^{60}, corresponding to the accuracy required to hit a one-inch target on the other side of the observable universe.[35] The flat universe, predicted by Alan Guth in his inflation theory,[36] has been confirmed by analysis of the cosmic microwave background radiation.[37]

Contingency in prebiotic evolution

Several types of contingency also have occurred for the origin of life on Earth from inorganic matter, as it currently is thought to have taken place (chapter 2.4):

- The initially oxygen-free Earth's atmosphere had a double advantage. It allowed formation of biomolecules (for instance, amino acids) through solar ultraviolet radiation unhindered by an ozone layer. At the same time, the absence of oxygen protected these biomolecules from being destroyed by oxidation.
- Hydrothermal vents in the ocean bottom may have provided the right environment for the formation of the components of the first living cells.
- An initial "RNA world" probably overcame the chicken-and-egg problem of the present DNA replication system (chapter 2.4).
- Water has some very propitious and unique characteristics essential for life. It has high heat capacity, expansion on freezing, and maximum density at 4°C (which safeguards aquatic life). It has a high dielectric constant, which is important for nerve and muscle function. It can form hydrogen bonds, allowing DNA and protein molecules to adopt the right shape for their function. Its polarity allows the spontaneous formation of lipid bilayers in cell membranes. No other fluid with all these fortuitous properties is known.[38]
- The growth of microbes with a photosynthetic system in the ocean led to an oxygen-rich atmosphere with an ozone layer, allowing terrestrial organisms to emerge.
- The carbon cycle (uptake of carbon dioxide and release of oxygen by plants and the reverse by animals) maintains a constant 21 percent oxygen level in the atmosphere. This level is high enough to permit the existence of large, advanced vertebrates and low enough to prevent spontaneous, large-scale forest fires.
- The distance of Earth to the sun and the nearly circular orbit of Earth provide a suitable and sufficiently constant temperature on Earth. The radiation of the sun increased by about 30 percent during the past 4 billion years, but algal photosynthesis gradually lowered the

atmospheric carbon dioxide level, so Earth's surface temperature has remained remarkably constant.[39]

- Earth's strong magnetic field (eight hundred times stronger than for Mars) diverts harmful cosmic particle radiation.
- The presence of massive Jupiter in the solar system diverts asteroids from Earth.
- Earth has a suitable surface gravity. If it were stronger, too much ammonia and methane would have been retained. If it were weaker, insufficient water would have been retained.

All these contingencies have provided the right conditions for the origin and maintenance of life on Earth.

Contingency in biological evolution

Additional examples of contingency involve biological evolution. One is evolution's unpredictable course. In 4 billion years of biological evolution, billions of species have arisen, but only about one-thousandth of these have survived. Evolution has been a meandering process in which all possibilities seem to have been tried out.

Another contingency is the Cambrian evolutionary "explosion," which occurred 540 million years ago. After 3 billion years of sluggish evolution, generating virtually only unicellular organisms, all currently existing animal phyla arose in a mere 5 million years.

In addition, unpredictable catastrophes have played a decisive role in the course of the evolutionary process. About 250 million years ago, the greatest mass extinction in history took place (80 percent of marine species and 70 percent of terrestrial species lost). It was caused by a series of massive volcanic eruptions in Siberia, possibly triggered by an asteroid impact,[40] which caused global cooling and oceanic oxygen depletion from the massive discharge of carbon dioxide.[41] Another asteroid impact 65 million years ago led to the extinction of the dinosaurs,[42] permitting primate development and eventually the appearance of humans.

Contingency in human evolution

Three notable contingencies involve human evolution. First, the Rift Valley tectonic event turned East Africa (Ethiopia, Kenya, and Tanzania) some 8 million years ago into a dry, open savanna without great forests.[43]

This environment led to bipedalism in *Australopithecus*, the ancestor of chimpanzees and humans. Bipedalism had important consequences. New activities of the hand (for defense and for gathering seeds and berries) had to be coordinated with the eye, which led to increased size and complexity of the brain (the visual system supplies 39 percent of the neuronal input of the brain). The freeing of the hands relieved the jaw from the task of grasping objects, which permitted the development of throat, tongue, and mouth, later permitting the development of speech. All hominids (*H. habilis, H. erectus,* and *H. sapiens*) appear to have originated and emigrated from East Africa.[44]

Second, through the population bottleneck of *Homo sapiens* (10,000 or fewer individuals until some 50,000 years ago),[45] the survival of humankind hung on a thread until better stone-tool technology, ending of a glacial period, and the advent of agriculture led to a population explosion. This population bottleneck made *Homo sapiens* a single family (genome varying only by 0.1 percent), in contrast to the several families of gorilla and chimpanzee.[46]

Finally, the evolution of *Homo sapiens* appears to end. The evolutionary rate (mutations per nucleotide per billion years of noncoding DNA sequences) decreases in the sequence rat $\rightarrow$ dog $\rightarrow$ monkey $\rightarrow$ human.[47] The use of medicine and technology has in the last two centuries eliminated natural selection for humans.

9.5 Attempted explanations of contingency

Physical theory cannot explain the fine-tuning of the fundamental constants that has permitted the development of human life. Two attempts at a nontheistic explanation have been made: anthropic principles and the multiworld hypothesis.

Anthropic principles

John Barrow and Frank Tipler have proposed the four so-called anthropic principles:[48]

1. The universe we observe must be compatible with our existence as observers (weak anthropic principle).
2. The universe must have the properties that allow intelligent life to develop, or else we would not exist (strong anthropic principle).

3. The universe exists in a definite state, because it is observed by conscious beings (participatory anthropic principle).
4. The life that now exists in the universe will continue to evolve until reaching the point at which it is omnipotent, omnipresent, and omniscient (final anthropic principle).

To this, John Polkinghorne quite rightly remarks that the weak anthropic principle is merely a tautology (a senseless repetition of a meaning in different words), while the others are a form of teleology (belief in a purpose), which is just what the drafters wanted to escape.[49] The anthropic principles cannot provide a satisfactory explanation for the "improbability" of our universe. Moreover, they do not constitute a scientific theory, because they cannot be proven wrong.

Multiworld hypothesis

A little more sophisticated is the hypothesis that there exists an infinite number of universes with different sets of fundamental constants, one of which happens to be the right set for the development of the universe in which we live and the only one we can observe. Richard Gott has suggested that the big bang produced such an infinite number of universes.[50] Lee Smolin claims that every time a black hole is formed, a new universe is spun off deep within it, each with a different set of constants.[51] However, the latter scenario appears to violate accepted astrophysical theory on several points.[52] Max Tegmark presents four different models without a shred of proof that any of them exists.[53] To the contrary, recent observations of the cosmic microwave background radiation suggest that there is only a single universe.[54]

The abundant evidence for contingency in the evolution from big bang to *Homo sapiens* that cannot be explained by science appears to be the nearest thing to a proof of God's existence that we as mere creatures will be able to find. A purposeful Creator seems to be a more reasonable assumption than the "explanations" offered by anthropic principles and multiworld hypotheses.

9.6 Intelligent Design

While anthropic principles and multiworld hypotheses are an attempt to provide a nontheistic explanation for the contingencies observed in cosmic and biological evolution, the reverse is the case for the Intelligent Design hypothesis (chapter 1.5). Biochemist Michael Behe claims in *Darwin's Black Box* that a Darwinian series of mutation-selection steps would be too slow for the formation of complex biological systems including the visual system, blood-clotting system, immune system, and bacterial flagella.[55] So he invokes Intelligent Design (ID), presumably meaning God's intervention in the evolution process, but does not indicate how and when such interventions would take place. Behe calls these biological systems "irreducibly" complex, meaning that removal of one component makes them lose their function.

However, they are not quite so irreducible:

- The visual system has as its key component the visual pigment rhodopsin, which consists of retinene bound to the protein opsin. It is found in all three eye types (insect, mollusk, and vertebrate) and also in *Halobacteria*, where it serves as the light-sensitive element of a proton pump. The rhodopsin design must thus be more than 600 million years old and flexible enough to serve two quite different functions and operate in three different eye types. The marine worm *Platynereis* has both insect-type (for vision) and vertebrate-type photoreceptors (in the brain, for circadian rhythm control).[56] This worm descends from an annelid ancestor *Urbilateria* that has changed little over 500 million years and presumably already possessed both types of photoreceptors. These findings strongly suggest a gene-based evolution of the rhodopsin photoreceptor. It is not "irreducible" in Behe's sense, since the various opsins differ in amino acid composition and the retinene moiety exists in a few different types.
- The blood-clotting system of the dolphin misses Factor XII, but the animal has normal blood clotting, while humans missing this factor are hemophiliacs.[57] It appears that 450 million years ago, jawless vertebrates (hagfish, lamprey) already had a primitive blood-clotting system, with tissue factor, prothrombin, fibrinogen, and possibly some proteases, which has since then evolved to the present, more complex mammalian system.[58] So here again, evidence supports evolution, and the system is not "irreducibly" complex.
- The immune system also lacks "irreducibility." A crucial component of the immune system is immunoglobulin G (IgG), which is responsible for the production of antibodies against harmful intruders. In humans, the IgG is made up of four protein chains, two heavy ones and two light ones. Each of these consists of an invariable and a variable part,

which permits the production of millions of different antibodies. The IgG of camels has no light chains,[59] which reduces the number of possible antibodies to a few thousand. Yet the camel lives happily with this restricted system.

- The bacterial flagellum has a circular base consisting of ten proteins and is located in the cell membrane. To this base, the flagellum tail, consisting of twenty other proteins, is attached. The base with its ten proteins is found in gram-negative bacteria, where it forms the type III secretion system (TTSS) by which the bacteria squirt their toxins into the cells of the host.[60] This suggests that the flagellum was formed by joining preexisting components, more suggestive of an evolutionary origin than a single, sudden operation of Intelligent Design.

- An example of the rapid replacement of a complex system by another is the motility system of *Myxococcus xanthus* bacteria. These bacteria normally move collectively over a solid nutrient medium by means of *pili* (digital extrusions). When the gene for pili formation is destroyed, the bacteria develop within 32 generations a novel motility system consisting of an extracellular matrix of fibrils, which allows them to move even more rapidly.[61] Would we have to believe that the Designer was looking over the shoulders of the microbiologists and then designed a new motility system for the manipulated bacteria?

In addition, recent progress in molecular genetics shows that "gene play" is much more complex and flexible than a linear sequence of mutation-selection steps (chapter 2.5). It seems to me that Intelligent Design is an argument from ignorance. Our rapidly increasing insight into gene play suggests that the Intelligent Design hypothesis will become superfluous and is thus an example of God-in-the-gap theology. It is much more reasonable, scientifically as well as theologically, to assume that the Creator laid down the design of the entire creation in the very beginning by a judicious choice of laws, forces, and constants (section 9.3).

9.7 Summary

God interacts with the creation transcendentally and immanently. The transcendent action is seen in the initial creation, when God lays down laws, forces, and constants and turns immaterial chaos into ordered universe. In the continuing creation, God allows cosmic and biological evolution a great degree of freedom, retaining the possibility to intervene at critical moments in immanent action through the "nudging" of a chaos event. A transcendent-only or immanent-only action model is shown to be unsatisfactory.

Three candidates have been proposed for the role of God's creative agent: *Logos*, Spirit, and Wisdom. The idea that the *Logos*, the Word of God, is God's creative agent rests directly on John 1:1-14 and Ps 33:6 and indirectly on Genesis 1, and it is upheld by Philo and the early church fathers and councils. The idea that the Spirit functions as such cannot be based on Gen 1:2b, because *ruach* stands here for wind, a strong wind that swept over the face of the waters, making it an element of the primordial chaos. The idea that a personified Wisdom is the creative agent is not supported by biblical evidence; wisdom should rather be seen as a quality of God's creative work.

A distinction should be made between the *Logos* before and after the incarnation. The non-incarnate *Logos* initiated creation, while the incarnate *Logos*, Jesus Christ, brings the creation to fulfillment and redemption. Cosmological theory suggests that the initial *Logos* supplied the energy needed for the big bang (initial creation), while a fraction of a second later, the Spirit provided the information required for the cosmic and biological evolution (continuing creation). A similar cooperative action of *Logos*, now as the cosmic Christ, and the Spirit will deflect the universe from its route to complete degradation to the formation of a new kingdom. This provides a trinitarian definition of creation: the Father sends through the *Logos* the energy needed for initial creation, the Spirit infuses the information required for continuing creation, and Christ the incarnate *Logos* completes and redeems creation.

The contingency of creation is noticed in cosmic evolution in the "fine-tuning" of the fundamental constants and in the "flat" universe, as well as in several incidents in prebiotic and biological evolution. Nontheistic explanations of such contingency by anthropic principles and multi-world hypotheses are unsatisfactory. The Intelligent Design hypothesis for the origin of complex biological systems also is unsatisfactory.

10

The Cosmic Christ: Person and Work

In this chapter I consider what chaos theology and science can contribute to our understanding of the person and work of Jesus Christ, the most central topic of the Christian faith.

10.1 The person of Jesus

Notwithstanding the limited historical information from non-Christian and biblical sources, the historicity of Jesus of Nazareth is not seriously doubted nowadays. The amazing fact is that after only three years of teaching and healing, ended by his execution at age thirty-three, this man could give rise to a worldwide religion that has persisted for two thousand years and now counts 2 billion adherents, 33 percent of the world's population (compared with 22 percent for Islam, 15 percent for Hinduism, 6 percent for Buddhism, 10 percent for other religions, and 14 percent nonreligious including agnostics).[1] Yet Jesus lived in a remote corner of the Roman Empire, and knowledge about him remained hidden from most of its inhabitants. He did not leave a single written word, as far as we know. The earliest Christian writings about him date from fifteen to thirty years after his death, having been passed on by word of mouth in the meantime.[2]

Biblical witness

Nearly the only sources for our understanding of the person of Jesus are the gospels and the letters of Paul. The first three gospels—Matthew, Mark, and Luke—have much in common in content and structure, so they are called the Synoptic Gospels. Matthew and Luke contain many parts derived from Mark, but they also have common parts not found in Mark, which are ascribed to a lost source, called Q (for *Quelle*, German for "source"), consisting mostly of sayings of Jesus. Finally, there are passages that occur in only one gospel. For example, the birth story in Matthew centers on Joseph, and the one in Luke on Mary, while Mark has no birth story. The Fourth Gospel, the Gospel according to John, is distinguished by a more advanced theological insight in proclaiming Jesus to be the incarnate Word of God (John 1:1-18). When a saying of Jesus is found in all four gospels, it is generally considered "authentic" in the sense that it is attributed to him by all witnesses whose oral accounts have later been recorded by the gospel authors.

The primary intention of the gospel authors was not to write a biography of Jesus, but rather to proclaim the belief he inspired in his followers by his life and work. For this purpose, they collected sayings, parables, debates, anecdotes, and miracle stories without much detail about dates, places, or historical circumstances. These were joined together by means of short introductory and connecting phrases, indicating time ("next," "a few days later") or place (mountain, road, house, lake).

The gradually emerging insight that Jesus was more than a mere human teacher is first of all reflected in the titles given to Jesus:[3]

- Lord (Greek *kurios*)—in the Old Testament mostly used for Yahweh; in the New Testament frequently for Jesus.
- Christ (Greek *Christos*, Hebrew *Messiah*)—the Anointed One, set apart for a special office, such as that of a prophet or king.
- Son of Man—a name used for the Messiah in the Old Testament book of Daniel (7:13-14). Jesus applies the term to himself, and it is used in reference to his suffering, death, and resurrection.
- Son of God—used for Jesus in the Gospels and by Paul. This title is never directly claimed by Jesus, though he frequently speaks about God as "my Father." The term is implied in Matt 11:25-27: "All things have been handed over to me by my Father; and no one knows the Son except the Father, and no one knows the Father except the Son and anyone to whom the Son chooses to reveal him."
- Word of God—used in the prologue of John's gospel, which says the preexisting Word of God became flesh in Jesus.

Another indication of this emerging insight is the frequent use of the expression "being in," both in the gospel and letters of John and in the letters of Paul.[4] For John, there is a reciprocal indwelling: Father in Son, Son in Father, each of them in the believer, and the believer in each of them (e.g., John 14:11: "Believe me that I am in the Father and the Father is in me"; John 17:21: "As you, Father, are in me, and I am in you, may they also be in us"). Paul frequently speaks about "being in Christ" to indicate the state of the believer (e.g., Rom 8:1: "There is therefore now no condemnation for those who are in Christ Jesus"). Paul also introduces the term "the body of Christ" (1 Cor 10:16).

Thus, it can be said that the Gospels and Paul's letters present an image of the human Jesus, which may be called Godlike, being one with God as humans can never expect to be. Some further development in the thinking about the person of Jesus is noticeable in Paul's idea about *kenosis* (Phil 2:7), which implies that Jesus during his earthly life laid aside some of his divine attributes, and in John's idea of the *Logos*, discussed under the topic of the incarnation (section 10.2).

From Nicea to Chalcedon

The discussion about the person of Jesus continued during the second century. The Ebionites (a Jewish-Christian sect) taught that Jesus was a mere man, who by scrupulous observance of the law was justified and became the Messiah. In contrast, the Greek Docetists did not believe in Jesus' full humanity, but considered him a divine manifestation in human form. The Apologists (c. 120–220) elaborated John's *Logos* idea, saying that beside the Creator God, there was a different and secondary God, the Son. They considered the Holy Spirit to be divine and third in rank after Father and Son.

By the late third century, the three great centers of Christian thought— Alexandria, Antioch, and Rome—were more or less agreed that Jesus is the Son of God, born of Mary through the operation of the Holy Spirit, that God is three in one, and that Jesus is both divine and human. But each center of thought had its own characteristic form of explaining this belief. Alexandria was strongly influenced by Greek philosophy. Antioch was more aligned with Hebrew thought. And Rome, as the capital of the Roman Empire, tried to keep the balance between the two.

The ongoing discussion about the relation between the human Jesus and the divine Christ produced during the fourth century four theologies: those of Arius, Apollinarius, Nestorius, and Eutyches, each of which met with opposition.[5] The persecution of Christians ended when Emperor Constantine embraced the Christian faith (in 312). Since he and his successors felt that unity in the church would further the unity of the empire, these teachings were debated at four major councils: Nicea (325), Constantinople (381), Ephesus (431), and Chalcedon (451). In each case, the teaching discussed was condemned as a heresy, and the accepted teaching was formulated in the Nicene Creed. This development is of paramount importance, because it fixed the central teaching of the church about Christ that is still held by all major denominations.

To summarize very briefly, Arius taught that *Logos* is less than perfect God, and Jesus is more than mere human but created. The council of Nicea rejected this in favor of teaching that the Son is of the same substance (*homoousios*) as the Father yet also fully human. The Nicene Creed was adopted. However, a question remained: How can Christ be both fully God and fully human?

Apollinarius held that in Christ the human spirit was replaced by the divine *Logos*. The council of Constantinople rejected this thesis and affirmed the full divinity of *Logos*, Spirit, and Christ, as well as the full humanity of Jesus. The Nicene Creed was augmented.

Nestorius taught that in Christ there is a voluntary association of the human and divine nature into a new person. The council of Ephesus rejected this thesis and stated that Christ is one person with two natures. The council reaffirmed the Nicene Creed. An unsolved question was, How can there be two natures in one person?[6]

Eutyches said that in Christ there was one nature, that of the incarnate *Logos*. The council of Chalcedon stated that Christ is one person, perfect God and perfect human, of one substance with the Father in his divinity and of human substance, having two natures without confusion and separation (the two-natures doctrine).

All four councils upheld the idea that Jesus Christ could be the Savior of the world only if he was both fully human and fully divine. However, the Greek philosophical terminology used in the Nicene definition of Christ as "one person in one substance with the Father and with two natures" is confusing for us. There substance meant the essence, in this case, divinity. Today we tend to think of substance in chemical terms as a material (which would make Christ identical with God and thus lose his humanity) and of nature in psychological terms (leading to a "schizophrenic" Christ).

For many centuries, it remained rather quiet around Christology. This changed with the eighteenth-century Enlightenment, which brought forth German liberal theology and later Roman Catholic modernism. In an earlier book, I have reviewed these movements and the effects of biblical criticism and recently found manuscripts.[7] My conclusion is that these developments have not abolished the Nicene-Chalcedonian teaching but in some cases have contributed some useful new insights.

10.2 The incarnation of the cosmic Christ

Incarnation

We have two stories on the origin of Jesus: the virgin birth story in the Gospels of Matthew and Luke (Matt 1:16-25; Luke 1:26-38) and the incarnation of the Word in the prologue to the gospel of John (John 1:1-14). In chapter 1.5, I presented scientific, biblical, and theological grounds for considering the virgin birth story as a pious legend, which cannot contribute to our theological understanding of the person of Jesus. What I actually rejected is that a virginal Mary would have been made pregnant by the Spirit. Although Matthew seems to proclaim this, Luke says, "The Holy Spirit will come upon you, and the power of the Most High will overshadow you; therefore the child to be born will be holy; he will be called Son of God" (Luke 1:35). The "power of the Most High" could well be taken to refer to the *Logos*. Then we would have another example of a concerted action of Spirit and *Logos* (chapter 9.3), the *Logos* instilling God's power into the baby Jesus, and the Spirit transmitting God's wisdom to him. The *Logos* power we notice in the healing acts of Jesus, the Spirit's wisdom in his teaching.

John's idea of the incarnation of the *Logos*, the creative Word of God, in the human Jesus of Nazareth emphasizes that Jesus thereby becomes fully divine while remaining fully human. Bishop John Robinson notes that John 1:1 implies neither an identity between God and Christ nor a simple likeness between them.[8] The Greek version *kai theos en ho logos* has usually been translated "The Word was God," which suggests identity. However, says Robinson (who was a New Testament scholar), then the Greek would have had the article with God: *ho theos*. Nor is John saying that Jesus is a "divine" human, in the sense of the Greeks, because then *theios* would have been used instead of *theos*. Robinson translates instead, "What God was, the Word was" (as in the New English Bible), which is not an identity but rather suggests a common quality. In Jesus we see God (John 14:9); he is the complete expression of God, which is how Phillips translates John 1:1: "At the beginning God expressed himself. That personal expression, that word, was with God, and was God."[9] It should be noted that this does not entail the idea of a preexistent Christ.[10]

In 1977 the doctrine of the incarnation came under severe attack in Anglican circles in a volume of seven essays, entitled *The Myth of God Incarnate*.[11] The authors feel that the doctrine needs to be reconsidered in the light of a "growing knowledge of Christian origins." Their arguments are based on New Testament texts, linguistic analysis, the problem of explaining a fully human and fully divine Christ, and the hypothesis that the incarnation idea was taken over from the Samaritans. The incarnation is seen as "a mythological way of expressing Jesus' significance for us." This led to a book with critical essays[12] and a conference of the seven authors paired with seven "conventional" theologians, with published proceedings.[13] In the latter publication, Brian Hebblethwaite and Nicholas Lash point out that the authors of *The Myth of God Incarnate* mistakenly assume that "incarnation" used in a literal sense cannot be true. To John Hick's claim that atonement is achieved by a "metaphorical incarnation" of divine love in each human, Charles Moule replies that this idea is foreign to the New Testament, that the incarnation is the *Logos* becoming a man of flesh and blood in Jesus rather than a divine inspiration, and that an appeal to truth and nobility in each of us—without resurrection, church, and Eucharist—is an insufficient explanation of Christ's saving work.

Another modern voice on Jesus

Roman Catholic theologian Edward Schillebeeckx has presented an extensive, critical study of Christology, in which he restudies the sources and then rephrases traditional formulations, adding depth without abandoning crucial elements.[14] He emphasizes the humanity of Jesus over against his excessive divinization by earlier theologians. Jesus was a human in divine manner, thus becoming a manifestation of God. Schillebeeckx considers *Abba* one of the most authentic words of Jesus, which leads him to claim that in his humanity Jesus is so intimately "of the Father" that he is "Son of God." The divinity must not be sought *behind, above, or below* the human Jesus, but appears *in* his humanity. His actions are thus free of human limitations, obtain universal validity, and live on in the sacraments.

The heart of the Christian message, according to Schillebeeckx, is that human history with its successes, failures, illusions, and disillusions is surmounted by God in the personal and bodily resurrection of Jesus. The resurrection confirms that God was constantly with Jesus throughout his life, right up to the human dereliction of his death on the cross, which

Schillebeeckx considers to be a judicial murder. The resurrection *precedes* the Easter experience of renewed life in the disciples and is not merely a symbolic expression of this experience, as Bultmann claimed.

On the two-natures doctrine, Schillebeeckx remarks that the concepts of nature and person are inadequate terms to describe God's absolute freedom. In Jesus there is not an identity of two finite modes of being, but the presence of a finite human mode of being and an infinite divine mode of being. He summarizes his view of Jesus in the apt phrase "Jesus parable of God and paradigm [model] of humanity."

10.3 Death and resurrection

Death of Jesus

The death of Jesus by crucifixion receives prominent attention in all four Gospels and is even mentioned by non-Christian authors. Roman historian Tacitus (c. 110 CE), writing about Nero's persecution of the Christians, mentions that the latter were followers of "Christ, whom the procurator Pontius Pilate had executed in the reign of Tiberius." The Jewish historian Flavius Josephus writes in his *Jewish Antiquities* (vol. 18, c. 95) about Jesus:

> Pilate condemned him to be crucified and to die. And those who had become his disciples did not abandon his discipleship. They reported that he had appeared to them three days after his crucifixion and that he was alive; accordingly, he was perhaps the Messiah concerning whom the prophets have reported wonders.

Some scholars have assumed this passage to be a later Christian insertion. However, in 1972 Jewish scholar Shlomo Pines found the passage in an old Arabic translation, on which no Christian scribe could have laid hands.

The Gospels record that Jesus foretold his own death. Death by crucifixion was the cruelest form of execution, reserved by the Romans for slaves and foreigners to punish robbery, tumult, and sedition. The execution was the result of an incidental collusion between those who hated and feared Jesus for quite different reasons: Sanhedrin and Sadducees saw in him a danger for the religious establishment, the Pharisees hated Jesus for his attacks on their self-righteousness, King Herod feared him as a rival to the throne, Pontius Pilate feared for his own position if a popular revolt broke out, and the people were bitterly disappointed when Jesus after the Palm Sunday events turned out not to be the political Messiah who would liberate them from Roman rule. Thus, Jesus' death on the cross was a judicial murder. Those who had followed him for his teaching and healing during his three years of ministry abandoned him; one of his disciples betrayed him; the other disciples fled after his arrest; and Peter followed him to the court of the Sanhedrin but in the end disowned him. As a common criminal, Jesus died on the cross.

Resurrection of Christ

The resurrection of Jesus on the third day after his death is reported in all four Gospels (and by Flavius Josephus, as mentioned in the discussion of Jesus' death). But unlike his death, this event is difficult to grasp with our human understanding. Calvinist theologian H. M. Kuitert, who in his later years has repudiated most tenets of the Christian faith, sneers, "A corpse doesn't come to life again."[15] Others maintain that it is merely a symbolic expression of the post-Easter experience of renewed life in his disciples. No, says Schillebeeckx, the resurrection *precedes* the Easter experience.[16] The heart of the Christian message is that human history with its successes, failures, illusions, and disillusions is surmounted by God in the personal and bodily resurrection of Jesus.

Simple logic suggests that the resurrection of Christ from death was inevitable; otherwise, remaining chaos would have won out against God. Yet the disciples did not expect the resurrection on the third day after the crucifixion, as shown by their reaction to the empty tomb (Luke 24:11; John 20:2). This makes it unlikely that the belief in the resurrection was wishful thinking on their part, as some claim. Moreover, if the post-Easter appearances of Jesus had merely been subjective experiences of the disciples, as some have proposed, then these would have worn off in time and would not have been transmitted to us as a reality. And the fearful disciples, hiding behind closed doors, would not have turned into fearless witnesses of the resurrection on the day of Pentecost (Acts 2).

What about the biological fact that a corpse doesn't come back to life? To this I say that in the resurrection, Jesus' dead body was transformed into a new body, the resurrection body. This is borne out by the details about the burial cloths in John 20:6-8, which suggest that Jesus' dead body had been transformed, leaving the cloths behind. This is quite different from the description of the raising of Lazarus, who came out of the tomb with the cloths still around him (John 11:44). In this case, it appears to be a resuscitation of Lazarus's human body (like that after a cardiac arrest nowadays), and he later presumably died. The resurrection body of Christ is also noticeable in the post-Easter appearances to his disciples, where the risen Jesus can walk through a closed door, appear and disappear momentarily, and reappear at another place (as in the story of the men of Emmaus, recorded in Luke 24:13-35).

Science cannot add much beyond suggesting that the resurrection places Jesus outside space and time. This implies that the natural laws governing life in this world do not apply to the risen Christ, as witnessed by the post-Easter appearances and the ascension account. This is in contrast to Arthur Peacocke, who speaks about a "trans-mutation . . . consonant with and culminating the series of biological mutations," a continuity from the earthly Jesus to the risen Christ in the "molecular, material aspect."[17] Although I agree with the continuity, I would say that the resurrection is a revolutionary rather than an evolutionary event, and I wouldn't like to include the molecular, material aspect in the continuity (for more on this, see chapter 14).

The significance of the resurrection is manifold. It led to the founding and the rapid growth of the church, as recorded in the book of Acts and subsequent history of the church. It gives Christians the experience of union with the living Christ, sacramentally expressed in the Eucharist. It sets Christ free for his task in the fulfillment and redemption of the creation. And it ushers in the new age, the messianic age, with the promise of the triumphant return of Christ on the last day (*Parousia*), the establishment of the new kingdom, and the resurrection of the dead (see chapter 14).

10.4 Jesus Christ and reconciliation

What does the reconciliation between God and humans mean, and how is it brought about? The answers given to this question in the course of time have resulted in many serious conflicts, particularly in the continental Reformation. Even today, in our secularized age, the subject can arouse emotions. In 1997 Dutch theologian C. J. den Heyer, then professor of New Testament theology at the Calvinist Kampen University, caused quite a stir with his book on reconciliation.[18] He presented an extensive discussion of what the New Testament tells us about "reconciliation," and at the end, he admits that he can no longer accept traditional Calvinist teaching about it.[19] He merely says that in this teaching, God seems to have become a prisoner of God's self, so entrapped in God's own justice that blood must flow to effect reconciliation. Finally, he states that he wants to be guided and inspired by the Bible, but that he finds there a multiplicity of images and opinions coming across a gap of two thousand years. He also expresses reservations about the resurrection, saying, "Jesus 'rises' in those people who dare to walk in his way. Thus he 'lives' on, not only in the remembrance, but also in our time."[20]

Within a year, several books on the topic appeared,[21] including one by H. Baarlink, den Heyer's predecessor and teacher at Kampen University.[22] In it Baarlink repeats the Bible study and concludes that the New Testament witness is less diverse than suggested by den Heyer. He then cites Anselm's *Cur Deus Homo* (Why Did God Become Man?),[23] but leaves the interpretation to the dogmatists, so the reader is left uncertain what to think about the "mechanism" of reconciliation.

Here I shall briefly discuss the biblical images and later theological interpretations, including the doctrine of original sin, followed by an interpretation of reconciliation from chaos theology.

Reconciliation in the Bible

In the Old Testament we read about the covenant that Yahweh made with Moses and his people, and the law God gave them. Anyone who fully and steadily keeps the law is assured of God's acceptance. But over the centuries, the question arose how God could forgive the transgressor of the law without compromising God's own perfect justice. It became clear, particularly to the prophets, that this was impossible. Jeremiah speaks about a new covenant (Jer 31:31-34), but without solving the problem that, for the Israelites, this required blood—the blood of oxen in the first covenant, but whose blood in the new covenant? Isaiah suggests a solution when he writes about the Suffering Servant: "He was wounded for our transgressions, . . . he bore the sin of many" (Isa 53:5, 12). The Old Testament prophets also realized that, without repentance, the offering of sacrifice for sins was futile: "I have had enough of burnt offerings of rams. . . . I do not delight in the blood of bulls" (Isa 1:11); "I desire steadfast love and not sacrifice, the knowledge of God rather than burnt offerings" (Hos 6:6).

In the New Testament, Jesus starts his ministry with a call to repentance for sin, saying, "The kingdom of God has come near; repent, and believe in the good news" (Mark 1:15). He affirms the uselessness of animal sacrifices as a substitute for repentance, repeating the words of Hosea: "I desire mercy, not sacrifice" (Matt 9:13). The image of ransom (a metaphor of the slave market, as is the case for "redemption") appears in his words "the Son of man came . . . to give his life as a ransom for many" (Mark 10:45). At the institution of the Eucharist, Jesus answers Jeremiah's problem by declaring, "This is my blood of the covenant, which is poured out for many for the forgiveness of sins" (Matt 26:28). He also applies to himself the words of Isaiah 53 about the Suffering Servant: "For I tell you, this scripture must be fulfilled in me" (Luke 22:37). John the Baptist describes Jesus as "the Lamb of God who takes away the sin of the world" (John 1:29). His death is thus compared to the killing of the paschal lamb at the Passover.

Paul proclaims, "Christ died for our sins" (1 Cor 15:3). For him, Christ's death and resurrection are the means by which we are redeemed from the effects of our transgression of the law, our sins. By baptism we share mystically in Christ's death and his victory over death in the resurrection and acquire justification as God's free gift. Faith in Christ is what is required of us, rather than works, as these can never meet the standard of the law (Gal 3:10-14). Peace was made between God and humans through the blood of the cross (Col 1:20). Paul also uses a "substitution" image: "For our sake he made him to be sin" (2 Cor 5:21). Once Paul uses the image of the paschal lamb: "For our paschal lamb, Christ, has been sacrificed" (1 Cor 5:7), although he knew very well that the paschal lamb was only killed in the temple for consumption at the family Seder meal, rather than for a sacrifice. In Hebrews (author unknown), we find the image of the high priest who offered up himself (Heb 7:27). The Bible tells the story of our redemption in various metaphors, which should not be literalized.

Subsequent theological elaboration

Through the centuries, theologians have attempted to combine the various biblical images into a comprehensive theology of reconciliation. Following are some of the main examples with a brief characterization:

- Origen (c. 200) formulated the ransom theory: the death of Christ is the ransom that had to be paid to Satan, who had acquired rights over all humans by Adam's fall.
- Augustine (c. 400) accepted the ransom theory and connected reconciliation with the idea of original sin (see next paragraph), the "hereditary" disease of humankind after Adam's fall.

- Anselm (c. 1100) developed in *Cur Deus Homo* (Why Did God Become Man?)[24] the satisfaction theory: as finite humans cannot make satisfaction to the infinite One, God had to take their place in the person of Christ and, by his death, make a complete satisfaction to divine justice.
- Thomas Aquinas (c. 1250) denied the necessity of this method of satisfaction but stated that the manner God chose was highly fitting ("congruous"). It shows forth God's omnipotence, goodness, wisdom, and the harmony between God's justice and mercy. Reconciliation to Thomas Aquinas is the free gift of God to us, who cannot redeem ourselves due to the loss of the supernatural gifts by original sin. Humans may cooperate (by faith and works) with God's grace in receiving justification and sanctification. This became the traditional Catholic teaching on reconciliation.
- Luther vigorously denied the possibility of human cooperation with grace other than by faith alone (*sola fide*). Claiming to return to Pauline teaching, he rejected the satisfaction theory and replaced it with the substitution theory: Christ, bearing by voluntary substitution the punishment due to us, was reckoned by God a sinner in our place.
- Calvin went even further with his penal theory: Christ bore in his soul the tortures of a condemned and ruined man.

From all this emerges, in my opinion, a gruesome image of a God who is so hopelessly imprisoned in God's own perfect justice that the only possibility to save humankind is by sacrificing God's own Son. How could theologians from Origen to Calvin slip up so badly? Five errors were made: (1) biblical metaphors were literalized; (2) the death of Christ was isolated from the incarnation and resurrection; (3) continuing creation as God's ongoing battle against evil—or, in terms of chaos theology, the remaining chaos element—was neglected; (4) the idea of the cosmic Christ, who is reconciling the entire cosmos and not only humans, was neglected; and (5) errors 3 and 4 led to an anthropocentric view of God's action in the world. This final error causes us to lose sight of the fact that God's creative work is aimed at the fulfillment and perfection of creation, of which humans can be a part only by repentance and faith in Christ.

Original sin

The doctrine of original sin was formulated by Irenaeus (c. 190) in order to absolve God from responsibility for moral evil, necessitated by his adoption of *creatio ex nihilo*. He interpreted Paul's words "As sin came into the world through one man [Adam], . . . many died through the one man's trespass" (Rom 5:12-21) as meaning that evil came into the world through the sin of Adam. Didymus of Alexandria (c. 350) taught that Adam's sin was transmitted by natural propagation, and Chrysostom (c. 390) attributed this to sexual lust. Augustine (c. 400) affirmed Chrysostom's idea about sexual lust as the driving force, claiming that Adam's guilt turned humanity into a *massa damnata* (condemned multitude). Anselm (c. 1080) defined original sin as the "privation of the righteousness which every human ought to possess," thus separating it from sexual lust. Thomas Aquinas (c. 1270) taught that Adam through his sin lost the ability to keep his inferior impulses in submission to reason, but without losing his reason, will, and passions. He rejected the role of sexual lust. Since 1856 this is the official Roman Catholic teaching. Luther and Calvin adopted the Augustinian view, attributing transmission of original sin to sexual lust and claiming that it completely destroys human freedom and persists even after baptism.

Five objections can be made against the doctrine of original sin. First, it offers a fatalistic view of human life by portraying human sinfulness as an inherited disease, as indicated by the German term *Erbsünde*. Second, it can be said that Paul in Rom 5:12-21 only wants to illustrate the superiority of grace over the power of sin.[25] A third objection is that the author of Genesis 3 is only expressing his experience that all humans are prone to sin in the powerful myth about a first human pair, so it is not permissible to literalize the myth and turn it around by claiming that all subsequent human sin was derived, inherited, from Adam. Fourth, science tells us that humans developed gradually over a period of 6 million years from *Australopithecus* via *Homo habilis* and *Homo erectus* to *Homo sapiens*, in body as well as mind (see chapter 2).[26] Finally, the evolution theory tells us that a new species does not originate in a single pair but in at least hundreds of individuals, making the idea of the literal existence of a human protopair untenable.

10.5 Reconciliation in chaos theology

The cosmic Christ

Over the centuries, popular Christian belief has regrettably narrowed down the significance of the incarnation to being merely the prelude to human salvation, with blithe disregard for the fate of all other creatures. However, Paul already recognized in Jesus the cosmic Christ when saying, "In Christ God was reconciling the world [Gk. *kosmos*] to himself" (2 Cor 5:19). And John writes, "That the world [Gk. *kosmos*] might be saved through him" (John 3:17).

The idea of Jesus as the cosmic Christ is supported by our knowledge of cosmic evolution, popularly expressed in the phrase that "we are made of stardust." The hydrogen and helium, resulting from the big bang, condensed into stars, which through nuclear fusion produced the heavier chemical elements (see chapter 2). After the exhaustion of their nuclear fuel, these stars turned into supernovas, which exploded and ejected these elements into interstellar space as "cosmic dust." Eventually, in one galaxy, sun and Earth were formed through condensation and accretion of these elements from a cloud of cosmic dust. In the prebiotic evolution, living cells were formed from these elements, and in the biological evolution, all living beings, including humans, are formed from these elements through the uptake of food. The saying "We are made of stardust" means that we humans are part of, are united with, the entire cosmos. The human Jesus also shares in this cosmic union, so through the incarnation, he becomes the cosmic Christ. This has decisive consequences for our understanding of his reconciling work.

Reconciliation by the cosmic Christ

In chaos theology (chapter 6), I hold that God in the continuing creation is involved in an ongoing battle against remaining chaos. That has gone on for 13.7 billion years already, whereas humans have existed only during the last two hundred thousand years. So the need for reconciliation is not only a human predicament, but a cosmic drama. Paul senses this, when he says, "The whole creation has been groaning in labor pains until now" (Rom 8:22) in expectation of liberation. Therefore, in this ongoing battle, God is not redeeming humans alone, but the entire cosmos. Paul glimpses this when he speaks about God reconciling the world in Christ (2 Cor 5:19), as does John when writing about the world to be saved through Christ (John 3:17). This is the idea of the cosmic Christ, who fulfills the entire creation and reconciles it with God.

The entire creation with all its creatures, including humans, is being reconciled by the cosmic Christ. Of course, it is not a trivial matter that God's top creatures, God's image bearers, have succumbed to the remaining chaos element and become habitual sinners. Thus, God takes our entire being, our body-mind unity, into God's self in the incarnation of Christ. Then remaining chaos, "in a desperate effort," leads humans to kill Christ in the crucifixion, as many martyrs have been killed in the course of history. However, God turns the apparent defeat against chaos into victory by the resurrection of Christ. This is an initial victory, which will become definitive on the last day, when God will banish the remaining chaos element forever (Rev 21:1). It is the total action of Christ, rather than merely his death, that brings reconciliation to the cosmos and all its inhabitants. The only difference between humans and all other creatures is that (at least as far as we know) only humans can distinguish between good and evil and have (in principle) the freedom of will to make the right choice, thus bearing the responsibility for making wrong choices. When we humans repent in faith in Christ, we may share in the benefits of his cosmic reconciling work (Rom 4:1-16).

This theology of reconciliation avoids literalizing biblical metaphors, integrates crucifixion with incarnation and resurrection, and places reconciliation in the continuing creation on the way to its fulfillment on the last day. Moreover, it does not picture God as a captive of divine justice. Crucial for us humans is our acceptance of the freely offered reconciliation in and through faith. Briefly put, Jesus did not die *for* our sins, but through our sins; Jesus brings reconciliation not through his death, but through his resurrection. I hope that this fresh view on reconciliation will be helpful to those who cannot find themselves anymore in the doctrinal statements of the Reformers on this topic.

10.6 Summary

The New Testament shows that the disciples came to see Jesus as more than a mere human, as one who is Godlike, united with God as humans can never expect to be. During the next few centuries, the person of Jesus Christ was discussed at the four great councils, leading to the Christology enshrined in the Nicene Creed: Jesus Christ is fully human and fully divine, of one "substance" with the Father (*homoousios*), and with two natures. Further discussions from the eighteenth century onward and newer manuscript findings have not abolished the Nicene-Chalcedonian Christology but made it more intelligible for later generations.

Since the virgin birth story (Matthew, Luke) presents both biological and theological problems, I prefer to follow John's account of the incarnation of the *Logos* (God's creative Word) in Jesus of Nazareth, which makes him the Christ, the Son of God. This fits the Nicene definition, with the note that it does not imply a "preexistent" Christ.

The crucifixion was a judicial murder brought about by an incidental collusion of several diverse parties. This made the resurrection an inevitable action of God, unexpected by the disciples, only gradually recognized by them through the appearances of the risen Christ. It was not a resuscitation, but rather the transformation of the earthly body into a resurrection body unbound by space and time. The resurrection ushers in the new age with the triumphant return of Christ on the last day.

Christ's reconciling work is presented in the New Testament in various metaphors. Later attempts to construct a theology of reconciliation have led to the ransom, satisfaction, substitution, and penal theories. From them arises a picture of a God who is so entrapped in divine justice that the only way to redeem humans is by sacrificing God's Son. These theories suffer from four flaws: they literalize biblical metaphors, isolate the crucifixion from incarnation and resurrection, neglect the continuing creation as God's ongoing battle against chaos, and neglect the idea of the cosmic Christ.

After criticizing the doctrine of original sin, I present a revised theology of reconciliation based on chaos theology. On both biblical and scientific grounds, we may speak of the cosmic Christ, who is united with the entire cosmos and not only with humanity. Remaining chaos leads to the crucifixion, but God turns the apparent defeat against chaos into victory by the resurrection. The cosmic Christ brings fulfillment and reconciliation to the entire cosmos. Only humans must choose to receive the benefits of this process by faith. Jesus did not die *for* our sins, but through our sins; Jesus brings reconciliation not through his death, but through his resurrection.

11

Human Ambivalence: Genetic Modification

11.1 Image bearer and sinner

In this chapter, I consider the question "Who are we humans?" in the light of our practice of genetic modification. Humans are, like plants, animals, and all inanimate structures, created and thus limited. Yet only humans are created in the image of God, who blesses them and tells them to rule over all the earth and its creatures (Gen 1:26-30). The Genesis stories make a sharp distinction between humans and all other creatures. Only humans have the likeness of God, so only they can communicate with God and think about themselves and their surroundings. In naming all the animals (Gen 2:19-20), humans interpret and order God's creation, pursue science and technology. They are cocreators with God, and their technology is, in principle, necessary and good. This is what I call human grandeur.

However, when God places the protohumans Adam and Eve in the Garden of Eden, telling them to cultivate it and to eat from any of the trees, except from the tree of the knowledge of good and evil, they succumb to the temptation to eat from the fruit of this tree (Gen 3:1-24). They are not satisfied to be God's image bearers but want to be equal to God. Greed and selfishness make us abuse other creatures and misuse our technology. This is human brokenness.

Humans are, therefore, ambivalent creatures embodying two opposing traits in one creature: grandeur and brokenness. Our grandeur is to be God's image bearers, who may rule over the entire created world as cocreators with God, in the pursuit of science and technology for the well-being of humanity and our environment and for the glory of God. Our brokenness makes us restless aspirers, who again and again are grasping for equality with God, misusing our God-given creativity, our science and technology, for our own glory, power, and wealth. Our ambivalence thus also taints our technology, so that every application of new scientific knowledge brings with it its own problems and potential for evil. Like Adam and Eve after their trespass were condemned to wander in the desert, we are doomed to wander in the desert of our high-technology society.

In this chapter, I consider this ambivalence in our technology in some depth for the field of genetic modification. The use of genetic modification is very much in public discussion for its great potential in promised benefits as well as for feared undesirable consequences and even abuses. I shall explain the principle of this technology, give examples of its applications, describe risk and opposition, and conclude with a discussion of the theological and ethical aspects.

11.2 Principles of genetic modification

Genetic modification is the alteration of the genetic makeup (genome) of cells for the purpose of producing biological materials or biological effects for medical, veterinary, agricultural, or other uses. The basic principle is to isolate the gene responsible for the production of the desired material or effect from the cell in which it normally occurs, and then to introduce it into the host cell, where one wants it to exert its effect.[1] (A brief description of the genetic system is presented in chapter 2.5.)

In the case of producing biological materials, the host cell is usually a bacterial or yeast cell, which multiplies fast and then secretes a large amount of the desired material into the cultivation medium. The material, most often a protein, is isolated from the medium and purified. When bacteria or yeast cells cannot produce and secrete the desired form of the protein, cultured vertebrate or invertebrate cells are used, although these require a more complex cultivation procedure and have a lower rate of production.

For producing biological effects, the genetically altered cell itself is used. The scientist either allows that cell to grow into a full plant or animal or implants it in a patient for the cure of a hereditary disease.

The crucial step in genetic modification is the introduction of the gene into the host cell in such a way that it will come to "expression." One way to introduce the gene is to link the gene to a vector, a carrier such as a virus that enters the host cell and inserts itself with the gene into the genome of that cell. A simpler but less reliable method is to microinject the gene into the host cell.

11.3 Production of biological materials

The biological materials produced by genetic modification are mostly proteins, namely, hormones, growth factors, vaccines, and antibodies. These cannot be produced on a commercial scale by chemical synthesis; they can only be obtained by complex and expensive isolation procedures from animal or cadaver organs. In contrast, once the genetically altered cell has been prepared in the laboratory, virtually continuous and relatively inexpensive production on a commercial scale is possible.

The first two products coming to commercial production were human growth hormone and human insulin. Human growth hormone used to be isolated in small quantities at high cost from cadaver pituitary glands. A batch was once found to cause Creutzfeldt-Jakob disease, a rare but fatal brain disease, and production was suspended. Fortunately, at that time, the genetic preparation became available and was found to meet all medical requirements. Now human growth hormone is produced at far lower cost and in sufficient quantity to treat all children with impaired growth due to a lack of this hormone. Human insulin is useful for the 5 percent of insulin-dependent diabetics who have developed resistance to the traditional animal product.

Many other medicinal compounds can be produced. They include erythropoietin, which cures anemia due to kidney disease; tissue plasminogen activator (TPA), which dissolves blood clots after a heart attack or stroke; factor VIII, a blood-clotting factor lacking in hemophiliacs; epidermal growth factor, which promotes wound healing; and nerve growth factors, which may protect cholinergic nerves from degeneration in Alzheimer's and Parkinson's disease and amyotrophic lateral sclerosis (ALS, also known as Lou Gehrig's disease).

Antibodies, produced by inserting the gene for the antibody into a bacterium, are widely used for diagnostic purposes. Their uses include AIDS virus tests, detection of melanoma (a fatal skin cancer), and detection of dead heart tissue after a heart attack. Antibodies can in principle also be used for therapeutic purposes, including prevention of kidney transplant rejection and selective tumor therapy, as in treatment of non-Hodgkin's lymphoma. In these applications, the antibody is linked with a chemotherapeutic agent or a radioactive isotope.[2]

11.4 Transgenic plants and animals

Animals or plants into which a foreign gene has been incorporated are usually called "transgenic."

Transgenic plants

Gene transfer can be used to produce crops with increased resistance to herbicides, drought, high soil salinity, insects, or disease.[3] Examples are soy and corn resistant to the herbicide glyphosate. This resistance allows farmers to spray for weeds much earlier and in smaller amounts, as the young transgenic crop plants are resistant to the herbicide, while the young weeds are more sensitive to the herbicide than mature weeds.

Another type of application is to change the metabolism of the plant by introducing a foreign gene. Transgenic sugar beets can produce, instead of sucrose, fructane, which can be used as a noncaloric sweetening agent or as a natural fiber. Raising such altered beets is more profitable to the farmer. A transgenic potato produces, instead of amylose (potato starch), amylopectine, which is used as a thickener for foods and again sells at a higher price. A pea that is the major protein supply for people in developing countries but lacks some essential amino acids has been enriched with the gene for the enzyme threonine deaminase. The modification causes the peas to contain the amino acids threonine, methionine, and lysine, which are missing from the native pea.

The worldwide acreage of farmland on which genetically modified (GM) crops are grown is steadily increasing: from 142 million acres in 2002 to 167 million in 2003 and 200 million in 2004. Of the 8 million farmers in seventeen countries who grew GM crops in 2004, 90 percent live in developing countries. However, the five largest producers are the United States, Argentina, Canada, Brazil, and China.

Transgenic animals

Animals with a desired trait are produced by microinjecting the chosen gene into the male nucleus in a fertilized egg cell before fusion of the male and female nuclei has taken place.[4] Many applications are possible. Modified cows may produce more milk or milk containing a medicinal substance. Chickens may be made resistant to infections so they can be raised with fewer antibiotics. Other modifications may produce leaner pigs and faster-growing salmon and trout.

An important laboratory application is the production of animal models for the study of a human disease by inserting the gene responsible for the disease into a mouse embryonic stem cell, which is then introduced into a developing mouse embryo. In this way, the genetic alteration will be transmitted to its progeny. Transgenic mice are used for studying diseases like cystic fibrosis, muscular dystrophy, Alzheimer's disease, sickle-cell anemia, and pancreatic cancer. Mice from which a crucial gene for development of the immune system has been removed acquire severe combined immune-deficiency disease (SCID). When cells derived from a child with leukemia are injected into SCID mice, the cells grow and spread in the same way as in diseased children,[5] allowing the researcher to develop the optimal chemotherapy protocol for the child. In SCID mice in which a human immune system has been implanted, AIDS vaccines and drugs are tested. Previously such testing was possible only in chimpanzees, the only animal susceptible to the human form of HIV, the virus that causes AIDS.

Another possibility is to insert human immune genes into piglets to produce organs for transplantation into humans that will not be rejected. This procedure could overcome the increasing shortage of human organs for transplantation. A concern is that a swine virus present in the organ might infect the patient, so experiments in humans are not (yet) permitted in the United States and the United Kingdom.

11.5 Human applications: Gene therapy

The main medical application is sought in gene therapy of hereditary diseases, of which 3,500 are known, 25 percent of all known diseases. In addition, many common diseases, including hypertension, diabetes, heart disease, allergies, mental illness, and several forms of cancer, have a genetic component that may involve several genes.

Two types of gene therapy must be distinguished: genetic repair of somatic cells (differentiated body cells, such as muscle cells) and of germ cells (egg cells and sperm cells, separate or combined after fertilization).

Somatic-cell gene therapy is possible when the disease is caused by a single missing or defective gene in cells that are still dividing. This limits the therapy primarily to bone marrow cells forming red blood cells and lymphocytes (white blood cells).[6] The normal gene is isolated from a suitable donor and then inserted into cells taken from the patient, which are then multiplied by cultivation and returned to the patient. Success requires a sufficient number of modified cells and sustained expression of the healthy gene so the modified cells can "overgrow" the defective cells. A problem is that the viral vector, used to introduce the gene, might infect the cells of the patient.[7]

Germ-cell gene therapy is required in the majority of hereditary diseases in which nondividing somatic cells are affected.[8] The functioning gene must be inserted into a fertilized ovum just prior to fusion of the male and female chromosomes. This will introduce the gene into all cells of the child and all the child's descendants. This type of gene therapy has not yet been permitted because of unknown risks to embryo and succeeding generations.

Unfortunately, after fourteen years and over a hundred clinical trials, researchers have achieved no proven cure with gene therapy for the prime candidates: sickle-cell anemia, thalassemia (a type of anemia), melanoma, ADA-immunodeficiency, and emphysema. One problem appears to be the vector used for gene insertion (it may land near a gene that is then affected); in a case of eleven children treated for SCID, three developed leukemia. Other possible problems are removal of the transformed cells by the patient's immune system and insufficient expression of the introduced gene. More laboratory research is needed to overcome these problems.

In the Human Genome Project, scientists of the United States, Europe, and Japan have mapped all genes (about thirty thousand) on the forty-six human chromosomes. They expect to have soon determined their complete DNA sequences.[9] The gene map is expected to be of great benefit for understanding the genetic basis of diseases, for genetic screening, for designing new drugs, and hopefully, for gene therapy.

11.6 Risks and opposition

Genetic engineering has met with more public scrutiny of its risks and with more opposition than any other area of high technology. This is due partly to fear of the unknown, partly to ethical objections, and, ironically, also to the responsible behavior of scientists who devised the technique. Paul Berg and colleagues called in 1974 for a moratorium on the use of the technique until guidelines for its safe application were formulated, accepted, and enforced. They recognized the remote possibility that genetic modification of a microorganism might turn it into a dangerous pathogenic (disease-producing) organism, which could cause an epidemic against which existing antibiotics would be ineffective.

Laboratory work and biomedical products

After careful studies by experts in microbiology, infectious diseases, epidemiology, and molecular biology, strict guidelines were formulated and imposed by the National Institutes of Health (NIH) and similar bodies in other countries. After more than twenty-five years of widespread application of genetic modification in laboratory studies without a single accident, it is now clear that the risk is extremely low. The guidelines for these applications (production of biological materials) have since been relaxed and in 1982 were made voluntary.

Administration of medicinal products of genetic modification to human subjects has not caused any undesirable effects. This was to be expected, since these products are chemically and biologically identical to their natural counterparts. Nevertheless, treating cows with genetically produced bovine somatotropin to increase milk yield has been opposed as posing a health risk for consumers. Although extensive investigations have shown no risk, the hormone's use is still not permitted in the European Union. Unfortunately, rational scientific arguments sometimes do not prevail against irrational fear or commercial interests.

Introduction of transgenic organisms into the environment

For the introduction of large numbers of transgenic organisms into the environment, additional rules and regulations exist. It is highly unlikely that genetic alteration of nonpathogenic bacteria will make them pathogenic,[10] and this has never been observed.

The same can be said of genetically modified (GM) plants and animals, when we consider that genetic modification has been occurring on a large scale in nature for billions of years (in the form of the random mutations involved in evolution) and has been practiced by humans in the crossing of animals as well as plants for centuries, without any catastrophic consequences. Yet there is still much opposition against GM food, particularly in Europe. Much of it is based on the irrational fear that eating GM food might be harmful. However, all food DNA, including the modified DNA, is hydrolyzed to its four constituent nucleotides in the digestive tract. In one kind of GM soy, the gene for albumin had been inserted to enhance its nutritional value, but after an allergic reaction was noted in some consumers, this practice has been discontinued.

A special risk is provided by crop plants with a medicinal-producing gene. Accidental mixture of such a "pharmacrop" with the food crop could harm consumers. This happened in 2002 with a pharma-soy crop. The accident was discovered by the U.S. Department of Agriculture, and the company was fined. This risk can be eliminated by restricting the growth of pharmacrops to greenhouses or by using nonfood crops, like tobacco. An objection against glyphosate-resistant soy and corn was that this might lead to increased use of herbicide, but the reverse is found to be true, as the herbicide can be administered earlier when the young weed plants are more sensitive to it.

Another objection is that the resistance gene might transfer to a weed, making the weed herbicide resistant. Although this is considered very unlikely in view of the large species difference, the matter is closely studied by the FDA. In GM corn, two additional genes besides the glyphosate-resistance gene have been inserted: one is a gene producing a protein killing the corn borer caterpillar, and the other is an anti-ampicillin gene that only serves to facilitate the genetic modification process. If the latter gene were to transfer to bacteria, it could make them resistant to the antibiotic ampicillin. This is again considered very unlikely, but the intestinal bacteria of cattle fed with GM corn are checked. If necessary, this gene could be omitted.

Another possibility is the transfer of the herbicide-resistance gene to the native variety of the crop plant. After a plant disease, the native variety could then not be used to breed a new hybrid. Gene transfer to native corn via pollen is claimed to have been observed in Mexico, but this has later been questioned. Moreover, native corn doesn't grow near the large cornfields in the United States. An extensive study conducted in England, the Farm Scale Evaluations, shows that the biodiversity (number of insects and plants) in lots grown with GM sugar beets and rapeseed (but not with GM corn) was decreased compared to lots with the unmodified crop plants. However, this is not an effect of the GM plants but of earlier administration of herbicide in the GM lots.[11] On the basis of this study, the U.K. government has given a two-year approval for growing an herbicide-resistant corn variety, a first in Europe.[12]

My conclusion is that, given a continued responsible attitude of scientists and industry and proper research and supervision by regulatory bodies staffed with qualified experts, the use of genetic modification for obtaining either desired biological materials or desired biological effects does not pose unacceptable risks for humans. Further study of undesirable gene transfer from GM crop plants is needed.

Human applications

In the United States and other Western nations, all human experimentation is strictly regulated and supervised. Experimentation with human embryos, from fertilized ovum onward, is forbidden in the United States and the United Kingdom, except for direct and important medical benefit to a diseased person.[13] This should remain so; scientific inquiry in these fields can be satisfied in animal experiments, which also are regulated. Human cloning—which, strictly speaking, is not a form of genetic modification—is discussed in the next section.

Gene transfer to somatic cells of a patient poses two risks. The first is that the inserted gene could become located on a chromosome in a position where it might interfere with the function of other genes. Second, the virus used for gene transfer might recombine with an endogenous viral sequence, producing an infectious virus or a tumor. In animal experiments carried out so far, neither of these possibilities has been observed. However, a French trial to treat eleven boys having SCID with a gene on a retrovirus vector, though successful in nine patients, caused leukemia in three patients. The cause was the insertion of the vector near a gene linked to leukemia.[14] Careful planning and checking of the procedure in an animal model before attempting a clinical trial is necessary in every new instance.[15]

Gene insertion in germ cells poses two additional risks. First, the inserted gene will be passed on to the offspring, which may be desirable in most cases but is undesirable if the insertion would lead to an unwanted effect. Second, insertion of genes by microinjection into a fertilized ovum has so far too high a failure rate and carries the risk of damaging the fetus. More research is needed before this technique can ever be applied in humans.

Through gene insertion in the embryo, it might theoretically be possible to select hair and eye color, stature, intelligence, and behavioral characteristics of a child. It might even be possible to extend the human life span through telomere lengthening. Telomeres are stretches of fifty to sixty nongenetic DNA molecules at the tip of a chromosome. In every cell division, one DNA molecule is removed from each telomere, which limits the number of cell divisions to the range of fifty to sixty. Our body cells have a gene for the enzyme telomerase, which can restore the telomere, but in adult cells, this gene is inactivated. Activation of the gene through genetic manipulation could theoretically increase the possible number of cell divisions and thus the life span of the individual. Such possibilities of genetic enhancement pose risks of social problems. Individuals endowed with desirable attributes through genetic modification might encounter negative reactions from "ordinary" people, particularly if the technique were available only to the rich. Life span extension, if practiced on a large scale, would have serious economic and social problems through over-population and upsetting of the actuarial basis on which social security, pension, annuity, and life insurance systems are based.

11.7 Cloning and stem cells

Cloning

Although cloning is not a form of genetic modification, I discuss it here as one more example of modern biotechnology. In cloning, a geneti-cally identical copy of an existing individual is produced without sexual reproduction. In the case of the sheep Dolly, the nucleus of an unfer-tilized egg of one sheep was removed. A cell of the udder of another sheep was fused with the enucleated egg, which was then implanted in the uterus of a third sheep, from which Dolly was born.

The problem to be overcome is that in a differentiated cell like the udder cell, many genes are inactive, while in the early embryo, all genes must be active. The latter state was achieved by first blocking cell divi-sion in the udder cell, then letting all its genes be activated in the dividing embryo. In each of these steps, damage may occur; hence, Dolly was the first success in 277 attempts.

Clones of mouse, rat, cat, pig, and horse have since been produced, with similar difficulties. A "virgin birth" (parthenogenesis) of a mouse has been achieved by fusion of two eggs from different female mice.[16] Failure to clone monkeys is ascribed to the loss of two proteins essential for cell division during nuclear transfer and to genes important for early devel-opment not being turned on.[17] However, South Korean scientists seem to have overcome these problems in producing cloned human embryos.[18] The few claims for the birth of human clones have not been substantiated by proper scientific information.[19]

Cloned animals appear to have a shortened lifetime, because the implanted chromosomes from an adult donor cell have already divided several times and have therefore shortened telomeres. Dolly suffered multiple morbidity and had to be killed at half the normal sheep's life span.[20] These problems are thought to be due to inappropriate expression of crucial developmental genes, particularly when nuclei of differentiated donor cells are used.

What is the use of cloning? The procedure may be useful for obtaining copies of prime livestock and transgenic animals, but at the expense of more morbidity and shortened life span. The advantage of human cloning is not clear to me, for several reasons:

- Cloning offers no advantage over existing in vitro fertilization techniques for artificial conception. Furthermore, it has the disadvantage that a cloned child would have the genes of only one parent.
- Cloning of a deceased child would require that the donor cells be removed very soon after death, as in organ transplantation. If the deceased child died at age twelve, then the cloned child would at birth be at least thirteen years younger. I doubt that the parents would see this child as a duplicate of the dead child, and if they still tried to raise it as a "duplicate," this might cause serious psychological harm to the new child, who already will have to deal with the knowledge that it is a clone of a dead child. If the deceased child died of a disease, this may be a contraindication to cloning it. The older the deceased child, the greater the chance that the mother would be unable to carry the clone, necessitating the use of a surrogate mother. Moreover, as shown by litters of cloned pigs, cloned children would present as much diversity as between normal brothers and sisters.[21]
- If the objective is to clone a child dying of leukemia to provide that child with a needed bone marrow transplant, the chance that the bone marrow could be obtained in time to save the sick child seems remote. The knowledge of this would place a burden of guilt on the cloned child.
- Cloning of a deceased spouse reminds me of the question of Naomi in the book of Ruth: "Even if I should have a husband tonight and bear sons, would you then wait until they were grown?" (Ruth 1:12-13).
- A person who is so pleased with himself that he wants to be cloned should be referred to a psychiatrist, in my opinion.
- With regard to cloning to produce human organs for transplantation, in vitro cultivation of a human embryo to full development is

technically impossible and will probably remain so for the foreseeable future. It seems very unlikely that any woman would be willing to carry a fetus to term for this purpose.

Stem cells

Stem cells are undifferentiated cells, which means that all genes are still active, as in an early embryo. Research is aimed at establishing stem cell lines by cultivating isolated stem cells and then obtaining organ-specific cells from them by adding a specific growth factor. After further cultivation for multiplication, these would be implanted in a patient with a deficient organ or tissue. This procedure would alleviate the shortage of donor organs or permit the repair of an organ that cannot be transplanted, such as the brain of a patient with Parkinson's or Alzheimer's disease or a spinal cord injury. Making a whole heart with functioning muscle, nerves, and blood vessels is still utterly impossible. However, there is some hope from a procedure that involves seeding stem cells onto a biodegradable polymer scaffold impregnated with growth factors for transplantation into a patient.[22]

Four- to five-day-old human embryos left over from an in vitro fertilization treatment are the main source of embryonic stem cells. In adults, stem cells occur in bone marrow, where they form red and white blood cells during life. Drawbacks of using adult stem cells are that they must be obtained by a bone marrow puncture, which is an unpleasant procedure for the donor, and they multiply much slower and have a more limited differentiation capacity than embryonic stem cells. The umbilical cord and placenta also could yield stem cells. Claims have been made that bone marrow stem cells can differentiate into heart muscle, nerve cells, and pancreatic beta cells, but these claims have been contradicted.[23] In any case, no reliable and repeatable cases of cures with any kind of stem cells have yet been reported.[24]

11.8 Theological and ethical considerations

Choice of approach

In considering the ethical aspects of genetic engineering, we must first choose an ethical basis. Instead of deducting answers from unalterable moral principles, as in the Roman Catholic approach, I choose the Anglican approach of detailed empirical study and interdisciplinary discussion to allow theological insight to illuminate the subject. With John Habgood,[25] I feel that central Christian beliefs can provide guidelines for the approach to various ethical aspects of genetic modification:

- The doctrine of creation reminds us of our creatureliness, warning us against assuming godlike powers over life and death and excessive interference with the conditions of human and nonhuman life. It also reminds us that we are cocreators with God, called to be responsible stewards toward the world of which we are part, while as God's image bearers essentially different from all other living creatures.
- The second great commandment to love our neighbor as ourselves implies justice, one of the principles of medical ethics.
- The doctrine of incarnation encourages us to respect the human potentialities of the unborn and of the sick and handicapped.
- The doctrine of salvation acts as a corrective to naive optimism and suggests the need for some skepticism about the ability of human beings to plan successfully for their own future, and thus the need for intelligent and effective laws and regulations.
- The doctrine of life after death reminds us that banishing all sickness is not to be our primary goal.
- The doctrines of forgiveness and grace indicate that any workable ethic must make provision for failure. Part of human brokenness is the fact that many of our decisions are choices between evils, and even the best actions leave many claims unmet.

I shall use these guidelines in considering the ethical questions raised by the application of genetic modification, taking note of the risks discussed in sections 11.6 and 11.7.

Nonhuman applications

Genetic modification in the laboratory has by now been shown to be quite safe. Likewise, the introduction of genetically modified microorganisms, crop plants, or livestock into the environment, with careful inspection that the proper rules are observed, seems unlikely to expose the population to any serious risks. Yet even if these various procedures can be carried out without serious risk for the population and the environment, ethical questions remain to be answered.

Is genetic modification "playing God," as some would have it? I do not think so. There is no unchangeable, sacrosanct genome, since the genome of all species, including humans, has been changing throughout the course of evolution, and that of crop plants and livestock additionally through breeding. The ordering of species will not be violated, as the biological laws of heredity make it impossible to produce entirely new species, like flying pigs. If we are willing to see genetic modification as merely an extension of conventional animal and plant breeding practices for the purpose of producing more and better food for an expanding world population, then this activity would seem to be in line with God's charge to us to exercise responsible stewardship over all the earth and its creatures, to make the earth habitable, to populate it and to cultivate it. If carried out for this purpose and with proper safeguards against harming other creatures and the environment, this is not assuming godlike powers over life and death.

The problem of justice is raised by the commercial production of GM seed material and the patenting of it. Small farmers in Western countries and particularly farmers in developing nations are disadvantaged by the higher cost of GM seed material.[26] When the main producer of GM seeds announced that it would insert three extra genes to make seed formed by the crop sterile, critics pointed out that 1.4 billion people worldwide depend on the use of seed derived from the previous harvest. The company then withdrew the development of its "terminator gene." Moreover, the latest figures show that GM crops are widely used in developing countries.

An unsolved case is that of the parasitic plant *Striga* (witchweed), which is endemic in Africa and destroys 40 percent of the grain harvests. A variety of sorghum that is resistant to the herbicide used to combat *Striga* was developed in the United States, but the company refrained from producing it when it learned that the inserted gene easily transfers to Johnson grass, a weed in the United States. Application in Africa with its much greater need was apparently not considered, possibly for fear of liability suits if Johnson grass became herbicide resistant.

In spite of the Green Revolution, which doubled and quadrupled crop yields between 1950 and 1983 through the use of hybridized crop plants, 3.7 billion people are currently malnourished (according to a World Health Organization report), and per capita cereal grain production has been declining since 1984 (according to the UN's Food and Agriculture Organization).[27] Genetic modification of crop plants for the purpose of increasing food production is much needed; it is faster and more versatile than hybridization. It is also needed in meeting the medical needs of the

Third World with its 1 billion people suffering from malaria, hookworm, and schistosomiasis while the advanced nations expend all their efforts on cures for their 10 million cancer patients.

Human applications

Genetic modification of humans raises sharper ethical questions in view of the unique position of humans in creation. Therefore, "tampering" with the human genome is not permissible, say some. But what could be wrong with curing those who are conceived with a serious genetic illness by means of gene therapy, which merely compensates (somatic cell repair) or replaces (germ cell repair) the defective gene? If we are willing to see genetic modification as an extension of conventional medical practice, then this activity would seem to be in line with God's charge to "love our neighbor" as ourselves, which throughout the history of the church has been interpreted to include the care of the sick for the relief of suffering. There is, however, the duty to weigh very carefully the expected benefits against the risks of possible harm to the treated individual, that person's offspring, and the community, bearing in mind that the doctrine of life after death implies that a diseaseless existence, even if it were achievable, is not the highest good in Christian thinking.

Three potential forms of the use of genetic technology in humans can be distinguished: genetic screening, gene therapy via somatic cells or germ cells, and genetic enhancement.

Genetic screening
In theory, genetic screening permits the diagnosis of every hereditary disease, pre- and postnatal. It poses little physical risk to the individual and none to others. Yet it raises a number of questions that need to be answered before it is widely applied:[28]

- If a faulty gene is found, what is the actual risk of disease, particularly if more than one gene is involved?
- In the case of prenatal testing, is it ethically permissible to seek an abortion to prevent the birth of a child who will suffer for life and die young? My view is that this is not permissible in the case of Down syndrome but that it is in a case like Lesch-Nyhan syndrome, which causes great suffering for the patient, leads to self-mutilation, and requires institutionalization until death at an early age.

- Is it ethically permissible for couples at risk of conceiving children with a genetic disorder to have several embryos produced in vitro, have one that is defect-free selected, have that implanted in the womb, and have the others destroyed?
- In the case of postnatal testing, should a person at risk of suffering a fatal or crippling disease for which no cure is available (for instance, Huntington's disease) be tested and be informed of the result?
- How can discrimination in employment and insurance be prevented? Employers and insurance companies might demand genetic testing (or to see results of prior testing) and refuse employment or insurance to persons with a genetic predisposition to a serious illness.[29] Protective legislation is needed, and laws have been adopted or are pending in many countries.
- How will the potential benefits of genetic diagnosis and therapy be made available to all who need it, regardless of financial status?

If these questions can be satisfactorily resolved, then genetic screening could greatly reduce the incidence of hereditary disease, prevent much suffering, and reduce the need for costly gene therapy.

Gene therapy
The risk of physical harm in somatic-cell gene therapy is limited to the patient, and the diseases involved are serious and in some cases fatal at an early age. However, the disappointing results to date and the occurrence of leukemia in one trial imply that much more laboratory research is needed. If the risk can be limited acceptably, and if the therapy can be made available to all who need it without curtailing other medical treatment to other patients, then there would seem to be no ethical prohibition for this type of gene therapy.

Germ-cell gene therapy still carries too much risk for the resulting child and its offspring to consider application at this time.

Genetic enhancement
Is it ethically acceptable to confer desirable physical or behavioral traits, such as high intelligence or increased life span, to individuals by means of genetic modification, once it becomes technically feasible? Here the risk of societal harm dominates any risk of physical harm to the treated individual. The doctrine of creation teaches us not to assume godlike powers over life and death, not to interfere unnecessarily with the conditions of human life (there is no suffering in this case), and to entertain some

skepticism about our ability to design our future. The Christian position would thus suggest that genetic enhancement, as discussed here, should not be practiced. This position has also been taken by a presidential commission in the United States.[30]

Cloning and stem cells

There are serious theological and ethical objections to reproductive cloning of humans. In the biblical vision, each human being, unlike animals, is a unique person. That uniqueness pleads against producing human clones. Therefore, it is not surprising that the U.S. National Bioethics Advisory Commission has proposed a ban on human reproductive cloning[31] and that the Council of Europe is considering the same. Animals are not assigned a unique individual identity in the biblical vision. On that basis, if there are no indications of serious suffering of cloned animals, cloning of animals seems to me to be permissible if this serves a considerable interest, like the production of important medicinals.[32]

Another matter is therapeutic cloning for the production of human cells for implantation. This could reduce the shortage of transplantable organs and obviate the need for lifelong usage of immunosuppressive drugs to prevent rejection of the transplanted organ. Although the technique is still in a developmental stage, two British advisory bodies have reported favorably.[33] The ethical problem is that, however beneficial the aim may be, (early) human embryos would be produced and destroyed in the process. I consider an embryo to be a form of potential human life only after its implantation in the uterus (this is still the only way that an embryo can develop to a living human being), and thus the use of an early embryo for the cure of a serious disease would not be unethical. In Britain and the Netherlands, therapeutic cloning is permitted. In the United States, only the use of cell lines existing at the time of the presidential decision in 2001 is allowed.[34] The European Commission made a similar ruling, but the European parliament wants a full permission for therapeutic cloning. The UN legal committee proposed a declaration encouraging countries to develop their own laws to regulate human cloning, and the UN General Assembly approved a non-binding resolution in March 2005 urging countries to pass laws prohibiting cloning where it was incompatible with "human dignity."

11.9 Summary

Genetic modification is a prime example of the role of humans as cocreators. Theology sees humans as ambivalent creatures: as God's image bearers and cocreators, but also as grasping for equality with God.

The principle of genetic manipulation, as explained in this chapter, has applications in the production of biological materials and of effects in plants, animals, and humans. Research has identified possible risks of these activities, and some have opposed genetic modification, as well as cloning and the use of stem cells (which are described here as examples of biotechnology, though not involving genetic modification).

In my consideration of the ethical aspects of current and future applications of genetic modification, I conclude that current applications, including genetic diagnosis and gene therapy, are not contrary to Christian ethics, if all relevant rules and regulations are adhered to. However, I consider human cloning and genetic "enhancement" of humans in terms of physical and behavioral characteristics to be in conflict with Christian ethics.

12

Disease:
Punishment for Sin or Chaos Event?

12.1 Body, mind, spirit

Recent polls indicate that health is the primary concern of people in the Western world, rated above family life, work, money, and religion. This shows how essential it is to address the topic of health and disease in any attempt to reconcile the scientific and theological worldviews. Remarkably, few theologians have given attention to this topic. There is a great need for a theology of disease in view of the continuing tendency of many to ascribe disease to sin or to divine punishment for sin, leading to misplaced guilt feelings in many seriously ill people. This chapter addresses this matter and presents a theology of disease after a brief discussion of "hominization," body, mind, and soul.

Hominization

Evolution shows that there is a transition from animal to hominid, as well as a gradual development of both body and mind in the hominids (chapter 2.6). This raises the question, When did hominids become human? In other words, when did hominization take place? The older creation story suggests that first the human body was created "of dust from the ground," and then "the breath of life" was breathed into him, which made him a living being (Gen 2:7). Traditional theology assumes that God introduced a soul at the creation of the first human and repeats this at the birth of each human being.[1] Brunner tries to reconcile this with the evolutionary view by assuming, without much argument, the introduction of the human soul (*humanum*) at some point in the hominid line—for example, when reverence for the dead arose.[2]

However, the parallel evolutionary development of mind and body suggests that hominization is a gradual process (chapter 2.6, Table 2.5). Milestones along this evolutionary road are construction of a dwelling, indicating forethought (*Homo habilis*); making and use of fire (*Homo erectus*); burial of the dead with ritual, indicating religious awareness (Neandertals); and appearance of art and language (Cro-Magnons). The awareness of self as part of the cosmos and of transcendent spirit and power, together with the ability to manipulate nature, appear to have gradually developed during human evolution. The evolution of the mind is repeated in broad outline during individual human development. Self-awareness is gradually established in the first two years of life and then continues to develop toward adulthood. Hominization is a continuous process of physical and spiritual development in human evolution as well as in individual human development.

The crucial distinctions between animals and humans appear to be self-awareness and transcendental awareness. The statement in Genesis 1 that only humans are God's image bearers is in line with the fact that they and their nearest animal cousin, the chimpanzee, show an opposite mental development. At birth, the chimpanzee and human have about the same brain size and perform about equally in various tests, but after about eighteen months, the human baby leaves the chimpanzee far behind in brain size (adult human at 1,350 cubic centimeters versus the chimpanzee at 385 cubic centimeters) and mental performance.

Mind rather than soul

"Soul" is an ambiguous concept that is often confused with God's life-giving spirit and incorrectly thought to be immortal, which leads to mistaken ideas about resurrection.[3] I prefer to replace it with the term *mind*, defined as our combined intellectual, moral, and spiritual capacity and activity (which, according to neurobiological studies, utilize largely the same neuronal circuits).

What I call mind is represented by the Hebrew word *leb*, meaning the seat of vital energy, sensation, emotion, inclination, disposition, and will. The Hebrew words *neshama, nephesh,* and *ruach,* which are virtually synonymous, may be translated as "spirit."[4] In Gen 2:7, *neshama* is the breath of life breathed by God into Adam, which makes him a living being. In Gen 1:20, 21, and 24, *nephesh* is used for the same concept, both for animals and humans, the life principle. In Eccl 3:21 and 12:7 and in Ezek 37:1-10, *ruach* is the life-giving breath of God. In the New Testament, the term *psyche* (derived from *psycho*, "to breathe") is used in the sense of the Old Testament *nephesh*. In the Gospels, it is often translated as "life" (for instance, in Matt 6:25; Mark 8:35; and John 10:11). Paul sometimes uses *psyche* as a synonym of *pneuma* (spirit), but in 1 Thess 5:23, he uses the combination *pneuma, psyche, soma* (translated "spirit, soul, body") to denote the whole living person. The term *nous* in Rom 11:34 and 1 Cor 2:16 parallels the Old Testament *leb* for the self as the subject of its thinking, feeling, and willing (mind), while the body (*soma*) is the same self as the object of these activities.[5]

So we can say that the human mind (Hebrew *leb*, Greek *nous*) has developed during evolution in close association with the body (*soma*) and develops again in each new human being from embryo to adulthood. In both processes, it is made alive by God's life-giving spirit (*nephesh, pneuma*), which is withdrawn at death. By thus employing the words *mind* and *spirit*, as defined here, we can eliminate the ambiguous term *soul*.

Body-mind interaction

In Judeo-Christian thinking, humans are a unity of body and mind, an animated body, rather than an embodied mind as in Greek philosophy. With modern scanning techniques, we can trace the operation of the mind in neuronal activities in specific areas of the brain. This shows us the physical substrate of our mental processes, but it doesn't explain the processes.[6] We also know that the mind can interact with the body by means of the so-called hypothalamic-pituitary-adrenal axis. This means neuronal impulses from the cerebral cortex of the brain go to the hypothalamus (a gland at the bottom of the brain), which secretes certain compounds to the pituitary gland, which in turn releases certain hormones that stimulate the adrenal glands to secrete other hormones. In this way, our mind can influence the functioning of various physiological functions, as when stress affects the immune system.[7] Conversely, the condition of the body can influence the state of the mind. Body and mind act as a complex unified system.

12.2 Health and disease in biblical view

Old Testament

In the time of the kings and the exiles, physicians were merely pharmacists (Jer 8:22), and God was the acknowledged Healer (Exod

15:26).[8] The prophets predicted the outcome of sickness, as with Nathan (2 Sam 12:14), Elijah (1 Kings 17:17), and Elisha (2 Kings 5:3), but they also treated disease. Elisha neutralized poisonous herbs (2 Kings 4:41), purified the waters of Jericho (2 Kings 2:20-21), and cured Naaman (2 Kings 5:3-14) and the son of the Shunammite (2 Kings 4:18-37). By the second century BCE, the prestige of physicians had increased considerably. God is still seen as the Healer but is thought to have committed gifts of healing to physicians and to have provided medicines for the cure of sickness (Sir 38:1-15).

Health was seen primarily in terms of physical strength and well-being, needed for sheepherding and agriculture.[9] The ideals of bodily vigor and health were cherished (1 Sam 16:18). Health was regarded as the greatest of all earthly blessings (Sir 30:14), and longevity was one of the most frequently requested benefits in blessings. However, the infirmity of advanced age was dreaded (Eccl 12:1-8).

While health was seen as a divine gift, disease was regarded as divine punishment for sin or disobedience (Exod 4:11; Deut 32:39) but was also attributed to the devil under divine permission (Job 2:7). Since God is the divine Physician, healing was seen as a token of divine forgiveness. Health could be maintained by close observance of the divine commands throughout life (Exod 15:26). As sickness was seen as a spiritual matter, healing could only be expected from reconciliation with God. Disease was seen as conditioned largely by moral and spiritual, rather than physical, factors. By pursuing a life of spiritual fellowship with God, one had the best chance of avoiding illness.

New Testament

We owe to Luke, the "beloved physician" (Col 4:14), the accurate recording of the healing acts of Jesus. Healing is central to the earthly ministry of Jesus from the beginning (Mark 1:29-32, 40-45).[10] Luke says, "The power of the Lord was with him to heal" (Luke 5:17). His opponents attribute this power to Satan (Mark 3:22), but Jesus ascribes it to God (Matt 12:28; Luke 11:20) and claims that healing is a sign that the rule of God has been inaugurated (Matt 11:5; Luke 4:19; 7:22), as predicted by Isaiah (Isa 35:5-6; 61:1-2). Jesus sends forth his disciples with authority "to heal every disease and every infirmity" (Matt 10:1). Mark reports their success (Mark 6:13), and Luke sees this as evidence of the kingdom's nearness (Luke 10:9).

Jesus emphatically rejects the Old Testament idea that disease is divine punishment, for either personal sins or those of the parents (John 9:3).[11]

He sees the individual as an essential unity of body and mind, and disease as the result of evil producing an imbalance in the body-mind unity. Hence, in healing the body of the sick, Jesus always pays close attention to their mind and spirit, as when linking healing with forgiveness of sins (Mark 2:2-11). His encounter with the Samaritan woman (John 4:7-26) is a superb example of nondirective counseling. Jesus turns a casual conversation into a powerful therapeutic analysis of her emotional conflicts and reveals to her the person of the living Christ as the answer to her deepest needs. The healing acts of Jesus are a spontaneous expression of his compassion as well as a sign of the kingdom of God. Jesus does not suggest that the sufferer ought to remain ill in order to learn patience (Luke 5:12-13). In several instances, Jesus is said to heal by casting out a demon: the epileptic boy (Matt 17:14-18; Mark 9:14-27; Luke 9:37-42), the Syrophoenician's daughter (Matt 15:22; Mark 7:25), the Gerasene (Matt 8:28; Mark 5:2; Luke 8:27), the Capernaum demoniacs (Mark 1:23; Luke 4:33), and the blind and dumb demoniac (Matt 12:22; Luke 11:14). This reflects ancient belief, long held in Babylonia and Egypt, introduced into Judaism some centuries before Jesus' birth, and persisting in New Testament times.[12]

Jesus sees illness as a manifestation of evil, operating in the recesses of the mind or between a person and his or her environment. Disease violates the divinely established order. Since his primary mission is to destroy the works of the devil (Luke 13:16), Jesus makes every effort to heal the sick and disabled. His ministry is as much to the mind as to the body. He interrogates those who come for healing in order to obtain insight into their situation. When a degree of faith has been elicited, he proceeds not only to treat the illness, but also to resolve spiritual conflict. Jesus thus attempts to win people for the kingdom of God (Luke 7:21-22). This presupposes a degree of faith in the sick person, expressed in the words of Jesus, "your faith has made you well" (Luke 17:19; 18:42; Matt 9:29), or implied in the sufferer's response (Matt 9:1-8). Matthew sees Jesus' healing ministry as a fulfillment of Isaiah's prophecy about the Suffering Servant, who "has borne our infirmities and carried our diseases" (Isa 53:4), and translates this as "he took our infirmities and bore our diseases" (Matt 8:17). This suggests that Jesus' death and resurrection resolve not only our sins, but also our illnesses.

In the early church, healing of the sick becomes apostolic practice, in conformity with the expressed will of Christ, particularly in the period immediately after Pentecost (Acts 2:43; 5:12-16; 8:7).[13] The gift of healing is conferred by the Holy Spirit (1 Cor 12:9, 28). The mighty works, including healing, are signs of the messianic age (Acts 2:16-21); the powers of the new age have entered the present age (Heb 6:5). Christ's power has been delegated to all who believe in him. People are astonished at the healing work of Peter, Paul, and Philip (Acts 3:11; 5:15; 8:9-13; 14:8-10). When a demon from a soothsaying girl is troubling Paul and his companions (Acts 16:16), Paul casts out the demon. To the healing process belong faith in the name of Jesus (Acts 3:6, 16; cf. Matt 9:27-31; Mark 5:34; 9:14-27), prayer and anointing with oil (Jas 5:14-15; cf. Mark 6:13), and the laying on of hands (Acts 9:12, 17; 28:8; cf. Mark 5:23). Healing and forgiveness of sins also go together (Jas 5:16; cf. Mark 2:3-12; Ps 103:3). As time passes, the treatment becomes more uniform: laying on of hands invoking the name of Jesus in response to the expectant trust of the sufferer. Prayer with anointing by the elders comes to be used (Jas 5:14-15). However, the healing power of the apostles appears to have decreased with the passing of time. For example, Paul leaves Trophimus ill at Miletus (2 Tim 4:20). Yet the gifts of healing in the early church are an integral part of the mission and message of Jesus.[14]

In summary, it can be said that in the Old Testament, health is generally seen as a gift of God, disease as God's punishment for sin or disobedience, and healing as a token of God's forgiveness. Jesus rejects the idea of disease as the result of divine punishment, for either personal sins or those of the parents. Jesus' healing acts are seen as the expression of his compassion and a sign of the kingdom of God. Jesus sees illness as a manifestation of evil, a violation of divinely established order. His healing ministry is as much to the mind as to the body, an anticipation of current holistic medicine and psychotherapy. In the early church, this develops into an act of healing by laying on of hands with prayer invoking the name of Jesus.

12.3 Cancer: Cause and treatment

To illustrate the modern medical approach to disease, I choose neoplastic disease, the collective term for the one hundred or more forms of cancer, since it is the second leading cause of death (after cardiovascular disease) in Western nations and a source of much suffering. Notwithstanding our increasing understanding of the phenomenon of malignant cell growth and the new treatments that have become available, the cancer death rate keeps increasing. Between 1972 and 1992, the age-adjusted cancer death rate in the United States rose by 6.3 percent—and by 16 percent for people older than sixty-five. In recent years, the number of new cases has decreased by 0.5 percent per year and mortality by 0.7 percent.[15] Worldwide, 40 percent of all people will have cancer, and annually 6 million will die from it.

Death rates from some types of cancers greatly decreased in the United States from 1973 to 1992, due to advances in detection and treatment. Deaths from testicular cancer fell by 66 percent, Hodgkin's disease by 57 percent, cervical cancer by 43 percent, stomach cancer by 35 percent, uterine cancer by 26 percent, bladder cancer by 23 percent, thyroid cancer and oral cancer by 21 percent, and colorectal cancer by 17 percent. However, the death toll from lung cancer for women rose by 137 percent. For males it increased 17 percent and is beginning to come down, dropping 3 percent from 1990 to 1992. The difference in rates is probably because males started smoking cigarettes earlier than women, so the subsequent decline in smoking also comes first for men. The decline in smoking is taking effect for the males now, while for women it will come later.

How cancer arises and spreads

Much is known about the molecular biology of cancer. The first step is the malignant transformation of a normal body cell.[16] Normal cells in body tissue divide only when instructed to do so by surrounding cells. Two types of genes, proto-oncogenes and tumor suppressor genes, control the cell cycle, the process by which a cell grows and divides. A proto-oncogene forms a growth factor, which after secretion binds to a receptor on a neighboring cell, which then begins to grow. Mutation of this gene turns it into an oncogene, which causes the neighbor cell to multiply excessively. In a similar way, the tumor suppressor gene inhibits growth of a neighboring cell. Mutation of this gene cancels its growth-inhibiting activity. These two effects cause uncontrolled, rapid division of the neighboring cell, transforming it into a cancer cell.

Cells have two backup systems to prevent runaway growth:

1. Apoptosis, or cell suicide (essential for normal embryonic development), is activated by mutation of a proto-oncogene or tumor suppressor gene.
2. Telomere shortening, in which a telomere (a stretch of DNA molecules at the tip of a chromosome) is shortened a notch at every cell division, limits normal cells to 50 to 60 divisions.

"Successful" cancer cells are able to inactivate both processes. They inactivate the protein that triggers apoptosis and to activate the enzyme telomerase, which lengthens shortened telomeres.[17] Having disabled these two backup systems, the cancer cell continues to multiply and forms a primary tumor. Beyond a diameter of 1.6 millimeters, the tumor begins to suffer from oxygen deficiency, which stimulates angiogenesis, the formation of small blood vessels in the tumor, through the release of angiogenic protein.[18] The tumor can then continue to grow.

The next step is metastasis, in which the cancer spreads through the dislodging of one or more tumor cells. Cells normally produce certain proteins, which make them adhere to receptors on neighboring cells.[19] Cancer cells lack the adhesion proteins or the receptors for them, so they can slip out of the tissue in which they were formed. Normally this would expose them to death through apoptosis, but cancer cells can inactivate this process. The escaped cancer cell adheres to the basement membrane of a blood or lymph vessel. The enzyme metalloproteinase in the tumor cell is then activated and excreted.[20] This enzyme digests the collagen of the basement membrane, making a hole in the membrane through which the tumor cell enters the vessel. It is then carried with the blood or lymph flow until it reaches a capillary bed, where it is stopped, adheres, and forms a secondary tumor. This process can be repeated with other tumor cells and thus lead to widespread metastasis. When this disrupts essential organ functions, the patient dies.

Treatment of cancer

The three standard forms of cancer treatment are surgery (for solid tumors only), radiation, and chemotherapy, often applied in combination.[21] Technical advances have increased the effectiveness and reduced the undesirable side effects of these treatments. Surgery provides quick and effective removal of the tumor, but a few tumor cells may be missed, leading to recurrence. For this reason, surgery is often followed by radiation treatment. Radiation kills cells directly by mutation or indirectly by apoptosis. It is particularly successful in cervical and early prostate cancer and Hodgkin's disease. The linear accelerator, together with CT scanning for accurate beam positioning, maximizes the effect on the tumor while minimizing damage to healthy tissues. Thus, larynx cancer can be treated without impairing speaking ability. Proton and neutron beams may permit even better focusing, allowing treatment of small spinal tumors and salivary gland tumors. However, radiation may not kill all cells in a solid tumor. Also, it is unsuitable in cases of widespread metastasis, as the whole-body radiation needed would destroy vital tissues.

Chemotherapy acts on cancer cells the way antibiotics do on pathogenic bacteria; it aims at inhibiting DNA replication. It may do this directly, as in the case of doxorubicin, which inhibits the enzyme that splits the two strands of the DNA double helix in replication. Or it may work by inhibiting a prior metabolic step; for example, methotrexate inhibits the conversion of folic acid to adenine and guanine, building blocks of DNA. The problem is that the metabolic differences between human cells and bacteria do not exist between malignant and healthy cells, so cancer chemotherapy causes much more damage to healthy cells than antibiotics do, resulting in side effects, including anemia, infections, clotting problems, diarrhea, nausea, and hair loss.[22] Like bacteria after antibiotic treatment, tumor cells may develop resistance, so it is best to use a mixture of chemotherapeutic agents. A special form of chemotherapy is antihormone treatment, based on the finding that a hormone that stimulates the normal cells of an organ also stimulates the growth of tumor cells deriving from it. Thus the antiestrogen tamoxifen is used against breast cancer,[23] and an antitestosterone drug against prostate cancer. Chemotherapy (to treat systemic micrometastases) before radiation yields good results for cancers of head, neck, prostate, lung, and bladder.

The problem with all cancer treatments is that complete removal or destruction of all cancer cells in the patient is usually impossible. A true cure is therefore rare, but with the available therapies, life expectancy can often be greatly increased with an acceptable quality of life.

New therapeutic approaches are based on what is known about the steps in tumor development.[24] These therapies include blocking of tumor angiogenesis,[25] activation of the immune system,[26] use of tumor-specific antibodies,[27] interference with gene activities,[28] and triggering apoptosis of tumor cells. A general problem in the treatment of solid tumors, in addition to damage to healthy cells, is poor penetration of therapeutic agents to the tumor cells. Antibodies with a radioactive or cytotoxic "payload" are being developed in the hope of overcoming this problem.[29]

12.4 Theological interpretation

Before speaking about disease, we should recognize that normally our body-mind unity is maintained in a state of health by a very complex, orderly, coordinated functioning of thousands of genes, regulators, enzymes, hormones, messenger molecules, receptors, and neurons in our cells and tissues. This order has been established by the Creator in the course of evolutionary creation and is established anew in each individual by means of the genetic system.

Yet this order is contingent—always in danger of falling back into chaos, the remaining chaos present in the unfinished creation. Only God's loving hand can protect us against this threat. Waking up in good health in the morning is reason for us to thank God and to ask for God's continued protection during the day and, after we retire, during the night. However, chaos remains in this world and in our lives. We know that at a given moment disease may strike us, as chaos overcomes order.

In chapter 8 I already noted that disease is a form of physical evil that was present in the world since long before the appearance of human beings. Studies of fossil bones show that dinosaurs already suffered from arthritis and cancer.[30] In fact, the evolutionary process appears to have played an important role in the development of disease.[31] From the description of the origin and development of cancer in the preceding section, we can conclude that the primary event is the random mutation of a single gene in one body cell. This event has several important consequences: unlimited cell division, dislodging of the transformed cell, growth of blood vessels in the early tumor (angiogenesis), secondary tumor formation (metastasis), and death of the patient when growing tumors disturb vital organ functions. While I have illustrated this for the example of cancer, the same can be said for all diseases in which a normal physiological mechanism is derailed. Various types of psychiatric disease are ascribed by psychiatrist-theologian Eugen Drewermann to the fear of being thrown back into primordial chaos, of which he sees a remaining element in our world.[32]

In chapter 7 I have described how all living beings, being "nonlinear systems," are subject to chaos events. The random mutation that turns one body cell into a malignant cell with a cascade of further effects can, in my opinion, be seen as such a chaos event. This makes created order degenerate into chaos on the cellular level with potentially fatal consequences. Here we see the operation of the "double chaos" in the title of this book.

This theological interpretation of disease is in accord with the teaching of Jesus (section 12.2) that disease is a manifestation of evil, a disturbance of divine order, rather than a punishment for sin of the sick person or that person's parents (John 9:3) or a means to make us grow spiritually through suffering (although spiritual growth may be a salutary result of suffering).[33] Guilt—but not divine punishment—can be considered only when the disease is due to our negligence, say, by alcohol abuse or unprotected sex with multiple partners.

In chapter 7 (sections 7.5 and 7.6), I have argued that chaos events are open to being influenced by God, just as two laboratory-created cases of chaotic behavior can be influenced by human intervention. Where chaos events play a role in disease, we may assume that divine and human spirit can influence onset and course of the illness. This legitimates prayer and the use of the sacrament of healing. It may explain medically unintelligible cures and remissions. These are discussed in the next two sections.

12.5 Curing or healing

Current cancer treatment is almost exclusively directed against the tumor, so it neglects to a great extent the fact that we are a body-mind unity (section 12.1), where our state of mind may play an important role in protecting us against disease or, negatively, in contracting a disease. This is illustrated by the case history of a Dutch oncological surgeon.[34] In 1988, in the midst of a successful (and stressful) surgical career, he was at age forty-five diagnosed with non-Hodgkin's lymphoma. Light chemotherapy treatment resulted in a remission, but in 1992 there was a recurrence, and he was given heavy chemotherapy. In 1993 he received the ultimate treatment: bone marrow transplantation with heavy radiation and chemotherapy, but again there was a recurrence. Medicine could offer no further treatment. Then in 1994 he received psychotherapy at the Helen Dowling Institute, aimed at release of stress and stimulation of the body's self-healing capacity. He gave up his surgical career and adopted a new lifestyle. In 1995 he received light chemotherapy, and two years later, he was still symptom-free. He was not necessarily "cured," but he was healed. He died in 2003 after having enjoyed a decade of a more meaningful lifestyle.

How can the mind affect the occurrence and course of cancer? It is assumed that fairly regularly a cell in our body becomes malignant through random mutation. Our immune system should recognize such a cell as abnormal and kill it. The immune system is known to be influenced by the brain via the hypothalamic-pituitary-adrenal axis (section 12.1). If the mind is in a poor state due to fatigue, stress, conflict, anxiety, depression, or unresolved guilt feelings, then immune function is known to be impaired. A malignant cell may then escape detection, survive, and form a tumor, as has been demonstrated in animal experiments.[35] Psychogenic effects on apoptosis and metastasis have also been observed. In humans, the influence of the immune system is demonstrated by the finding that kidney transplant patients, who must be kept on immunosuppressive drugs to prevent rejection, have a highly increased rate of cancer incidence (a 10 percent increase after one year and 50 percent after ten years). Conversely, social support and psychotherapy increase immune function and survival of patients with breast cancer and melanoma.

These observations and the growing awareness that the current treatment of cancer is too exclusively aimed at "curing" (removal or destruction of malignant tissue) suggest that more attention needs to be given to "healing." Institutes like the Commonweal Cancer Help Program in Bolinas, California, and the Helen Dowling Institute in Utrecht, the Netherlands, offer programs to stimulate the patient's recovery of emotional and spiritual well-being by stress reduction (through relaxation meditation) and individual or group therapy (aimed at integration) to supplement—not replace—conventional medical treatment.[36] The patients are assisted in liberating themselves from wrong ideas about guilt, sin, and punishment and in expressing their feelings of anger and anxiety, allowing them to become an integrated person, a unity of body and mind, again. This is reflected in an enhancement of the immune function observed in some studies. Although these institutes work on a nonreligious basis, it is remarkable how well their approach agrees with Jesus' practice. Expressing anxiety, anger, and guilt feelings before a compassionate therapist resembles the forgiveness offered by Jesus in his healing acts.[37]

Jesus teaches that human wholeness and reconciliation are God's purpose, so healing of the sick forms an essential part of his earthly ministry (section 12.2). He sees the individual as a unity of body and mind, and illness as an imbalance in the personality due to the effect of evil—due to remaining chaos, to use the terms of chaos theology. Jesus ministers as much to the mind as to the body, interrogating those who come for healing in order for the patients to obtain insight into their state of mind. When Jesus has elicited a degree of faith, he proceeds not only to treat the physical affliction, but also to resolve the spiritual conflict, to bring reconciliation. Jesus heals in the sense that he makes the body-mind unity whole, thus anticipating the holistic approach of the present cancer help programs. There is a wealth of statistical evidence for the importance of religious commitment (measured as attendance and participation) in combating cancer and other diseases.[38] Recent polls indicate that in our secularized Western world, a relation between faith and healing is still widely recognized.[39]

12.6 Sacrament of healing

In the early church, healing of the sick became apostolic practice, in conformity with the expressed will of Christ and as a sign of the messianic age to come (section 12.2). The ritual practice was the laying on of hands by a priest with prayer invoking the name of Jesus. In subsequent centuries, the practice declined, and around 800, the Western church came to reserve the rite for the dying. In the Church of England, anointing of the sick was included in the first Prayer Book (1549) but was omitted in later revisions. However, it is included in the Common Worship Book (2000). In the American Episcopal Church, it returned in the 1928 Prayer Book and, in expanded form, in the 1979 Prayer Book. Other churches abolished it completely, in part because of the abuse of the sacrament of healing by various sects and faith healers in a desire for spectacular miracles.[40]

Three positions can be taken on the sacrament of healing: One view is that it is superfluous in light of the great capacity for curing disease by modern medicine. However, as pointed out before, these treatments are often inadequate, as in many forms of cancer, since they are purely physical and do not treat the whole person. Others think the church should disregard medical curative treatment and offer the sacrament of healing instead. This position, taken by the Christian Science movement, disregards the capacity we have developed as God's cocreators for curing many diseases. The third position is that the church should offer the sacrament of healing to the sick to complement the medical treatment they may receive.

This third position is the one I take. As I have argued in this chapter, disease is more than a physical ailment. It occurs in the body-mind unit, and our state of mind has a great influence on the origin and progress of illness. Even if, after we have received the sacrament of healing and proper medical treatment, a "cure" does not result, we may be healed in the sense of receiving peace of mind and the assurance that God will guide us through the final stage of earthly life toward eternal life, the ultimate life for which we are created and destined.

Bearing this in mind, I feel that the proper place for the sacrament of healing is—if not at the sickbed—in the Sunday Eucharist after the distribution of the consecrated elements, in the midst of the congregation. The use of separate healing services limits the opportunities for receiving the sacrament of healing and tends to place too much emphasis on a cure. For the latter reason, I prefer to use a fixed prayer with the laying on of hands and not to ask the recipients for which ailment they want healing. In subsequent conversations with the recipients, there is opportunity to learn more about their particular concerns and to support the healing process by proper counseling. A form that shows a right balance between curing and healing is provided in the 1979 American Prayer Book.[41]

Notwithstanding my thoughts about place and time for administering this sacrament, we should not forget that Jesus' healing work usually occurred outside a religious building or service and often involved the disadvantaged, those shunned by society (like today's AIDS sufferers), and others who are unlikely to attend church services.[42] This means that priests should go out to these persons and administer the sacrament of healing when and where this is desired.

12.7 Summary

Although health is a primary concern, at least among Western people, theologians and even scientist-theologians have not given much attention to the topic of health and disease. In the Old Testament, health is generally seen as a divine gift, disease as divine punishment for sin, and healing as a token of God's forgiveness. Jesus firmly rejects the idea of disease as divine punishment for sin. He is convinced of the Father's purpose for human wholeness and salvation, so he heals the sick and disabled. Jesus sees the individual as a unity of body and mind, and disease as the result of an imbalance between them, so he ministers to both mind and body to resolve spiritual conflict.

Modern medical understanding and treatment of disease is illustrated by a discussion of cancer, the second leading cause of death in Western nations. Cancer is now understood in terms of a loss of the orderly, coordinated function of many genes and enzymes in a normal body cell, changing it into a rapidly dividing cancer cell. Cancer cells inactivate two processes for the elimination of abnormal cells. They also induce the formation of blood vessels, which provide nutrition to the growing tumor. Activation of certain enzymes leads to metastasis, the spreading of tumor cells with the formation of tumors in other locations. The three main forms of treatment are surgery, radiation, and chemotherapy, often used in combination. Since total eradication of every cancer cell is usually impossible, a total cure is rare. New therapies, such as blocking of tumor angiogenesis, immune system activation, and tumor-specific antibodies, offer hope for further advances.

Cancer can be seen as a case of finely tuned order reverting to chaos on the cellular level. In terms of chaos theology, the remaining chaos is acting against the order established in the evolutionary creation process. This implies that ideas about guilt, sin, and divine punishment in cancer and other diseases are unfounded. Guilt can exist only when the illness is due to negligence on our part.

Modern medical treatment attempts to "cure" cancer by removal or destruction of malignant tissue. This view neglects the fact that humans are a body-mind unity, in which the state of mind plays an important role in protecting against disease by influencing the hormonal control of the immune system, which normally should destroy a cancer cell before it can form a tumor. The healing acts of Jesus are aimed at the healing of the body-mind relationship. Curing is only a part of healing, of making the body-mind unity whole, which is the aim of current cancer support programs. The sacrament of healing by the laying on of hands with prayer is also directed toward healing, so it can be meaningfully employed in supplementing conventional medical treatment. Even if a cure does not result, it may provide healing in the sense of receiving peace of mind, reconciliation, and the assurance that God will guide us through the final stage of earthly life toward eternal life, the ultimate life to which we were created and destined.

13

Are We Alone?
Theological Implications of Possible
Extraterrestrial Intelligent Life

13.1 From speculation to search

Humans are fascinated with the topic of extraterrestrial life. Consider the great popularity of books, movies, and television programs that tell science-fiction stories about extraterrestrial beings. And there are the thousands of claims of sighting unidentified flying objects (UFOs) and the tenacious belief of so many people in UFOs against all rational explanations.[1] With a mixture of curiosity and fear, people wonder, "Are we alone in this vast universe or not?" In this chapter I shall address the question: If advanced beings elsewhere in the universe do exist, what does this mean for Christian theology?

Ancient speculation

The Greek philosophers Leucippus, Democritus, and Epicurus (480–270 BCE) already speculated about the existence of life outside Earth.[2] The Roman poet Lucretius wrote in *De Rerum Natura* (c. 70 BCE), "So we must realize that there are other worlds in other parts of the universe, with races of different men and different animals. In the totality of creation no thing is unique."[3] In contrast, Plato (c. 310 BCE) and Aristotle (c. 330 BCE) opposed the possibility of extraterrestrial life. Their thinking led the early Christian theologians Augustine (c. 400), Albertus Magnus (c. 1250), Thomas Aquinas (1273), and his contemporary Roger Bacon to reject the idea as well.

This changed after Étienne Tempier, bishop of Paris, issued in 1277 a list of condemnations of doctrines that seemed to limit God's power, one of them being the idea that God could not create many worlds. This led to renewed discussion of the matter in the fourteenth century. After critical consideration of the arguments of Aristotle and Aquinas, William of Ockham (c. 1320), Jean Buridan (c. 1340), Nicole Oresme (c. 1350), and others judged that a plurality of worlds was not impossible. Later Willem van Vorilong (d. 1463) and Nicholas of Cusa (1440) published treatises in which they defended the idea of a plurality of worlds.

After Copernicus

The Copernican view of the solar system seemed to make the existence of extraterrestrial life more likely. While Galileo, Descartes, and Kepler retained a cautious attitude, Giordano Bruno heartily embraced the idea in his 1584 treatise *On the Infinite Universe and Worlds*.[4] Other seventeenth-century pluralists were Tommaso Campanella, John Wilkins, Bernard de Fontenelle (1686), Richard Bentley (1693), and Christiaan Huygens (1698). Voltaire, in his satirical work *Micromégas* (1752), has two giants, one from the star Sirius and the other from the planet Saturn, visit Earth in order to impress upon the reader how small Earth must be in relation to the rest of the cosmos.[5] During the nineteenth century, the idea of plural worlds became popular, among both atheists like Thomas Paine and evangelicals like Thomas Chalmers and Thomas Dick. Great defenders of extraterrestrial life were the astronomers Richard Proctor (1870) and Camille Flammarion (1862). Their attitude is well summarized by American astronomer and popularizer of science Simon Newcomb. He argued in an article for *Harper's* magazine titled "Life in the Universe" (1905) that if Earth is a representative planet orbiting a representative star, then life must be abundant throughout the universe.[6]

In a recent book titled *If the Universe Is Teeming with Aliens . . . Where Is Everybody?* Stephen Webb considers three possibilities:[7] Perhaps aliens don't exist, or they exist but don't communicate, or they are here already. He believes the first possibility but does not consider that we are still technically incapable of interstellar travel and so they might exist.

In another recent book, Jack Cohen and Ian Stewart claim that our scientific way to answer the question is wrong.[8] Their approach is, however, more like science fiction. They claim that our present cosmology is wrong. Instead, there exists a multitude of universes, and they write, "The (initial) vacuum of space-time might possess sufficient complexity to organize itself into some form of life by carrying out a complete thermodynamic work cycle," such that aliens might have lived through the inflation (the rapid and large expansion generally assumed to have occurred immediately after the big bang, as described in chapter 2.2). The idea that living beings could exist, let alone survive, in the very early universe is highly unlikely. Moreover, they neglect the fact that we cannot observe other universes, if existing, so our search for extraterrestrial life must be limited to our universe.

Search for extraterrestrials

During the twentieth century, the advent of modern observational techniques and space travel changed the picture considerably. We now know that in our solar system, no advanced life exists outside Earth, although microbial life may perhaps have arisen on early Mars in an ancient salty sea, later dried up due to climatic change.[9] For the existence of advanced extraterrestrial life, we must look to planets beyond the solar system. About 120 extrasolar planets have so far been detected.[10] Visiting an extrasolar planet to look for advanced life is technically impossible, however. A manned round-trip flight to the nearest star, Alpha Centauri, at 20 percent of the speed of light (the highest speed attainable with any current spacecraft) would take forty-four years and require for its launch three hundred times the total annual earthly energy production.[11]

Therefore, the search for extraterrestrial intelligence uses a simpler but indirect approach. It is based on the assumption that advanced extraterrestrials, if they exist, have radio and television broadcasts like ours (no irony intended!). Radio and television carrier waves and radiation from large radar installations are known to spread into space to a great depth. There is also the possibility that the extraterrestrials may transmit directed signals. The Phoenix project is a targeted search for microwave signals from one thousand selected sunlike stars within 150 light-years from the Earth, which might have an Earthlike planet that might have permitted the development of intelligent beings.[12] The double "might have" indicates how great the uncertainty is, not even counting the problem of synchronicity (or lack of it) of any extraterrestrial civilization with human civilization. Observations are made using a radio telescope equipped with an ultrasensitive detector that uses a smart software system to process signals automatically.[13] A frequency range of 1 to 3 gigahertz (1 to 3 billion vibrations per second) was chosen, since in this range, there is minimal interference from celestial and terrestrial microwave radiation. In ten years of operation, 710 of the 1,000 targeted stars have been fully observed without any significant signals being detected.[14] This project is now continued with the Allen Telescope Array, a dedicated system of ultimately 350 small (6 meters in diameter) radio telescopes, allowing researchers to check out a few million stars in 20 years. Another project carries out an optical search for nanosecond laser flashes that an alien population might emit for communication with spacecraft.

13.2 Paucity of theological data

Bible and early thinkers

Biblical and nonbiblical creation stories do not refer to extraterrestrial life, if we exclude angels, the immaterial messengers between heaven and earth.[15] John 10:16 ("I have other sheep that do not belong to this fold") is commonly thought to refer to the Gentiles, while 1 Peter 3:18-20 ("in which also he went and made a proclamation to the spirits in prison, who in former times did not obey") refers to people who died before the time of Jesus, rather than to extraterrestrials. Tradition (the body of teaching of the early church) also is silent about extraterrestrial life.

This silence is hardly surprising. The biblical message is "economic" in the sense that it is directed to our life on this planet in preparation for the future life. In addition, the geocentric worldview dominated until the sixteenth-century work of Copernicus, Kepler, and Galileo. The scientific insight into the prebiotic formation of life and the possibility of its arising elsewhere in the universe dates from only the last fifty years. As mentioned earlier, in the pre-Copernican era, only Nicholas of Cusa and his contemporary Willem van Vorilong clearly expressed a belief in advanced extraterrestrials.[16]

Even after the overturn of the geocentric model in the sixteenth century, the picture does not change much. Bruno (1584), who ended at the stake in 1600 on the accusation of pantheistic immanentism (belief that God is part of the universe), maintained the likelihood of the existence of extraterrestrial beings "no less noble" than humans. In his *On the Infinite Universe and Worlds* (1584), he presents a fictitious dialogue between Burchio (B) and Fracastorio (F):

> B: Then the other worlds are inhabited like our own?
> F: If not exactly as our own, and if not more nobly, at least no less inhabited and no less nobly.[17]

Tommaso Campanella, in his *Apologia pro Galileo* (1622), rejected Aquinas's objection against a multitude of worlds with the argument that it concerns many small systems within one large system. He claims that the inhabitants, because they did not descend from Adam, do not need salvation unless they have committed other sins. Fontenelle, in his *Conversations on the Plurality of Worlds* (1686), maintains, "The moon . . . is inhabited, because she is like the earth; and the other planets are inhabited, because they are like the moon."[18] Christiaan Huygens (1629–95) left a very speculative work, *Cosmotheoros,* in which he claims the presence of water on Jupiter, Saturn, Venus, and Mercury, and thus of all kinds of plants and animals, and even creatures endowed with reason, created as described for humans in Genesis 1 and having both virtues and vices as we do.[19]

Contemporary theologians

Few contemporary theologians show much interest in the matter of possible extraterrestrial life. This may be because the geocentric model has lingered on in our thinking as a result of our human self-centeredness, and because the divorce between science and theology since Darwin's time has placed the question of extraterrestrial life outside the view of most theologians.[20] These two factors may well explain why such prominent contemporary theologians as Karl Barth, Emil Brunner, Hans Küng, John Macquarrie, Wolfhart Pannenberg, Jürgen Moltmann, Edward Schillebeeckx, Keith Ward, and even scientist-theologians Arthur Peacocke and John Polkinghorne have not considered the possibility of extraterrestrial life in their theological works. Willem Drees mentions only T. M. Hesburgh, E. L. Mascall, Paul Tillich, H. Berkhof, A. Ford, and S. L. Jaki as contemporary theologians willing to accept the possibility of extraterrestrial life.[21] To them may be added Teilhard de Chardin, who left an unpublished and not very helpful paper on the topic.[22] Over against them, Drees cites several lesser-known theologians, including U. Köhler, L. J. van Holk, J. J. Buskes, E. A. Milne, P. J. Roscam Abbing, and A. J. Burgess, who argue for the physical and/or theological uniqueness of life on Earth.[23]

The near absence of sound theological reflection on this topic in Bible and tradition and by prominent contemporary theologians necessitates some pioneer work in formulating a theology of extraterrestrial life. In particular, the implications for Christ's redemptive work should be considered. A book edited by Steven J. Dick offers little help in this.[24] The chapters by Ernan McMullin and George V. Coyne only list the questions to be addressed,[25] and the principles for a "cosmotheology" offered by Dick hardly represent a Christian theology.[26]

Before turning to the theological implications of possible advanced life beyond Earth, I first consider the likelihood of its occurrence and the characteristics such life might acquire.

13.3 Possibility of extraterrestrial life

Since we can be fairly certain that no extraterrestrials exist on any of the other planets in our solar system, we must look for extrasolar planets where conditions similar to those on Earth exist. The intermediates in the formation of amino acids and of ribose (component of RNA) are present in interstellar space, and amino acids of extraterrestrial origin exist in meteorites. These conditions suggest that life can have arisen elsewhere in the universe through a process resembling the prebiotic evolution on Earth (chapter 2.4).

Beyond the solar system, there are billions of stars, some of which resemble the sun in size, age, and luminosity, and these may well have planets. Direct observation of such planets is difficult because the bright light of the star overshines the faint emission of the planet.[27] Indirect evidence can be obtained from the detection of small motions ("wobble") or small light fluctuations of the star due to the orbiting planet. So far, all that this technique has detected are "hot Jupiters"—planets with a mass equal to or larger than that of Jupiter and with elliptical orbits bringing them at times very close to their star.[28] Advanced life could not have arisen on any of these planets. Also, three Neptune-sized extrasolar planets (with masses fourteen to twenty-one times that of Earth) have been observed, but lacking data on their density, there is doubt whether they are rocky planets like Earth.[29] This doubt is fed by the idea that the formation of the planets in our solar system by agglomeration of dust particles left from the sun's formation is special; in contrast, the hot extrasolar Jupiters may have condensed directly from the gaseous material surrounding their star.[30]

In addition, any Earthlike planet will have to satisfy some thirty-two requirements in order to permit development and maintenance of life on it. For example, its star must be between 0.4 and 1.4 solar masses, and it must be stable in radiation for at least 4 billion years (the length of time needed for the development of human life on Earth). Also, the distance of the planet to its star must have been constant within 5 percent.[31] The requirements for star mass and planet–star distance alone may eliminate 99.9 percent of all candidates.

There also needs to be some synchronicity in their appearance with that of Earth. However, 75 percent of the sunlike stars in our galaxy are at least 1 billion years older than the sun.[32] It is therefore uncertain whether any of their planets would still harbor advanced life. This may leave few fitting candidates, but in view of the very large number of stars, we cannot rule out that there are some.

13.4 Nature of extraterrestrial life (if existing)

What can we predict about the nature of the advanced life that could have developed on such a planet? Everywhere in the universe, the same chemical elements are present as on Earth, because hydrogen and helium were formed in the big bang, the elements up to iron by nuclear fusion in early stars, and the elements heavier than iron probably by neutron capture during early supernova explosions. As far as we know, the earthly physical and chemical laws are valid throughout the universe. We can therefore make some predictions about extraterrestrial life. Such life will be based, like all earthly life, on carbon chemistry, since carbon is the only element able to form the long-chain compounds (including DNA, RNA, and proteins) that are essential for the complex processes of growth and replication of living cells (chapter 2.4).

It is estimated that during 4 billion years of biological evolution on Earth, some billion species arose, of which fewer than one in a thousand have survived the process of natural selection. This suggests that in the evolutionary process, all possible life-forms have been explored. Moreover, all existing species on Earth have basically the same biochemistry, the same DNA-based replication system, and an identical genetic code. Thus, it seems likely that in extraterrestrial evolution of life, the same DNA replication/transcription system would evolve. In all earthly DNA, only four (labeled A, T, G, and C) of sixteen possible nucleotides occur, apparently because these four provide the lowest incidence of replication errors.[33] Hence, I would expect the same four to be selected in extraterrestrial life.

Another interesting point is the chirality of amino acids and many other biomolecules (chapter 2.4). The Murchison meteorite was found to contain a preponderance of the L-form over the D-form of certain amino acids. This suggests that the preference for the L-form already existed in the universe before life on Earth originated.[34] Therefore, the amino acids of extraterrestrial beings would probably also have the same chirality as those of earthly creatures.

Considering all this, it seems likely that advanced extraterrestrial beings (if existing) would not be radically different from *Homo sapiens* in physiology and biochemistry. I would expect these creatures to have brains and neuronal systems resembling ours, so they would have similar thought processes. Stanley Jaki comes to the same conclusion on theological grounds.[35] Further, we may expect these creatures to be mortal as we are, since without the life cycle, biological evolution cannot take place.

On the basis of our present scientific evidence, I consider the development of intelligent life elsewhere in the cosmos, resembling that on Earth, a definite possibility. However, I shall refrain from assessing its probability, since I think we cannot reliably calculate it. Chaos theory shows that it is difficult, if not impossible, to predict the behavior of complex nonlinear systems over a long period of time (chapter 7.4). Moreover, multiplying the probabilities of each separate step in a process like the origin of life may greatly underrate its actual likelihood, because of the occurrence of self-organization (chapter 7.3). We must also bear in mind that the methodology used in the SETI project allows the detection only of advanced extraterrestrials that have developed television or radar one or more centuries ahead of us, the amount of time the signal would take to reach us.

13.5 Bottom-up theological considerations

I have presented arguments for assuming that advanced extraterrestrial beings, if they exist, would show considerable likeness to us humans in physiological and even mental processes. Because religious awareness is common to all humans through the ages, we may then expect this to arise also in extraterrestrials. This makes it meaningful to trace the development of religious awareness in humans. I call this discussion "bottom-up theological considerations," because we look at the process from the creaturely side, from nature to supernature.

Animism and polytheism

The earliest evidence for religious awareness in humans is presented by Neandertal burial places with evidence of ritual, dating from about one hundred thousand years ago.[36] Three stages of religious development are commonly distinguished: animism, polytheism, and monotheism.[37]

Primitive, nomadic humans were utterly dependent on nature, and they saw nature as sacred and every natural object—trees, rocks, streams—as endowed with a spirit. These spirits were thought not only to control the existence of its object (a tree spirit makes the tree grow and spread its branches; a stream spirit makes the water flow) but indirectly also to influence human life by providing shade, water, and other benefits. Rituals were used to ensure the favor of these spirits and to ward off evil. This is animism.

Gradually, the spirits of animism came to be seen as deities with a personality, whom one had to please with gifts, sacrifices, in order to survive. Deities were then given a name and were usually associated with forces of nature, such as storm, rain, and thunder. In addition, tribes commonly adopted a territorial god, like the Canaanite Baals and Els in the Old Testament. In a further development, one deity came to be seen as more powerful than the others, and that one was featured as a creator god in the creation stories.[38] This is polytheism.

Monotheism

In the Old Testament, we can trace the extended struggle that it took the people of Israel to advance from polytheism to monotheism.[39] It is interesting to note that this transition occurred only in tiny Israel, rather than in the great nations of Egypt, Greece, and Rome. During the Exodus, the Israelites chose Yahweh, the territorial wilderness god from Mount Horeb, as their guide and protector, but still only as a tribal god. After many instances of apostasy (see the books of Judges, Kings, and Chronicles), their experience during the Babylonian exile led to the conviction that Yahweh is the universal, omnipresent God, the God of all peoples (Isa 49:6), the Creator of everything that is, the eternal and only God (Isa 43:10; 45:5-7, 18), to whom the cosmic forces are small and insignificant (Isa 40:12-15, 28). Yet they also come to experience Yahweh as a loving and caring God (Isa 40:11), who seeks to have a personal relationship with his human creatures and who gives them the law to live by.

This posed a question: How can the perfect Yahweh forgive transgressions of divine law without compromising the perfect divine justice? Initially, this led to the image of a vengeful god, who ruthlessly punishes the sinner. The prophet Jeremiah sought the solution in replacement of the old covenant of Mount Horeb with a new covenant "written upon the heart" (Jer 31:31-34), but he failed to solve the problem that, to the ancient mind, a valid covenant requires the blood of a sacrifice. Other prophets predict the coming of a Messiah (Mic 5:2-5; Zech 9:9-10), the suffering servant in Second Isaiah (Isa 42:1-4; 50:4-9; 52:13—53:12), who will bring reconciliation between Yahweh and his people. Here ends the evolution of religious thinking in the Old Testament period, which brought the crucial transition from polytheism to monotheism.

Trinitarian monotheism

Six centuries later, the Jewish followers of Jesus of Nazareth (again, a small minority) recognize in this Jesus the promised Messiah, who through his death on the cross brings reconciliation, a new covenant. Through their experience of his resurrection, they come to see him as the incarnate Son of God. The Pentecostal experience in Jerusalem leads to the awareness of the Holy Spirit as our lasting link with God the Father. The Christian church is born, and it grows rapidly and spreads over the entire world. Ten centuries of evolving religious experience of Jews and Christians are recorded in the books of the Bible, Old and New Testaments. During the first four centuries of the Christian era, the experience of the apostles is formulated by the church in the trinitarian monotheistic doctrine of the one God in three persons, Father-creator, Son-redeemer, Spirit-communicator. To me, this is the deepest understanding of God that so far has developed in the human mind. Even though the trinitarian nature of God may remain a mysterious concept, the trinitarian doctrine of creation developed in chapter 9 (sections 9.2 and 9.3) makes it more tangible.

Morality

Along with this evolution of religious thought in humans went the evolution of moral awareness.[40] The first notion of morality can be seen in higher animals in the form of kin concern, reciprocity, and altruistic behavior[41] and in primitive humans. The first moral codes were developed by Egyptians and Babylonians. The precept of "eye for eye, tooth for tooth" in the Babylonian Code of Hammurabi, where it was restricted to the elite, is taken over into Jewish law, where only foreigners are excluded (Exod 21:23-25). The Jewish code of law is summed up in the Decalogue (Exod 20:1-17), which is based on the covenant of Israel with Yahweh.

Jesus affirmed and at the same time radicalized the law (Matt 5:21-48), so that no human can hope to comply fully with it. From a moral code, the law has thus became a mirror showing us our brokenness, from which we can only be rescued by God's intervention in the saving death and resurrection of Jesus Christ. Having accepted this message, we may in joy and gratitude for our salvation follow the guidelines of the radicalized law, knowing that the decisive step has been taken by God in Christ (Rom 3:20-26; 8:1-17). Morality has thus developed from group morality, without clear transcendent basis, first to morality from a divine law and then to morality out of gratitude for God's saving act in Christ. Christian morality, rooted in the life, death, and resurrection of Jesus, invites all members of the human family to imitate Jesus in their lives, and thus to share in his work of salvation. In this way, kin concern, reciprocity, and altruism have evolved into a communal ethic with an emphasis on love (*agape*).

From these considerations, it appears that evolving religious experience with an associated moral awareness is a universal phenomenon among humans. It seems to me quite reasonable to assume that a similar religious evolution will take place in the development of any extraterrestrial advanced creatures. However, religious evolution on Earth has led to other faiths beside the Christian faith. Among them are continuing Judaism and Islam as closely related monotheistic religions, and Hinduism and Buddhism as other forms of religion. Which kind of religion(s) may eventually have developed in any extraterrestrial culture can thus not be answered by bottom-up considerations. So I shall now move to top-down considerations, based on the Judeo-Christian image of God.

13.6 Top-down theological considerations

Cosmic revelation and salvation

Religion can be seen as the result of the interaction between divine revelation and human experience. This means the development of religious thinking among humans, described in the preceding section, can be considered to reflect the interaction of God's progressive self-revelation with increasing human understanding in the evolution of the human race. The experience of the presence of Yahweh with them during the Babylonian exile led the Jewish prophets, particularly Second Isaiah, to the conclusion that Yahweh is not only the God of Israel, but the Creator of the entire universe. (Genesis 1 was written in the same period.) Thus, we may say that

God is also the creator of any possibly existing extraterrestrials. God is the universal, omnipresent God of all peoples, Jews and Gentiles (Isa 49:6), and thus also of any extraterrestrials. In the early church, as described in chapter 10.5, Christ came to be seen as the cosmic Christ (Eph 1:20-23; Col 1:15-20; Heb 2:7-9), as the universal Redeemer: "that the world [*kosmos*] might be saved through him" (John 3:17); "in Christ God was reconciling the world [*kosmos*] to himself" (2 Cor 5:19).

This means that the creative work of the Father, the saving work of Christ, and the communicative action of the Holy Spirit will apply just as much to any creatures on another planet as they do to us. Van Vorilong (c. 1450) already stated that Christ's death on Earth can bring salvation to the inhabitants of other worlds, even if there were an infinite number of these worlds, that is, extrasolar planets on which advanced life has arisen.[42] Then we may also expect that the one God of the universe will have made himself known to them, as God has progressively revealed himself to us humans.

Would they be sinful?

Would such beings also be sinful and in need of salvation? Thomas Campanella (1616) did not think so: "They do not descend from Adam and thus are not tainted by his sin, so they do not need salvation, unless they have committed another sin."[43] In this somewhat simplistic reasoning, he bases himself on the doctrine of original sin, which is untenable in the light of our scientific insights about the origin of humankind and the weakness of its biblical and theological foundation (chapter 10.4). Over against this, I claim, in agreement with most current theologians, that the story of the fall in Genesis 3 does not concern a unique, historical event but describes in mythical form the condition common to all humans—namely, the human ambivalence of being both image bearers of God and sinners grasping for equality with God.

It is likely that this condition would also apply to any extraterrestrial creatures. One reason is that such beings will have a way of thinking that is similar to ours. In addition, such creatures will also have received freedom of will as an expression of God's love, giving them the possibility for disobedience. And third, in view of the operation of remaining chaos in the entire universe (chapter 6.3), these creatures will also be subject to chaotic thinking, to temptation. Thus, there seems to be good reason to expect extraterrestrials to be sinners just as much in need of salvation as we are.

I would even claim that salvation and reconciliation will come to them at the same time as to us, namely, when Christ at his triumphant return will definitively banish the remaining element of chaos from the universe.

Would this require multiple incarnations?

The question has been raised whether their salvation would require a repetition of Christ's incarnation, death, and resurrection for our extraterrestrial brothers and sisters on their planet. Van Vorilong said that it would not be "fitting" if Christ had to go to another world to die again.[44] However, this is the expression of a sentiment, rather than a rational theological statement. E. L. Mascall has discussed the question in a more theological way.[45] He first rejects the "extreme kenotic view," according to which Christ in the incarnation would have scaled down his divinity to the limits of humanness. In that case, the incarnation could hardly have taken place simultaneously on two different planets. He also rejects the idea of a second incarnation after Christ had already been taken up in glory. But, Mascall says, the orthodox view is that the incarnation is not the conversion of Godhead into human flesh, but rather the taking up of humanness into Godhead, so there is no reason why another finite rational nature of inhabitants of another planet could not also be taken up in this way—in other words, that several incarnations would be possible. Brian Hebblethwaite has argued against the possibility of multiple incarnations, but strangely, he believes that this also rules out the existence of advanced extraterrestrial life.[46]

My answer to the question about multiple incarnations follows a different line of thinking but also leads to the uniqueness of Christ's incarnation. Over the centuries, popular Christian belief has narrowed down the significance of the incarnation to being merely the prelude to the salvation of us humans. I rather recognize, with Paul (2 Cor 5:19) and on the basis of our insight into cosmic and biological evolution, Jesus as the cosmic Christ (chapter 10.5). The human Jesus, like us made of "stardust," is united with the entire cosmos, and thus through the incarnation he becomes the cosmic Christ. Incarnation, death, and resurrection of Jesus Christ, taking place in Palestine two thousand years ago, are of cosmic significance and lasting validity. These epochal events bring salvation to us, who live two thousand years later in other parts of the planet, yes, to all humans who ever lived on Earth at any time and at any place. And not only to humans, but to the whole creation that "has been groaning in labor pains until now" and "waits with eager longing" for its final liberation, as Paul says (Rom 8:19, 22). Why not then to creatures on another planet? There is no need to assume multiple incarnations!

The universe is a single system, evolving in a process where the simple leads to the complex: inorganic matter leads to organic matter, organic matter to living matter, living matter to mind or spirit. The highest principle of unity in our universe is spirit. This insight led William Temple to introduce the concept of the "sacramental universe."[47] In a sacrament, the spiritual and the material are intimately related, with spirit being first and last and with matter being the effective expression of spirit. Likewise, in the universe, God expresses God's self in absolute supremacy and freedom through the evolution of matter to life and of life to human spirit, which is then united to God through God's love in the new kingdom.

On the basis of my earlier argumentation that extraterrestrials, if they exist, will strongly resemble us in body and mind, I suggest that they also will participate in the reconciliation brought about by Christ's incarnation, death, and resurrection two thousand years ago in Palestine, without requiring a repetition of these events on their planet. And as God has made the message of Christ's saving work heard in all times and in all corners of our planet, so God will also bring it in an appropriate way to any of God's creatures on another planet: God's communicative Spirit fills the entire world. These creatures will then also be offered the opportunity to participate in the New Creation that we expect to be part of. If we should never succeed in meeting them in this world, then we shall certainly meet them in the next world—at least if they exist! This will not require any radical change in our theology, merely the willingness on our part to share with them not only the unique place in the cosmos that we had assumed for ourselves, but also our salvation. All this I believe to follow logically from our present scientific insights and a reasonable extrapolation of Christian theology.

If our search is in vain

And what if none of the ongoing search projects detects any signal from an advanced civilization outside our solar system? A negative finding would not be conclusive: we may have to look farther into the universe with its billions of stars or find entirely different ways of searching for the existence of extraterrestrials. And what if the findings continue to be negative and the scientific community comes to the conclusion that we do seem to be alone in this vast universe? Then we must remind ourselves of the fact that even if advanced creatures arose only on Earth, this still required the vast universe of which we are part: gravity would have made a smaller universe collapse far too soon to permit biological evolution to proceed to the point of the arrival of *Homo sapiens.* Then we may praise and thank God for the willingness to create this immense cosmos in order to allow us to arise.

13.7 Summary

Could advanced beings exist elsewhere in the universe, and if so, what does this mean for Christian theology? Since no advanced life appears to exist on the other planets in our solar system, we must look for extrasolar planets. Search programs are in progress in which scientists use radio telescopes with ultrasensitive detection systems to watch for microwave signals broadcast by extraterrestrial civilizations on planets of sunlike stars within one hundred light-years from Earth. So far, no significant signals have been received.

Meaningful references to extraterrestrial life are absent in biblical and nonbiblical creation stories and in other biblical writings. Medieval theologians, including Albertus Magnus and Thomas Aquinas, rejected the existence of extraterrestrial life mainly on philosophical grounds. Only Nicholas of Cusa and van Vorilong (c. 1450) accepted the possibility. Even after Copernicus, not much interest was shown by theologians. This means that formulating a theology of extraterrestrial life requires some pioneer work.

As to the likelihood of extraterrestrial life, our present ideas about the origin of life on Earth suggest that life can have arisen on other Earthlike planets. Such planets have not yet been detected, but with more refined techniques, they will probably be detected. In view of the many requirements to be satisfied by star and planet, the number of suitable candidates will be small, though not zero.

What can we predict about the life that could have developed on such a planet? Everywhere in the universe, the same chemical elements and physical and chemical laws exist. Extraterrestrial life will then be based on carbon as the only element able to form the long-chain compounds (DNA, RNA, proteins, lipids) essential for growth and replication of living cells. Since all earthly species have basically the same biochemistry, DNA-based replication, and genetic code, I suggest that advanced extraterrestrials (if they exist) will resemble humans and have similar brains and thought processes.

The development of religious awareness in humans is likely to apply to the process that would occur in any extraterrestrials. From a Christian point of view, God is the Creator of the entire universe and thus also of any extraterrestrials. Likewise, the cosmic Christ is the universal Redeemer, and the Spirit will communicate with extraterrestrials as with us. The one God of the universe will have made himself known to them, as God has to us.

Would such beings be in need of salvation? They would be affected by the cosmic-wide remaining chaos and thus be sinners, as we are. Their salvation would not require a repetition of Christ's incarnation, death, and resurrection on their planet, since these events in Palestine two thousand years ago are of cosmic significance and lasting validity. As God brought the message of Christ's saving work to humans in all times and in all corners of our planet, so God will bring it to creatures on another planet. Their salvation will coincide with ours on the last day, when Christ will definitively banish remaining chaos from the entire universe. All this logically follows from our present scientific insights and from a reasonable extrapolation of Christian theology.

14

Future and Destiny: Eschatology and Chaos Theology

14.1 Scientific view of the future

In this final chapter, I consider what science and theology can tell us about the future of the universe and ourselves. Science can provide insight in the future by extrapolating from the known development to the present, but without recognizing a destiny or purpose. The theological view of the future, called eschatology (from *eschata*, the last things), deals not merely with the future, but with the destiny of creation. This implies that eschatology should be based on creation theology, for which I shall use chaos theology.

Cosmic degradation

Science offers a bleak picture of the future of the universe and its creatures. The cosmos is expected to go to complete degradation some 24 billion years from now, when its accelerating expansion due to the so-called dark energy is taken into account (chapter 2.2).[1] Rather than collapsing in a "big crunch," the universe is now expected to fly apart in a "big rip."[2] Galactic clusters will drift apart ever faster. In the final billion years, galaxies and solar systems will break up. In the final thirty minutes, stars and planets will disintegrate. In the final split second, molecules and atoms will tear apart, and their constituent particles will "evaporate," leaving only a cold, dark, lifeless, and matterless cloud of photons.[3]

Much earlier, some 5 billion years from now, our sun will have exhausted its nuclear fuel and expanded into a red giant, touching Earth. Earth's surface temperature will rise to about 1,300°C, extinguishing all life on Earth. Any advanced community on an extrasolar planet will suffer a similar fate when its star turns into a red giant. But before all this happens, a large asteroid may hit Earth, as happened at least twice during the history of biological evolution, and destroy life in the direct impact and by subsequent cooling from dust clouds encircling Earth.[4]

This bleak picture of the future of the universe made the nonbelieving cosmologist Steven Weinberg exclaim that the more he understood the universe, the more it seemed to him to be pointless.[5]

Ecological crisis

There is now a widespread awareness that humanity is threatened by a severe ecological crisis, largely of its own making. A major factor is the ever-increasing world population (6.37 billion in 2004, 9.19 billion in 2050), although the worldwide growth rate has been steadily decreasing since 1990.[6] Earth, with its land, water, and atmosphere, resembles the closed ecological system of a space station. Apart from solar radiation, nothing comes into the system, and nothing goes out. We have to make do with the remaining resources and try to survive with the waste we produce. An increasing world population and a shortage of resources, including water in Africa, make this progressively more difficult. Our ecological balance is in a very precarious state.

Threats to land and water are caused by toxic industrial and household wastes dumped in sea and rivers and on land, agricultural pesticides left on the land and washed into surface water, and radioactive waste from military and civilian nuclear reactors. Such pollutants can cause diseases, miscarriages, and birth defects among those living near toxic waste dumps or eating contaminated food.[7] Though disastrous to those affected, this problem does not appear to be a global threat to the survival of humankind. The effects are being contained by environmental laws and agencies, sensitive detection methods, improved technology, and recycling of waste.

The massive burning and cutting of tropical forests—the green lungs of the earth and host to millions of plant and animal species—is causing a serious loss of biodiversity and of human life and property through landslides from deforested areas after heavy rains. Loss of biodiversity is serious because it upsets the ecological balance among species that has been established during evolutionary history. Burning the forests aggravates global warming (discussed later) in a double way: by releasing carbon dioxide and by decreasing uptake of carbon dioxide through photosynthesis. Restriction of tropical forest cutting to a sustainable rate is greatly needed but difficult to enforce. Another possible remedy is large-scale reforestation in all countries, but this is difficult in the face of the ever-growing world population.

Ozone depletion in the upper stratosphere leads to an increase in short-wavelength ultraviolet radiation on Earth's surface, causing an increased incidence of skin cancer and cataracts in humans, lower yields of crop plants, and a decrease in plankton and consequently in fish. Ozone depletion is due to a chain reaction of chlorofluorocarbons (CFCs) with ozone under the influence of solar ultraviolet radiation, which destroys some one hundred thousand ozone molecules per molecule of CFC.[8] CFCs have been widely used (and ultimately released into the atmosphere) as refrigerants in refrigerating equipment, as solvents for cleaning computer chips, and as driving gas in spray cans and production of foam plastic. Over the last fifty years, 1 million tons of CFCs have been released per year, leading to the annual destruction of 500 million tons of ozone. Over the Antarctic every winter, an ozone hole of several million square miles forms with a maximum loss of 60 percent, larger than anywhere else, due to the presence of stratospheric ice clouds that promote the chain reaction. It is ironic that the ozone layer, which for 2 billion years has protected life on Earth, including that of humans, is now being destroyed by them, thus endangering all life on Earth! In the Montreal Protocol (1987), it was internationally agreed to abolish the use of CFCs by 2020; in 1990 this was advanced to 2000. However, the CFC lifetime in the atmosphere is about one hundred years, so it will take till well into the next century for ozone depletion to be effectively abolished.

Global warming

The greatest threat to life on Earth is presented by global warming, the so-called greenhouse effect. Global warming results from the trapping of infrared radiation (heat) from Earth's surface by atmospheric gases that strongly absorb infrared light, particularly carbon dioxide (CO_2). Through our massive use of fossil fuels, the atmospheric CO_2 concentration has risen from 250 parts per million in 1800 to 358 parts per million in 1995. It will reach 500 parts per million in 2050.[9] The effect on the climate is now noticeable from the temperature records, and the computerized climate models agree with the records. In its third report, the Intergovernmental Panel on Climate Change (IPCC) of the United Nations predicts a temperature increase of 1.7°C to 4°C and a 0.25- to 0.8-meter rise in sea level by the year 2100.[10] The ever more refined models offer more precise predictions: 2.5°C to 3.0°C for doubling of the CO_2 level by 2050.[11] These models also permit predictions for regional areas—for example, hotter and drier summers in the western United States, the same and colder and wetter winters in Europe, more cyclones in the United States and the Caribbean.[12] A side effect of global warming could be a threefold increase in ozone depletion over the Arctic.[13]

The main reason for the predicted rise in sea level is the melting of polar ice, which is now in progress in both the Antarctic and the Arctic.[14] It will cause frequent and eventually permanent flooding of low-lying lands (for example, the Mississippi and Nile deltas, the Maldives, and Bangladesh). The cold, sweet melting water will submerge the warm, saline water of the Gulf Stream, which may result in colder winters in northwestern Europe.[15] A significant warming of the bottom waters in the north Pacific Ocean since 1985 has been observed,[16] perhaps due to the same process. This shows that global warming is affecting not only Earth's surface, but also its oceans.

Effects on flora and fauna are already noticeable. In the northeastern Atlantic Ocean, phytoplankton now blooms twenty-one days earlier than in 1987, but zooplankton (which feeds on phytoplankton) blooms only ten days earlier. This seriously disrupts the food chain, affecting fisheries.[17] An analysis of breeding, flowering, and migration of 1,700 species of birds, butterflies, plants, shrubs, and trees over sixteen or more years concluded that plants and animals move every decade six kilometers toward the poles, and more than 95 percent of this movement must be attributed to global warming in the twentieth century.[18] A similar analysis of 143 studies of 1,468 plant and animal species found that 81 percent show the expected effects on local population density, shift toward the poles or higher location, time of migration, flowering or egg-laying, and others.[19] In Britain between 1970 and 1999, 71 percent of butterfly species and 28 percent of native plant species disappeared.[20] A modeling study concluded that by 2050, from 18 to 35 percent (depending on assumed temperature rise) of species will be lost.[21]

Global warming is clearly the greatest threat to the future of humanity and to all life on this planet. Can anything be done against it? The obvious solution—and really the only one—is to replace all fossil fuels with energy sources that do not emit greenhouse gases. A sobering thought is that this would not abolish global warming, but merely fix it at its present level: the current atmospheric level of carbon dioxide will not be diminished. The proposals in the Kyoto Protocol (1997), even if observed by all nations, will merely reduce the rate of increase. The renewable sources of wind power, earthly solar power, and tidal power can at most supply about

20 percent of our needs. Either we shall have to greatly expand the use of nuclear power[22] or we shall have to launch solar power panels in geosynchronous orbit to beam power to ground-based receiving stations.[23] In the latter option, the advanced nations jointly would have to construct and maintain the solar power satellite belt, allowing developing nations to build relatively simple and cheap receiving stations for their power needs. In any case, fossil fuel production is expected to pass its peak sometime during this century.

In conclusion, the scientific picture of the future of the universe and of life on Earth is somber indeed. From the order that has been built up in 14 billion years of cosmic and biological evolution out of the chaos of the big bang, the universe seems doomed to return to complete, lifeless chaos. And we humans seem to speed up this process of disintegration for our planet through the ecological crisis. If this were the last word, then the entire evolutionary creation process would indeed be utterly pointless, as Steven Weinberg said.

14.2 Biblical view of the future

Old Testament view

In sharp contrast to the somber view that science offers us, the biblical view of the future is hopeful. In the biblical perspective, future becomes destiny, the end of our time, the last day. The creation in its present state is seen as threatened by remaining chaos symbolized as sea (chapter 6.3 and 6.4) and by human evil (Jeremiah 5–6), which in chaos theology is also ascribed to remaining chaos (chapter 8.6). Nowhere, not even in the apocalyptic writings, is there an indication of a complete disintegration of the cosmos, as science predicts. There may be catastrophes, desolation of the land, drought, starvation, disease, and warfare, but the Lord says, "Yet I will not make a full end" (Jer 4:27).

The prophet Isaiah predicts a brighter future when he proclaims the message of a new creation (Isa 41:17-20; 43:18-21): "I am about to do a new thing; now it springs forth, do you not perceive it?" (Isa 43:19). He speaks about the new heaven and the new earth that God will make (Isa 66:22) and has God call himself the first and the last (Isa 44:6; 48:12). The Old Testament prophets also forecast the coming of a Messiah, who will bring healing to broken humanity and the entire universe (e.g., Isa 9:1-7; 11:1-9; Dan 9:25-26).

New Testament view

The New Testament proclaims Jesus Christ as the Messiah who will appear on the last day. This is mentioned in all four Gospels (e.g., Matt 13:40-43; Mark 14:62; Luke 12:35-40; John 6:40; 21:22-23) and is often expressed by Paul (e.g., 1 Cor 15:20-28; Phil 3:20-21; 1 Thess 3:13; 4:16; 5:23), as well as by James (James 5:7-9) and Peter (1 Peter 1:5-7, 13, 4:5—5:11) and in Revelation (Rev 22:12-13). The return of Christ and the attending definitive fulfillment became a focal point of belief in the early church and should be for us today.

The New Testament authors integrate the idea of a new creation with their understanding of the central role of Christ in salvation. The title applied by Isaiah to God is given to Christ: "I am the Alpha and the Omega, the first and the last, the beginning and the end" (Rev 22:13). Christ stands at the beginning as the creative *Logos* and at the end as the inaugurator of the new creation: Alpha and Omega, the first and last letters of the Greek alphabet. The central New Testament message is that in the resurrection of Jesus, the new creation that the Old Testament prophets were expecting has already arrived, yet it is also a promise for the end of time, when there will be a new heaven and a new earth and no more evil and death: "Then I saw a new heaven and a new earth; for the first heaven and the first earth had passed away, and the sea was no more" (Rev 21:1). The "sea" symbolizes remaining chaos that will be abolished at that time. The paradox of a new creation, already introduced and yet to come in the future (aptly called "realized eschatology" by Charles Dodd), can be resolved only by seeing the resurrection as the decisive victory, which in God's good time will bring the fulfillment and final liberation of God's creation.

The resurrection changes *e*volution into *re*volution. Death will change into eternity life (which term I prefer to the customary "eternal life"), remaining chaos into perfect order. We are now living between the decisive event of the resurrection and the final event of the coming kingdom. Through Christ, this world is transformed into the new kingdom, in which humans may live in a new relation to God and therefore to their fellow humans and to the entire creation. Looking backward, the Christian community can say, "In Christ [*Logos*] all things were created," and looking forward, it may joyfully exclaim, "God will sum up all things in Christ, and will make all things new." In chaos theology terms, on the last day, the Creator will abolish remaining chaos, thus ending both moral and physical evil, and will fulfill God's original intention by perfecting creation. In this way, future will become destiny.

The new creation includes humanity, as expressed by Paul: "So if anyone is in Christ, there is a new creation: everything old has passed away; see, everything has become new!" (2 Cor 5:17). In Jesus, God has elevated humans to the state for which they were destined. Jesus is the New Man, the image of God (2 Cor 4:4), the firstborn of all creation (Col 1:15). Each human, as a unique creation of God, will participate in this process. Through Christ we may accept this new status and live in a new relationship to God, to other people, and to the entire creation—in preliminary, limited fashion in this life, but in fullness in the future life.

When will this come about? Jesus says, "About that day or hour no one knows, neither the angels in heaven, nor the Son, but only the Father" (Mark 13:32). So, although it is not given to us to know the time, I think we can safely assume that God will bring this about before the universe disintegrates and before all life will be destroyed by ecological catastrophes. Is this "pie in the sky" thinking? No, for the simple reason that it is unthinkable that God would allow this universe, created out of love in a marvelous and extensive process of cosmic and biological evolution, to disintegrate fully before bringing about the new kingdom. That would amount to declaring the first creation a failure, necessitating a second attempt.

Why such different views of the future in science and theology?

Science predicts a nihilistic ending that through a "big rift" leads to an eternal, cold, and silent cloud of photons. The Bible predicts the fulfillment of creation with the establishment of the new kingdom and the resurrection of all living beings to eternity life. Why such different views of the future? The simple answer to this question is that science, observing only this world, sees the universe as a thermodynamically closed system without any external input of energy and information that could reverse its ever-increasing entropy. Thus, according to the second law of thermodynamics, the universe must wind down following the arrow of time and eventually return to maximal entropy, to utter chaos.

The biblical view, in contrast, assumes that the Creator will not abandon the creation and will remain in interaction with it, making the universe a thermodynamically open system. At the proper moment, God will deflect the creation from its path toward degradation by sending energy through Christ, the *Logos*, and information through the Holy Spirit. This will bring about a state of full order from which remaining chaos has been abolished. For us, as the only beings created in the likeness of God, there is the challenge to believe this and thus to become part of the perfected creation. Three points are worth noting: First, the perfection of the creation is God's work, not that of humans. Second, it will not be a smooth, gradual transition, but a revolution rather than an evolution. Finally, we humans should, as God's cocreators, do what we can to assist in this revolution.

14.3 Interim state and judgment

Interim state

We cannot expect science to inform us about the intermediate state between our death and the last day, since science deals with this world only. A glimpse of insight about this topic can be obtained from the reports of persons with a near-death experience, to which I shall return later. The Bible doesn't speak much about an intermediate state. In the Old Testament, it is held that the dead go to Sheol, the abode of the dead, where there is darkness and silence and from where there is no return (Gen 37:35; Job 10:21-22; 11:8; Ps 115:17; Isa 38:18-19). A hesitant belief in a personal survival arose only during the Greek period (300–100 BCE), attested to by only two references in the canonical books of the Old Testament: "Your dead shall live, their corpses shall rise" (Isa 26:19); and "Many of those who sleep in the dust of the earth shall awake, some to everlasting life, and some to shame and everlasting contempt" (Dan 12:2).

The New Testament authors do not speak explicitly about the period between our death and the last day, probably because they expected the return of Christ in the very near future. In the words of the author of Hebrews: "A sabbath rest still remains for the people of God" (Heb 4:10). To fill this gap, Clement of Alexandria and Origen introduced the doctrine of purgatory, based on the apocryphal text 2 Macc 12:39-45, according to which Judas Maccabeus "made atonement for the dead, so that they might be delivered from their sin." The doctrine was further developed by Augustine and affirmed by the Roman Catholic Church. It was rejected by the Reformers, although this meant giving up the ancient tradition of praying for the dead. Anglicans commonly speak about an intermediate state for spiritual growth and development.[24] I suggest that in this state there is no remaining chaos but instead the peace reported by many of those who had a near-death experience.[25]

Judgment

What to say about judgment on the last day? *Judgment* is an ominous word to many, who recall the lurid medieval pictures of hell. However, the image of a vengeful and retributive God is not the general message of the Old Testament, but rather that Yahweh is the merciful Lord who punishes sin but also saves (Exod 20:5-6; Isa 6:3, 5). Yahweh sits in judgment over all that is ungodly, not in blind wrath, but to destroy sin, over foreign gods (Zeph 2:11), over the heathen nations (Jer 25:15ff.; Ezekiel 25–32), but also over the sins of his own people (Hos 4:1-2; Mic 6:1ff.). Note that punishment in the form of war, hunger, pestilence, fire, and earthquakes is seen in events befalling the Israelites in this world. Only Amos speaks about punishment in the ultimate sense (Amos 3:2). And punishment is always connected with salvation.

The image of a vengeful and retributive God is certainly foreign to the New Testament (except 2 Thess 1:5-10 and Revelation), where God's justice is seen as loving, creative, restorative, reconciling, and healing. The early church believed in God's final judgment of all people, living and dead (Heb 9:27; 1 John 4:17; Jude 6). In John 12:48, Jesus says, "The one who rejects me and does not receive my word has a judge; on the last day the word that I have spoken will serve as judge." In other words, we judge ourselves by our attitude toward Jesus. The judgment scene in Rev 20:4 may be interpreted in the same way.

This view of judgment is supported by the reports of those who have had a near-death experience.[26] Up to 30 percent of them report that, having entered "the other world," they saw in a flash their entire life as in a 3-D movie with an experience of judgment. This leads me to the idea that at death we are not judged so much as that we judge ourselves, in answer to the question, Am I able and desirous to live in God's presence, thus to believe in God, or not? In the intermediate state, there would then be an opportunity for further spiritual growth until at the last day we shall judge ourselves definitively either to living eternally in God's presence (heaven) or to existing forever in God's absence (hell). In the presence of the light of Christ, there will be full disclosure, such that in our self-judgment we cannot fool ourselves. So this does not mean "universalism," acceptance of all humans. The Doctrine Commission of the Church of England came to a similar view.[27] It should be noted that from an extensive clinical study, it was concluded that medical factors (clinical death, cerebral anoxia, medication, psychological factors) cannot account for the occurrence of near-death experiences, particularly the judgment experience and the effects on later life.[28]

For sinful human creatures, God shows boundless mercy: "The Lord is ... patient with you, not wanting any to perish, but all to come to repentance" (2 Peter 3:9). There are only two essential demands on us: faith (that is, trust) in God and repentance for our shortcomings past and present. Paul says, "We are justified by faith" (Rom 5:1), and "in Christ God was reconciling the world to himself, not counting their trespasses against them" (2 Cor 5:19). So, if we respond in faith to God's free offer of mercy, then we shall indeed be able and desirous to live forever in God's presence. Fortunate are those who reach this state during this life, but even at our death it is not too late: there will be an interim period between our death and the last day.

14.4 Resurrection: Views of Tipler, Pannenberg, and Polkinghorne

How shall we, with all our scientific insight, understand the resurrection of the dead on the last day? Physicist Frank Tipler offers in *The Physics of Immortality* a nontheistic, "scientific" theory of human survival.[29] He thinks we shall turn ourselves into computers, which will colonize the entire universe and, as "information," survive the big crunch (which at the time of writing his book, he still expected to occur).

Wolfhart Pannenberg, in a lecture about Tipler's book, states that Tipler "certainly succeeds in developing a coherent argument that allows for connecting the idea of creation as well as the eschatological hope for the resurrection of the dead with the properties of point Omega as the final future of the universe."[30] He adds, "With regard to the resurrection of the dead Tipler comes close to the Christian doctrine." This comment is surprising, considering that Tipler eliminates God and Christ from the process and has us "resurrect" ourselves. In his *Systematic Theology*[31] Pannenberg states—rightly in my view—that the goal of all creation is to share in the life of God (p. 136), and that creation and eschatology belong together because only in the eschatological consummation will the destiny of all creatures, especially humans, come to fulfillment (p. 139).

John Polkinghorne, in his recent book on eschatology, neglects the connection between eschatology and creation theology.[32] This is noticeable in his discussion of judgment, purgatory, heaven, and hell (pp. 128–38) and of the question of continuity versus discontinuity (pp. 144, 149). Only at the end does creation theology enter into the picture: "If the universe is a creation, . . . it must be redeemed from transience and decay"

(p. 148). Polkinghorne's belief that the last day is billions of years away, long after the disappearance of all carbon-based life (p. 141), is based on the assumption of a closed universe. If he then says that the old creation will provide the "raw material" for the new creation (p. 116), then I ask whether a cloud of photons after the full degradation of the present universe can serve as such. In Polkinghorne's view, we seem to end up with two separate creations, rather than the perfection of a single creation. This calls into question the significance of God's present creation. With regard to the resurrection of the dead, Polkinghorne accepts the body-mind unity, but then, he says, "'the information-bearing pattern of the soul' will have a resurrection re-embodiment through God's act while the earthly body decays" (p. 107). In this way, he splits the unity in an immortal soul (denied on p. 108) and a discarded body, thus calling the bodily resurrection into question.

14.5 Alternative view of resurrection and eternity life

Premise

My premise is that God will not let the world and all present living beings, all of which were created out of love, go to complete degradation, since this would imply a failed creation requiring a new attempt, and this contradicts the belief in an almighty and loving Creator. I am inclined to see in the ecological crisis and the evidence for the ending of human evolution[33] indications for the approaching completion of the creation process. It will not be a painless transition, as is expressed in Mark 13 and Matthew 24, and as we can see with our own eyes in the increasing political, social, and ecological problems in the world. Over against this stands the hopeful expectation of the coming of Christ. This is the *cosmic* Christ, who is the Savior not only of humanity, but of the entire cosmos and all its creatures, a point sadly neglected in the traditional theology of salvation. As Keith Ward says, "Salvation is not a matter of humans being taken out of the realm of nature into a different, heavenly world, leaving this cosmos to decay."[34] God's purpose is in Christ "to reconcile to himself all things, whether on earth or in heaven" (Col 1:19); God's plan is to unite in him all things in heaven and on earth (Eph 1:9). God remains from the beginning in interaction with creation, by infusing into the creation energy through the *Logos* and information through the Spirit, in the beginning and later where needed (chapter 9.2 and 9.3).

In continuity with the present creation, of which we are a part, there will be a new creation, perhaps better termed a "renewed" creation. In Jesus, God has elevated humans to the state for which they were destined. Each human, as a unique creation of God, may expect to participate in this process. Through Christ we may accept this new status and live in a new relationship to God, to one another, and to the entire creation in a preliminary, limited fashion in this life and in fullness in the future life. The belief in our resurrection flows logically and irrefutably from the belief in a loving God, who has created all humans in the divine image as unique individuals with each of whom God maintains a relationship. How then could we think that God would let these persons go into oblivion after a relatively short earthly life?

Digital photography metaphor

How can we picture a resurrection of the dead in the face of the cynical remark that "A corpse doesn't come back to life"? After death, our body-mind unit rapidly decays. How then can the dead person "survive" for resurrection? I suggest that present-day digital photography can provide a useful metaphor. When I take, with my digital camera, a vacation picture in full color and high resolution (more than 3 million pixels) and transfer it as a series of millions of ones and zeros to my computer, then with a few mouse clicks I can present the picture in its full glory and relive the vacation experience. Also, if I like, I can make an enlarged printout and hang it on the wall. Now consider what makes me (and all of us) unique: it is my genome, the collection of all my genes, and my mind. So I suggest that the Creator makes a perfect digital picture of my genome and mind and stores it in the heavenly computer. During my lifetime, updated pictures are made to record my physical and spiritual development. This digital picture collection is retained in the heavenly computer. At my death and on the last day, the entire picture collection is shown to me for my "self-judgment." And if I say Yes! to God, it is "printed out" in heavenly format and quality in a single, three-dimensional form (like a hologram), to which God imparts his life-giving spirit. And there I am, come to life in the resurrection body. Admittedly, it is only a metaphor for the process of resurrection, but it may be helpful, at least to those familiar with digital photography and computers.

Obviously, I do not claim that this is a description of the actual mechanism of our resurrection; it is merely a metaphor to aid our understanding (in contrast to Tipler, who thinks that transforming ourselves into a computer is the actual mechanism). In any case, we should remember that resurrection is not a mere gloss in our Christian faith, but it is the backbone. Our resurrection is assured in that of Christ, without which the incarnation would be meaningless, without which there would be no fulfillment of the creation in a new heaven and earth, without which creation would indeed be meaningless, as Steven Weinberg feared.

Eternity life

Then, after passing our definitive self-judgment, we enter "eternity life." I prefer this term to the common term *eternal life*, because it expresses the fullness of the future life without suggesting an endlessly prolonged state that would seem to be rather boring. How are we to understand eternity life? Bible and science do not tell us much about it. As I said in chapter 13, the Bible is remarkably economic, in the sense that it concentrates on what is necessary to know for earthly life as a preparation for eternity life, and speaks about the future only within that sense. However, the emphasis on love and community in the Bible implies that we shall live there in a community of perfect love with God and with each other. Death and evil will be absent, since remaining chaos will have been definitively abolished through Christ. In our resurrection body, we shall have the same identity as here, but purged from the negative characteristics that have marred us in this life (aging, physical and mental disabilities). Free will remains, but it will be fully God-directed, liberated from the effects of remaining chaos. Since we are a unity of body and mind in this life, we may expect the same for the new life,[35] but without the marks of age and other bodily imperfections.[36] Thus, we shall recognize others, regardless of the age at which we knew each other here.

We shall meet and recognize our loved ones, but also all those who appeared before and after us on Earth. Overpopulation need not be feared, because the new world will not have the space-time restrictions of the present cosmos. Eternity life also means to be liberated from the tyranny of clock time with its continually shifting present moment, squeezed between an ever-lengthening past and an ever-shorter (earthly) future. The present time will not be continued in the new world. Yet there will not only be rest but also activity, meaningful activity without the dire necessity, raw ambition, and inescapable deadlines that drive so many of our current activities.[37]

It seems reasonable to assume that plants and animals will share in the resurrection, because they also are God's creatures and form an essential part of creation. There will be a real ecological harmony, which in the present world has been lost through our neglect and greed. Summarized in theological terminology, the Father promises us the fulfillment of his creation and all creatures in the future. This is the Christian message of hope for a world that, from a simplistic scientific point of view, seems to be without purpose and doomed to futility. In the fulfillment of God's promise, future becomes "destiny."

14.6 Summary

This last chapter deals with the future. Science presents the somber picture of a disintegrating universe, the sun turning into a red giant, possible asteroid impacts, and the human-made ecological crisis. In contrast to this, the Bible presents a hopeful view of a new heaven and a new earth, the kingdom of God, the perfection of creation. On the last day, the cosmic Christ will inaugurate the new creation. In the terms of chaos theology, remaining chaos will be abolished and with it all evil and death. The contrast between the two views arises from the fact that science can only consider this universe and does not know of any influence from beyond it, and a closed universe must degenerate to chaos. The biblical view assumes that God keeps "energizing and informing" the universe and thus driving its entropy to zero.

On the basis of the evidence of people who had a near-death experience, judgment is seen as self-judgment—a preliminary one at the time of death and a definitive one on the last day in which one answers the question: Am I able and desirous to live in God's presence or not? Between these two moments, there is thought to be an intermediate state for spiritual growth and development.

In contrast to the ideas of Frank Tipler, Wolfhart Pannenberg, and John Polkinghorne, my view of our resurrection takes the form of a metaphor from digital photography.

I conclude with ideas about eternity life, the life for which the cosmos and all life were created in an evolutionary process lasting billions of years. Death and evil—with remaining chaos—will have been abolished. In our resurrection body, we shall have the same identity as here, but purged from the negative characteristics that have marred us in this life (aging, physical and mental disabilities). We shall recognize others, regardless of the age at which we knew each other here. Free will remains, but it will be fully God-directed, liberated from the effects of chaotic thinking. We shall also meet all those who appeared before and after us on Earth. And we shall be liberated from captivity to clock time. There will be rest but also meaningful activity without the dire necessity, raw ambition, and inescapable deadlines that drive so many of our current activities.

For a world that, from a simplistic scientific point of view, seems to be without purpose and doomed to futility, this is the Christian message of hope.

Notes

Preface

1. Sjoerd L. Bonting, *Schepping en Evolutie: Poging tot Synthese* [Creation and Evolution: Attempt at Synthesis] (Kampen, The Netherlands: Kok, 1996; 2nd ed. 1997).

2. Sjoerd L. Bonting, Chaos Theology: A New Approach to the Science-Theology Dialogue, *Zygon Journal of Religion & Science* 34(2) (1999): 323–32. Sjoerd L. Bonting, *Chaos Theology, A Revised Creation Theology*, Ottawa: Novalis, 2002.

Chapter 1. The Science–Theology Dialogue: How?

1. However, Huxley's account of the discussion does not state that Bishop Wilberforce argued from scientific insight rather than from a theological position. See W. B. Drees, *Religion, Science and Naturalism* (Cambridge: Cambridge University Press, 1996), 64–66.

2. Andrew D. White, *A History of the Warfare of Science with Theology in Christendom*, 2 vols. (New York: Appleton, 1907).

3. Dorothy Nelkin, *The Creation Controversy: Science or Scripture in the Schools, a History of the Struggle between Creationists and Scientists from the Nineteenth Century to the Arkansas Trial* (New York: W. W. Norton, 1982). For the creationist arguments, see Henry Morris, *Scientific Creationism* (San Diego: Creation Life, 1974).

4. Jacques Monod, *Chance and Necessity* (London: Collins, 1972).

5. Otto Weber, *Karl Barth's Kirchliche Dogmatik* (Neukirchen, Kreis Moers: Verlag des Erziehungsvereins, 1958), 86–104.

6. Emil Brunner, *Dogmatics*, vol. 2, *The Christian Doctrine of Creation and Redemption* (London: Lutterworth, 1952), 79–88.

7. Hans Küng, *Theology for the Third Millennium: An Ecumenical View* (New York: Doubleday, 1988), 123–69.

8. John Macquarrie, *Principles of Christian Theology* (London: SCM, 1966), 194–218.

9. Stephen J. Gould, *Rocks of Ages: Science and Religion in the Fullness of Life* (New York: Ballantine, 1999).

10. Mia Gosselin, *Wetenschap & Geloof* [Science and Faith] (Antwerp: Hadewijch, 1995).

11. Sjoerd L. Bonting, *Tussen Geloof en Ongeloof* [Between Belief and Unbelief] (Zoetermeer: Meinema, 2000), 85–107. English translation available upon request to s.l.bonting@wxs.nl.

12. Sjoerd L. Bonting, "The Dialogue between Science and Theology: How Should It Proceed?" *Sewanee Theological Review* 47(4) (September 2004): 365–71. Full text available at www.chaostheologie.nl.

13. Ian Barbour, *Religion and Science: Historical and Contemporary Issues* (San Francisco: Harper, 1997).

14. Christian Berg, "Comments on Barbour's Concept of Creation," in *Studies in Science and Theology, ESSSAT Yearbook, 2001–2002*, ed. Niels H. Gregersen, Ulf Görman, and Hubert Meisinger, 263–76 (Aarhus, Denmark: University of Aarhus, 2002).

15. John J. Cobb Jr. and David R. Griffin, *Process Theology: An Introductory Exposition* (Philadelphia: Westminster, 1976); and David R. Griffin, *God, Power, and Evil: A Process Theodicy* (Philadelphia: Westminster, 1976).

16. Arthur Peacocke, *Theology for a Scientific Age* (London: SCM, 1993), 11.

17. John Polkinghorne, *Scientists as Theologians* (London: SPCK, 1996).

18. John Polkinghorne, *Science and Christian Belief* (London: SPCK, 1994).

19. Polkinghorne, *Scientists as Theologians*, 8.

20. Polkinghorne, *Science and Christian Belief*, 143–45.

21. Peacocke, *Theology for a Scientific Age*, 275–79.

22. Polkinghorne, *Science and Christian Belief*, 162–75, as in Barbour, *Religion and Science* (n. 13 above), 216–20.

23. Arthur Peacocke, *Creation and the World of Science* (Oxford: Clarendon, 1979; reprint with etensive supplement, Oxford: Oxford University Press, 2004).

24. Philip E. Ross, in "Draining the Language out of Color," *Scientific American* 290(4) (2004): 24–25, quotes linguist Paul Kay: "It is unlikely that the world's languages are so different from one another that their speakers think in ways that are incommensurable."

25. Ludovico Galleni, "Is Biosphere Doing Theology?" *Zygon* 36(1) (March 2001): 33–48.

26. Anthony B. Kelly, "An Evolutionary Christology: Teilhard de Chardin and Beyond," *Philosophy Journal* (September 2001).

27. "Metaphysics," *Encyclopaedia Britannica*, 2005, CD edition.

28. Nathan Ng, "Spirituality and Theology," *Theology* 104(818) (2001): 115–22.

29. Peacocke, *Creation and the World of Science* (n. 23 above), 86–146. See also Rodney D. Holder, *Nothing but Atoms and Molecules?* (Tunbridge Wells, U.K.: Monarch, 1993), 81–97.

30. Francis H. C. Crick, *Of Molecules and Man* (Seattle: University of Washington Press, 1966).

31. Arthur Koestler and J. R. Smythies, *Beyond Reductionism: New Perspectives in the Life Sciences* (London: Hutchinson, 1972); and Nigel Williams, "Biologists Cut Reductionist Approach Down to Size," *Science* 277 (1997): 476–77.

32. Monod, *Chance and Necessity* (n. 4 above).

33. William G. Pollard, *Chance and Providence* (London: Faber, 1958).

34. Michael J. Langford, *Providence* (London: SCM, 1981), 91–95.

35. Peacocke, *Theology for a Scientific Age* (n. 16 above), 115–23.

36. Nelkin, *The Creation Controversy* (n. 3 above); and Morris, *Scientific Creationism* (n. 3 above).

37. Michael J. Behe, *Darwin's Black Box: The Biochemical Challenge to Evolution* (New York: Touchstone, 1996); and William Dembski, *Intelligent Design: The Bridge between Science and Theology* (Downers Grove, Ill.: InterVarsity, 1999).

38. Gregory R. Peterson, "The Intelligent-Design Movement: Science or Ideology," *Zygon* 37(1) (2002): 7–23.

39. Sjoerd L. Bonting, "Intelligent Design and the Origin of Complex Systems," *Sewanee Theological Review* 47(4) (September 2004): 413–19. Full text available at www.chaostheologie.nl.

40. Peacocke, *Theology for a Scientific Age* (n. 16 above), 275–79.

41. Compare this with a psychotherapist, who—however highly qualified—can bring healing only when relating to the patient as a fellow human.

42. However, Luke 1:35 adds after the Holy Spirit "and the power of the Most High" (*dunamis*), which was interpreted by Justin to mean the *Logos*.

43. Polkinghorne, *Science and Christian Belief* (n. 18 above), 162–75; Polkinghorne, *The God of Hope and the End of the World* (London: SPCK, 2002), 8–9; and Barbour, *Religion and Science* (n. 13 above), 216–20.

44. Sjoerd L. Bonting, *Schepping en Evolutie: Poging tot Synthese* [Creation and Evolution: Attempt at Synthesis], 2nd ed. (Kampen, The Netherlands: Kok, 1997). English translation available upon request to s.l.bonting@wxs.nl.

45. Sjoerd L. Bonting, "Chaos Theology: A New Approach to the Science-Theology Dialogue," *Zygon* 34(2) (1999): 323–32; and Sjoerd L. Bonting, *Chaos Theology: A Revised Creation Theology* (Ottawa: Novalis, 2002).

Chapter 2. The Scientific Worldview

1. "Subatomic Particles," *Encyclopaedia Britannica*, 15th ed. Scientists express very large and very small numbers by using powers of 10; for example, 10^9 = 1,000,000,000, and 10^{-9} = 1 divided by 1,000,000,000. In a power of 10, the exponent equals the number of zeros behind the 1.

2. George Musser, "A Tale of Two C's," *Scientific American* 288(4) (April 2003): 12.

3. George Musser, "The Future of String Theory," *Scientific American* 289(5) (November 2003): 48–53.

4. Lee Smolin, *Three Roads to Quantum Gravity* (New York: Basic Books, 2001).

5. Adrian Cho, "Constructing Spacetime—No Strings Attached," *Science* 298 (2002): 1166–67; Quirin Schiermeier, "The Long-Distance Thinker," *Nature* 433 (January 6, 2005): 12. It makes gravitation at quantum level repulsive, which could explain inflation. However, it brings with it a mirror universe that runs backward from $t = 0$. The observed polarization of gamma rays from GRB 021206 seems to rule out loop quantum gravity. Igor G. Mitrofanov, "A Constraint on Canonical Quantum Gravity?" *Nature* 426 (November 13, 2003): 139.

6. Chet Raymo, "A Spin on Spin Foam," *Scientific American* 285(2) (August 2001): 80–81. He calls these theories "the modern equivalent of calculating how many angels can dance on the head of a pin." See also Graham P. Collins, "Fractional Success: A New Theory of Everything?" *Scientific American* 286(1) (January 2002): 19; Peter Woit, "Is String Theory Even Wrong?" *American Scientist* 90 (March/April 2002): 110–12; Sean Carroll, "An Astrophysical Constraint," *Nature* 424 (August 28, 2003): 1007–8; Freedom J. Dyson, "The World on a String," review of *The Fabric of the Cosmos*, by Brian Greene, *New York Review of Books* 51(8) (May 13, 2004); and Lawrence M. Krauss, "Questions That Plague Physics," *Scientific American* 291(2) (August 2004): 66–69.

7. Stephen W. Hawking, *A Brief History of Time* (New York: Bantam, 1988), 175.

8. John Barrow, *The Constants of Nature* (New York: Pantheon, 2002).

9. Lennox L. Cowie and Antoinette Songaila, "The Inconstant Constant?" *Nature* 428 (March 11, 2004): 132–33; Charles Seife, "Fundamental Constants Appear Constant—at Least Recently," *Science* 306 (October 29, 2004): 793.

10. George Ellis, "Einstein Not Yet Displaced," *Nature* 422 (April 10, 2003): 563–64.

11. Steven Weinberg, *The First Three Minutes: A Modern View of the Origin of the Universe* (Glasgow: Fontana/Collins, 1978). "Big bang" is a derisory term introduced by Fred Hoyle, who stubbornly adhered to his steady-state theory.

12. Alan H. Guth, *The Inflationary Universe* (Reading, Mass.: Addison-Wesley, 1997).

13. Neil J. Cornish et al., "Constraining the Topology of the Universe," *Physical Review Letters* 92 (May 19, 2004): 201302; A. C. S. Readhead et al., "Polarization Observations with the Cosmic Background Imager," *Science* 306 (October 29, 2004): 836–44. There is, however, a conflict between two conclusions drawn from the WMAP data: (1) the universe has a flat space-time surface, implying that it is infinite and open; yet (2) it is finite and closed (spherical). A conformally flat universe could not be spherical, but it could have a cylindrical or conical shape of finite circumference that would become open when slit up and rolled out as a flat sheet. Another possibility would be a toroidal shape.

14. David B. Cline, "The Search for Dark Matter," *Scientific American* 288(3) (March 2003): 28–36. Even for the 25 percent dark matter, the search is still on. Konstantin Zioutas et al., "What Is Dark Matter Made Of?" *Science* 306 (November 26, 2004): 1485–88; J. Diemand et al., "Earth-Mass Dark-Matter Haloes as the First Structures in the Early Universe," *Nature* 433 (January 27, 2005): 389–91.

15. Charles Seife, "Light from Most-Distant Supernovae Shows Dark Energy Stays the Course," *Science* 303 (February 27, 2004): 1271; and Andrew Watson, "Cosmic Ripples Confirm Universe Speeding Up," *Science* 295 (March 29, 2002): 2341–43.

16. Wendy Freedman, "The Hubble Constant and the Expanding Universe," *American Scientist* 91(1) (January/February 2003): 36–43.

17. Adam G. Riess and Michael S. Turner, "From Slowdown to Speedup," *Scientific American* 290(2) (February 2004): 50–55.

18. Charles Seife, "Galaxy Maps Support Theory That the Universe Is Flying to Pieces," *Science* 302 (October 31, 2003): 762–63.

19. Peter Coles, "The State of the Universe," *Nature* 433 (January 20, 2004): 248–56.

20. James M. Cline, "The Origin of Matter," *American Scientist* 92(2) (March/April 2004): 148–57; and Frank Wilczek, "In Search of Symmetry Lost," *Nature* 433 (January 20, 2005): 239–47. Wilczek proposes a pervasive symmetry-breaking field, which fills all space uniformly, rendering the universe a sort of exotic superconductor.

21. Garth A. Barber, "A New Self Creation Cosmology," *Astrophysics and Space Science* 282 (2002): 683–730; and "Self Creation Cosmology: An Alternative Gravitational Theory," in *Progress in General Relativity and Quantum Cosmology Research*, ed. Frank Columbus (New York: Nova Science Publishers, in press).

22. Thomas P. Greene, "Protostars," *American Scientist* 89(4) (2001): 316–25; and Alan Heavens, "The Star-Formation History of the Universe," *American Scientist* 93(1) (2005): 36–41.

23. Ronald J. Reynolds, "The Gas between the Stars," *Scientific American* 286(1) (January 2002): 32–41.

24. Volker Bromm and Abraham Loeb, "The Formation of the First Low-Mass Stars from Gas with Low Carbon and Oxygen Abundances," *Nature* 425 (October 23, 2003): 812–14.

25. Shigeru Ida et al., "Lunar Accretion from an Impact-Generated Disk," *Nature* 389 (1997): 353–57.

26. Erik Asphaug, "The Small Planets," *Scientific American* 282(5) (May 2000): 28–37.

27. However, serious doubt has been cast on the "cyanobacterial" origin of "microfossils" in 3.5-billion-year-old rocks. J. M. Garcia-Ruiz et al., "Self-Assembled Silica-Carbonate Structures and Detection of Ancient Microfossils," *Science* 302 (November 14, 2003): 1194–97.

28. Claude J. Allègre and Stephen H. Schneider, "The Evolution of the Earth," *Scientific American* 271(4) (1994): 44–51.

29. S. L. Miller, "Production of Amino Acids under Possible Primitive Earth Conditions," *Science* 117 (1953): 528–29.

30. Gregory R. Bock and Jamie A. Goode, eds., *Evolution of Hydrothermal Ecosystems on Earth (and Mars?)* (New York: Wiley, 1996).

31. A. J. Zaug and T. R. Cech, "The Intervening Sequence RNA of Tetrahymena Is an Enzyme," *Science* 231 (1986): 470–75; and P. Nissen et al., "The Structural Basis of Ribosome Activity in Peptide Bond Synthesis," *Science* 289 (2000): 920–30. Gerald F. Joyce, in "The Antiquity of RNA-Based Evolution," *Nature* 418 (July 11, 2002): 214–21, suggests that the RNA world must have existed from 4.2 billion to 3.6 billion years before the present. But a "DNA world" also might be possible. A. Sreedhara et al., in "Ligating DNA with DNA," *Journal of the American Chemical Society* 126(11) (2004): 3454–60, have managed to select bits of DNA that can link themselves together without a helping hand from other molecules. Creation of these links is an essential part of the process by which DNA replicates itself. By contrast, natural DNA needs enzymes to make these links, correct mutations, and make copies of itself.

32. Philip Ball, "Artificial Cells Take Shape," *Nature* news online (December 6, 2004). Although phospholipids may not have been present during the prebiotic phase, other amphiphilic molecules like the polyisoprenoids (that form the membrane of the ancient *Archaea* microbe) or myristoleates may have served the purpose.

33. L. Leman et al., "Carbonyl Sulfide-Mediated Prebiotic Formation of Peptides," *Science* 306 (October 8, 2004): 283–86.

34. A. Bekker et al., "Dating the Rise of Atmospheric Oxygen," *Nature* 427 (January 8, 2004): 117–20. There is evidence for earlier non-oxygenic photosynthesis (3.4 billion years before the present), which oxidized ferrous to ferric oxide. Nicolas Beukes, "Early Options in Photosynthesis," *Nature* 431 (September 30, 2004): 522–23.

35. Jeffrey L. Bada, "Extraterrestrial Handedness?" *Science* 275 (1997): 942–43; and John Horgan, "The Sinister Cosmos," *Scientific American* 276(5) (1997): 16–18.

36. Koji Tamura and Paul Schimmel, "Chiral-Selective Aminoacylation of an RNA Minihelix," *Science* 305 (August 27, 2004): 1253; and S. Pizzarello and A. L. Weber, "Prebiotic Aminoacids as Asymmetric Catalysts," *Science* 303 (February 20, 2004): 1151.

37. Elizabeth Pennisi, "The Birth of the Nucleus," *Science* 305 (August 6, 2004): 766–68. Originally proposed by Lynn Margulis, *Origin of Eukariotic Cells* (New Haven: Yale University Press, 1970).

38. Frederic D. Bushman, "Evolutionary Teamwork," *The Scientist* 18(9) (May 10, 2004): 33–34.

39. Christine Mlot, "Microbes Hint at a Mechanism behind Punctuated Evolution," *Science* 272 (1996): 1741 (*E. coli* bacteria were cultivated at a low food level for four years, ten thousand generations, sufficient to see evolution in action).

40. Virginia Morell, "Predator-Free Guppies Take an Evolutionary Step Forward," *Science* 275 (1997): 1880 (evolution observed in nature in guppies over seven to eighteen generations).

41. Peter R. Grant and B. Rosemary Grant, "Adaptive Radiation of Darwin's Finches," *American Scientist* 90(2) (2002): 130–39.

42. Stephen J. Freeland and Laurence D. Hurst, "Evolution Encoded," *Scientific American* 290(4) (2004): 56–63.

43. Gunter Meister and Thomas Tuschl, "Mechanisms of Gene Silencing by Double-Stranded RNA," *Nature* 431 (September 16, 2004): 343–49.

44. W. Makalowski, "Not Junk after All," *Science* 300 (May 23, 2003): 1246–47; and John S. Mattick, "The Hidden Genetic Program of Complex Organisms," *Scientific American* 291(4) (October 2004): 30–37.

45. Jacob-S. Seeler and Anne Dejean, "Nuclear and Unclear Functions of SUMO," *Nature Reviews Molecular Cell Biology* 4 (2003): 690–99.

46. Tom Misteli et al., "Dynamic Binding of Histone H1 to Chromatin in Living Cells," *Nature* 408 (December 14, 2000): 877–81.

47. Zhenglong Gu et al., "Role of Duplicate Genes," *Nature* 421 (January 2, 2003): 63–66. In some instances, the entire genome is duplicated, as in the puffer fish 200 million years before the present, though with massive gene loss and gene shuffling. John Mulley and Peter Holland, "Small Genome, Big Insights," *Nature* 431 (October 21, 2004): 916–17. In humans 1,183 genes were duplicated, and 37 genes disappeared. Lincoln D. Stein, "End of the Beginning," *Nature* 431 (October 21, 2004): 915–16.

48. Elizabeth Pennisi and Wade Roush, "Developing a New View of Evolution," *Science* 277 (1997): 34–37; and Nipam H. Patel, "Time, Space and Genomes," *Nature* 431 (September 2, 2004): 28–29.

49. Charles S. Zuker, "On the Evolution of Eyes," *Science* 265 (1994): 742–43. Two additional eye regulator genes, *ey* and *dac*, have been found in *Drosophila*, which suggests the existence of a hierarchy of such genes.

50. D. M. Wellik and M. R. Capecchi, "Hox 10 and Hox 11 Genes Are Required to Globally Pattern the Mammalian Skeleton," *Science* 301 (July 18, 2003): 363–67.

51. Ian C. Scott and Didier Y. R. Stainier, "Twisting the Body into Shape," *Nature* 425 (October 2, 2003): 461–62.

52. D. H. Erwin and S. L. Wing, eds., *Deep Time: Paleobiology's Perspective* (Chicago: Paleontological Society/University of Chicago Press, 2000).

53. Simon Conway Morris, "We Were Meant to Be . . . ," *New Scientist* (November 16, 2002), 26–29. See also his book *Life's Solution* (Cambridge: Cambridge University Press, 2004). For an example of the high degree of predictability exhibited by the evolutionary diversification of complex behaviors, see Todd A. Blackledge and Rosemary G. Gillespie, "Convergent Evolution of Behavior in an Adaptive Radiation of Hawaiian Web-Building Spiders," *Proceedings of the National Academy of Science USA* 101(46) (November 16, 2004): 16228–33.

54. Richard Fortey, "The Cambrian Explosion Exploded?" *Science* 293 (July 20, 2001): 438–39 (discovery of arthropods ranging from 700 million to 1,500 million years BP); and Jun-Yuan Chen et al., "Small Bilaterian Fossils from 40–55 Million Years before the Cambrian," *Science* 305 (July 9, 2004): 218–22 (fossil found in China: 0.2 millimeters, bilateral symmetry, gut with oral and anal openings, body composed of mesodermal, endodermal, and ectodermal layers, and localized sense organs).

55. John Whitfield, "Plants Detonated Cambrian Explosion," *Nature* news online, September 29, 2003). On a new theory that proliferation of land plants made the temperature drop from 30ºC to 15ºC through their utilization of carbon dioxide, and that this triggered the Cambrian explosion, see W. von Bloh et al., "Cambrian Explosion Triggered by Geosphere-Biosphere Feedbacks," *Geophysical Research Letters* 30 (2003): 1963.

56. Gregory M. Erickson et al., "Gigantism and Comparative Life-History Parameters of Tyrannosaurid Dinosaurs," *Nature* 430 (August 12, 2004): 772–75.

57. Erik Stokstad, "Four-Winged Dinos Create a Flutter," *Science* 299 (January 24, 2003): 491 (debate about which dinosaur species was the ancestor of birds).

58. L. Becker et al., "A Possible End-Permian Impact Crater Offshore of Northwestern Australia," *Science* 304 (June 4, 2004): 1469–76. However, this is still in doubt. Richard A. Kerr, "Fossil Count Suggests Biggest Die-Off Wasn't Due to a Smashup," *Science* 307 (January 21, 2005): 335.

59. Walter Alvarez, *T. Rex and the Crater of Doom* (Princeton, N.J.: Princeton University Press, 1997); David A. Kring and Daniel D. Durda, "The Day the World Burned," *Scientific American* 289(6) (December 2003): 70–77. On mammals, see Tim Flannery, "Mammals on the European Stage," *Science* 297 (July 5, 2002): 57–58.

60. Eric J. Sargis, "Primate Origins Nailed," *Science* 298 (November 22, 2002): 1564–65 (Wyoming, USA, 56 million years BP); Robert D. Martin, "Chinese Lantern for Early Primates," *Nature* 427 (January 1, 2004): 22–23 (China, 55 million years BP).

61. Grant and Grant, in "Adaptive Radiation of Darwin's Finches," observed inter-breeding between two species of Darwin's finches and claim that this explains their rapid evolution over a thirty-year period. Also, a marine stickleback loses thirty-five body plates and pelvic spines after transfer to freshwater in two generations in the laboratory, in ten years in a lake, and vice versa; a single gene is responsible for this. Elizabeth Pennisi, "Changing a Fish's Bony Armour in the Wink of a Gene," *Science* 304 (June 18, 2004): 1736–39; and David Secko, "'Big Cross' Lands Sticklebacks in the Spotlight," *The Scientist*, 18(21) (November 8, 2004): 14–18. Speciation occurs at widely different rates: *Xenoleberis*, a 5-millimeter lobster, did not evolve in 425 million years, but cichlid fishes in Lake Victoria formed 500 species in 12,000 years.

62. Nick Colegrave, "Sex Releases the Speed Limit on Evolution," *Nature* 420 (December 12, 2002): 664–66.

63. Careful studies of fossils uncovered four transitional forms in the evolution of the land snail *Cerion excelsior* to *C. rubicundum*, spanning a period of only 13,600 years. Glenn Goodfriend and Stephen J. Gould, *Science* 274 (1996): 13. A transition of the fish nostril to the vertebrate nostril has been found in a 395-million-year-old fossil of the *Kenichtys* fish, before it developed limbs and crawled ashore 45 million years later. M. Zhu and P. E. Ahlberg, "The Origin of the Internal Nostril of Tetrapods," *Nature* 432 (November 4, 2004): 94–97. A 370-million-year-old freshwater animal had gills and tails like a fish but looked more like a salamander. It had a unique type of humerus (upper arm bone), suggesting that it was doing something between swimming and walking while still living in the water, 20 million years before it went ashore. N. Shubin et al., "The Early Evolution of the Tetrapod Humerus," *Science* 304 (April 2, 2004): 90–93.

64. Michael Behe, in *Darwin's Black Box: The Biochemical Challenge to Evolution* (New York: Free Press, 1996), argues from the complexity of various biological systems (vision, immune system, blood clotting) for the operation of "Intelligent Design."

65. Salvador Moya-Sola et al., "*Pierolapithecus catalaunicus*, a New Middle Miocene Great Ape from Spain," *Science* 306 (November 19, 2004): 1339–44. Bones, including part of a skull, dated 13 million years BP, belong to an apelike creature that might be the common ancestor of apes and humans.

66. Sileshi Semaw, "Early Pliocene Hominids from Gona, Ethiopia," *Nature* 433 (January 20, 2005): 301–5.

67. Yves Coppens, "East Side Story: The Origin of Humankind," *Scientific American* 270(5) (1994): 62–69.

68. Allan C. Wilson and Rebecca L. Cann, "The Recent African Genesis of Humans," *Scientific American* 266(4) (1992): 66–73. For group size, see: H. A. Erlich et al., "HLA Sequence Polymorphism and the Origin of Humans," *Science* 274 (1996): 1552–54. See also Svante Pääbo, "The Y Chromosome and the Origin of All of Us (Men)," *Science* 268 (1995): 1141–42; Chris Stringer, "Out of Ethiopia," *Nature* 423 (June 12, 2003): 692–95 (Ethiopian skull fossils, 160,000 years old, provide fresh evidence for "out of Africa" theory); and Pat Shipman, "We Are All Africans," *American Scientist* 91(6) (November/December 2003): 496–99 (a review of three studies, concluding that the single-origin theory is correct).

69. Naama Goren-Inbar et al., "Evidence of Hominin Control of Fire at Gesher Benot Ya'aqov, Israel," *Nature* 304 (April 30, 2004): 725–27; and G. Verri et al., "Flint Mining in Prehistory Recorded by *In Situ*–Produced Cosmogenic [10]Be," *Proceedings of the National Academy of Science, USA* 101(21) (May 25, 2004): 7880–84.

70. Kate Wong, "Stranger in a New Land," *Scientific American* 289(5) (November 2003): 54–63 (on the 1.75-million-year-old Dmanisi, Georgia, skulls).

71. Ian McDougall et al., "Stratigraphic Placement and Age of Modern Humans from Kibish, Ethiopia," *Nature* 433 (February 17, 2005): 733–36. Migration 160,000 years BP is

concluded by Francisco J. Ayala, "The Myth of Eve: Molecular Biology and Human Origins," *Science* 270 (1995): 1930–36.

72. Richard G. Klein, "Middle Paleolithic People," *Science* 272 (1996): 822–23.

73. Takeru Akazawa et al., "Neanderthal Infant Burial," *Nature* 377 (1995): 585–86.

74. Constance Holden, "Neandertals and Climate," *Science* 303 (February 6, 2004): 759. Extinction of Neanderthals was mainly due to the southward migration of bison and deer. The same is true for the Aurignacians (*H. sapiens*), who also died out, but the Gravettians with better technology and social organization replaced both. See also Paul Mellars, "Neanderthals and the Modern Human Colonization of Europe," *Nature* 432 (November 25, 2004): 461–65.

75. Wil Roebroeks and Thijs van Kolfschoten, eds., *The Earliest Occupation of Europe*, Proceedings of the European Science Foundation Workshop (Leiden, The Netherlands: University of Leiden, 1995).

76. Nicholas J. Conard, "Palaeolithic Ivory Sculptures from Southwestern Germany and the Origins of Figurative Art," *Nature* 426 (December 18, 2003): 830–32. But their 35,000-year-old beads were preceded by 75,000-year-old beads found in Blombos Cave, South Africa. Constance Holden, "Oldest Beads Suggest Early Symbolic Behavior," *Science* 304 (April 16, 2004): 369.

77. Henry C. Harpending et al., "Genetic Traces of Ancient Demography," *Proceedings of the National Academy of Science, USA* 95 (1998): 1961–67; and L. A. Zhivotovsky et al., "Features of Evolution and Expansion of Modern Humans, Inferred from Genomewide Microsatellite Markers," *American Journal of Human Genetics* 72 (2003): 1171–86. From different types of DNA studies, both groups conclude the existence of a lengthy bottleneck in *H. sapiens* population of 10,000 or 6,000 individuals, ending around 50,000 BP by improved stone tool technology and beginning agriculture. As a consequence, there is only a single human race. Michael J. Bamshad and Steve E. Olson, "Does Race Exist?" *Scientific American* 289(6) (December 2003): 50–57.

78. Brendan A. Maher, "The 0.1% Portrait of Human History," *The Scientist* 17(13) (June 30, 2003): 28–29.

79. Ann Gibbons, "When It Comes to Evolution, Humans Are in the Slow Class," *Science* 267 (1995): 1907–8.

80. Andrew G. Clark et al., "Inferring Nonneutral Evolution from Human-Chimp-Mouse Orthologous Gene Trios," *Science* 302 (December 12, 2003): 1960–63. Comments by Elizabeth Pennisi, "Genome Comparisons Hold Clues to Human Evolution," *Science* 302 (December 12, 2003): 1876–77; and David Penny, "Our Relative Genetics," *Nature* 427 (January 15, 2004): 208–9.

81. Michael Morley et al., "Genetic Analysis of Genome-wide Variation in Human Gene Expression, *Nature* 430 (August 12, 2004): 743–47; comment by Nancy J. Cox, "An Expression of Interest," *Nature* 430 (August 12, 2004): 733–34.

82. Jean Weissenbach, "Differences with the Relatives," *Nature* 429 (May 27, 2004): 353–54, commenting on "The International Chimpanzee Chromosome 22 Consortium," *Nature* 429 (May 27, 2004): 382–88.

83. Hansell H. Stedman et al., "Myosin Gene Mutation Correlates with Anatomical Changes in the Human Lineage," *Nature* 428 (March 25, 2004): 415–18. Comments by Pete Currie, "Muscling in on Hominid Evolution," *Nature* 428 (March 25, 2004): 373–78; and Elizabeth Pennisi, "The Primate Bite: Brawn Versus Brain?" *Science* 303 (March 26, 2004): 1957.

84. Frans de Waal, *Good Natured: The Origins of Right and Wrong in Humans and Other Animals* (Cambridge: Harvard University Press, 1996); *The Ape and the Sushi-Master* (New York: Basic Books, 2001); and S. F. Brosnan and F. B. M. de Waal, "Monkeys Reject Unequal Pay," *Nature* 425 (October 23, 2003): 297–99.

85. Ernst Fehr and Urs Fischbacher, "The Nature of Human Altruism," *Nature* 425 (October 23, 2003): 785–91.

86. Gretchen Vogel, "Orangutans, like Chimps, Heed the Cultural Call of the Collective," *Science* 299 (January 3, 2003): 27–28.

87. Thomas J. Bouchard, "Genes, Environment, and Personality," *Science* 264 (1994): 1700–1701.

88. Pieter J. Drent et al., "Realised Heritability of Personalities in the Great Tit (*Parus major*)," *Proceedings of the Royal Society of London* 270(1510) (January 7, 2003): 45–52.

89. Susan M. Rosenberg and P. J. Hastings, "Modulating Mutation Rates in the Wild," *Science* 300 (2003): 1382–83.

90. Gene E. Robinson, "Beyond Nature and Nurture," *Science* 304 (April 16, 2004): 397–99.

91. Paul H. Silverman, "Rethinking Genetic Determinism," *The Scientist* 18(10) (May 24, 2004): 32–33.

92. Jack Lucentini, "Gene Association Studies Typically Wrong," *The Scientist* 18(24) (December 20, 2004): 20. For example, a claim that a mutation of a dopamine receptor gene leads to a two to four times higher risk of schizophrenia (Crocq, 1992) was subsequently shown to be wrong. It is suggested that in such studies there should be a prior probability of a link and larger sample sizes, that more family-based studies are needed, and that negative findings should be published.

Chapter 3. The Theological Worldview: Creation Stories

1. Ellen van Wolde, *Stories of the Beginning* (London: SCM, 1996).

2. Jo Nesbo, *De vleermuisman* [The Batman] (Baarn, The Netherlands: Signature, 2000), 61–63.

3. D. Goetz and S. G. Morley, *Popol Vuh: The Sacred Book of the Ancient Quiché Maya* (London: William Hodge, 1951).

4. E. A. Speiser, "Enuma Elish," in *Ancient Near Eastern Texts*, ed. J. B. Pritchard, 60–72 (Princeton, N.J.: Princeton University Press, 1968).

5. Claus Westermann, *Creation*, trans. John J. Scullion (London: SPCK, 1974).

6. Claus Westermann, *Genesis 1–11: A Commentary*, trans. John J. Scullion (London: SPCK, 1984), 186–278.

7. Ibid., 93–177.

8. Ibid., 76.

9. Ibid., 106–8.

10. Ibid., 121.

11. T. C. Vriezen, *An Outline of Old Testament Theology* (Newton, Mass.: Branford, 1958), 187.

12. G. von Rad, *Genesis: A Commentary*, trans. J. H. Marks (London: SCM, 1951), 49.

13. "Primitive Religion," in *Academic American Encyclopedia* (electronic version), 1996.

14. John A. T. Robinson, *Redating the New Testament* (London: SCM, 1976), 1–12, 336–58.

15. Westermann, *Genesis 1–11* (n. 5 above), 175.

Chapter 4. Creation out of Nothing: Origin and Problems

1. Ellen van Wolde, *Stories of the Beginning* (London: SCM, 1996), 217.

2. "Philo," in *Encyclopaedia Britannica*, 1989.

3. Ibid.

4. "Gnosticism," in *Encyclopaedia Britannica*, 1989.

5. Gerhard May, *Creatio ex Nihilo* (Edinburgh: T. & T. Clark, 1994), 178.

6. Ibid., 1–38, 156–77.

7. Theophilus, *Ad Autolycum* II.10 and 15.

8. May, *Creatio ex Nihilo*, 178.

9. David A. S. Fergusson, *The Cosmos and the Creator: An Introduction to the Theology of Creation* (London: SPCK, 1998), 25.

10. Professor Nico Schreurs, Catholic University of Brabant, Tilburg, the Netherlands, kindly provided me with this information.

11. Colin E. Gunton, "Between Allegory and Myth: The Legacy of the Spiritualising of Genesis," in *The Doctrine of Creation*, ed. Colin E. Gunton (Edinburgh: T. & T. Clark, 1997), 57.

12. F. C. Copleston, *Aquinas* (Hammondsworth, U.K.: Penguin, 1955), 136–37.

13. Karl Barth, *Church Dogmatics* III, 2, ed. G. Bromiley and T. F. Torrance (Edinburgh: T. & T. Clark, 1960), 154ff.; and Emil Brunner, *Dogmatics*, vol. 2, *The Christian Doctrine of Creation and Redemption*, 4th ed. (London: Lutterworth, 1960), 9–21.

14. John Polkinghorne, *Science and Christian Belief* (London: SPCK, 1994), 76.

15. Claus Westermann, *Genesis 1–11: A Commentary*, trans. John J. Scullion (London: SPCK, 1994), 109, 121.

16. W. H. Bennett, *Genesis*, Century Bible, (Oxford: Oxford University Press, n.d.), 73. R. Albertz also states that *bara* does not connote *creatio ex nihilo*. Joachim Ritter and Karlfried Gründer, *Historisches Wörterbuch der Philosophie*, vol. 8 (Basel: Schwabe, 1992), 1392.

17. Fergusson, *The Cosmos and the Creator* (n. 9 above), 23; and May, *Creatio ex Nihilo* (n. 5 above), 6–7.

18. May, *Creatio ex Nihilo* (n. 5 above), 26.

19. Westermann, *Genesis 1–11* (n. 15 above), 109–10.

20. Georg Singe, *Gott im Chaos* (Frankfurt: Peter Lang, 2000), 129–32.

21. Mark W. Worthing, *God, Creation, and Contemporary Physics* (Minneapolis: Fortress Press, 1996), 79–110.

22. The "quantum vacuum" is supposed to be an all-pervasive field that exists even in so-called empty space and at absolute zero temperature. In this field there would be a succession of so-called quantum fluctuations in which pairs of particles and antiparticles are formed. These immediately annihilate each other with return of the energy used for their formation. Jay M. Pasachoff and Alex Filippenko, in *The Cosmos: Astronomy in the New Millennium* (New York: Wadsworth, 2001), call this a zero-energy condition, a *nihil*, because the particles consist of positive energy that is balanced by the (negative) gravitational energy between them. To explain the origin of the universe from such a field, they assume that "all one needs is just a tiny bit of energy to get the whole thing started." They do not explain where this "tiny bit of energy" would come from. Nor do they explain the formation of a small excess of unpaired particles, required for the beginning universe to arise and persist. Thus, their contention that the universe is "the ultimate free lunch," as it develops from a *nihil*, is wrong on two counts.

23. John Polkinghorne, *Science and Creation* (London: SPCK, 1988), 59.

24. Arthur Peacocke, *The Idreos Lectures: The Quest for Christian Credibility* (Oxford: Harris Manchester College, 1997), 31.

25. Worthing, *God, Creation, and Contemporary Physics* (n. 21 above), 110.

26. Paul Tillich, *Systematic Theology*, vol. 1 (Chicago: University of Chicago Press, 1951), 188.

27. Worthing, *God, Creation, and Contemporary Physics* (n. 21 above), 75.

28. Keith Ward, *God, Faith and the New Millennium: Christian Belief in an Age of Science* (Oxford: OneWorld, 1998), 53–59.

29. Jürgen Moltmann, *God in Creation* (San Francisco: Harper, 1991), 86–93.

30. Fergusson, *The Cosmos and the Creator* (n. 9 above), 27; and Alan J. Torrance, "Creatio ex Nihilo and the Spatio-Temporal Dimensions, with Special Reference to Jürgen Moltmann and D. C. Williams," in *The Doctrine of Creation*, ed. Colin E. Gunton, 83–103 (Edinburgh: T. & T. Clark, 1997).

31. John Hick, *Evil and the God of Love* (Glasgow: Collins, 1979); Harold S. Kushner, *When Bad Things Happen to Good People* (London: Pan Books, 1982); Fergusson, *The Cosmos and the Creator* (n. 9 above), 77–87; Hermann Häring, *Das Böse in der Welt: Gottes Macht oder Ohnmacht?* (Darmstadt: Primus Verlag, 1999); Brian Hebblethwaite, *Evil, Suffering and Religion* (London: SPCK, 2000); John A. Sanford, *Evil: The Shadow Side of Reality* (New York: Crossroad, 1989); C. S. Rodd, *Why Evil and Suffering?* (Peterborough: Epworth, 1998); Susan Neiman, *Evil in Modern Thought: An Alternative History of Philosophy* (Princeton: Princeton University Press, 2002).

32. Hebblethwaite, *Evil, Suffering and Religion*, 110.

33. John Paul II, *Fides et Ratio*, chap. 6, par. 76 (Catholic Information Network, 1999), www.cin.org/jp2/fides.html.

34. Sanford, *Evil*, 129.

35. Fergusson, *The Cosmos and the Creator* (n. 9 above), 38.

36. Paul Copan and William L. Craig, *Creation out of Nothing: A Biblical, Philosophical, and Scientific Exploration* (Grand Rapids: Baker Academic; Leicester, U.K.: InterVarsity Press, 2004).

37. Claus Westermann, *Creation* (London: SPCK, 1974), 3.

38. S. Wesley Ariarajah, "Religion and Plurality: Central Theological Issues in the Christian Faith," *Current Dialogue* (Geneva: World Council of Churches, June 2001), 22–25.

Chapter 5. Contemporary Creation Theologies

1. Karl Barth, *Church Dogmatics* III, 2, ed. G. Bromiley and T. F. Torrance (Edinburgh: T. & T. Clark, 1960), 154ff.

2. Emil Brunner, *Dogmatics*, vol. 2, *The Christian Doctrine of Creation and Redemption* (London: Lutterworth, 1960), 9–21.

3. Ibid., 33–35.

4. Ibid., 35.

5. Ibid., 160–70.

6. Ibid., 175–85.

7. Ibid., 260–70.

8. Wolfhart Pannenberg, *Systematic Theology*, vol. 2, trans. G. W. Bromley (Grand Rapids: Eerdmans, 1994), 76–136.

9. Colin E. Gunton, *The Triune Creator: A Historical and Systematic Study* (Edinburgh: Edinburgh University Press, 1998), 161–62.

10. Mark W. Worthing, *God, Creation, and Contemporary Physics* (Minneapolis: Fortress Press, 1996), 120–24.

11. Frank J. Tipler, *The Physics of Immortality* (New York: Doubleday, 1994). For a critique, see Sjoerd L. Bonting, "Resurrection; In Discussion with Tipler and Pannenberg," *Bulletin of the Society of Ordained Scientists* no. 32 (2003): 4–12, full text at www.chaostheologie.nl.

12. Jürgen Moltmann, *God in Creation* (San Francisco: Harper, 1991), 86–93.

13. Ibid., 196.

14. Ibid., 209.

15. Ibid., 228–29.

16. Ibid., 276–96.

17. H. Berkhof, *Het Christelijk Geloof* (Nijkerk: Callenbach, 1973), 156–233, translated as *The Christian Faith* (Grand Rapids: Eerdmans, 1986).

18. John Macquarrie, *Principles of Christian Theology* (London: SCM, 1966).

19. Ibid., 198.

20. Ibid., 199, 219.

21. Ibid., 203–5.

22. Ibid., 234.

23. Ibid., 245.

24. Ibid., 313–30.

25. Colin E. Gunton, ed., *The Doctrine of Creation* (Edinburgh: T. & T. Clark, 1997).

26. David A. S. Fergusson, *The Cosmos and the Creator: An Introduction to the Theology of Creation* (London: SPCK, 1998), 23–36.

27. Ibid., 36–45.

28. Ibid., 77–87.

29. Ibid., 87–97.

30. Arthur R. Peacocke, *Creation and the World of Science* (Oxford: Clarendon, 1979), 81–85.

31. Ibid., 43.

32. Arthur Peacocke, *The Idreos Lectures: The Quest for Christian Credibility* (Oxford: Harris Manchester College, 1997), 31.

33. Arthur R. Peacocke, *Theology for a Scientific Age* (London: SCM, 1993), 168–70.

34. Peacocke, *Creation and the World of Science,* 166; and *Theology for a Scientific Age,* 125–27.

35. Arthur R. Peacocke, *Science and the Christian Experiment* (Oxford: Oxford University Press, 1971), 198–99.

36. John Polkinghorne, *Science and Creation: The Search for Understanding* (London: SPCK, 1988), 59.

37. John Polkinghorne, *Science and Christian Belief* (London: SPCK, 1994), 75.

38. Augustine, *The City of God*, XI.5 and 6.

39. Polkinghorne, *Science and Christian Belief*, 75–82.

40. Ibid., 83.

41. John Polkinghorne, "Is Science Enough?" *Sewanee Theological Review* 39(1) (2005): 11–26.

42. Polkinghorne, *Science and Christian Belief*, 85.

43. John Polkinghorne, *The God of Hope and the End of the World* (London: SPCK, 2002).

44. Worthing, *God, Creation, and Contemporary Physics* (n. 10 above).

45. Ibid., 75–76.

46. Ibid., 79–104.

47. Ibid., 104–6.

48. Ibid., 115.

49. Ibid., 146–56.

50. Philip Hefner, "God and Chaos: The Demiurge versus the Ungrund," *Zygon* 19(4) (1984): 483.

51. Worthing, *God, Creation, and Contemporary Physics* (n. 10 above), 159–98.

52. Pierre Teilhard de Chardin, *The Phenomenon of Man* (London: Collins, 1959); and *Le Milieu Divin* (London: Fontana/Collins, 1964).

53. Pierre Teilhard de Chardin, *Christianity and Evolution* (San Diego: Harcourt Brace, 1971), 40.

54. Teilhard de Chardin, *Le Milieu Divin*, 80.

55. Ibid., 53, 58.

56. Ibid., 75.

57. Ibid., 84.

58. Ibid., 147.

59. Teilhard de Chardin, *The Phenomenon of Man* (n. 52 above), 288.

60. Ibid., 311–13.

61. John J. Cobb Jr. and David R. Griffin, *Process Theology: An Introductory Exposition* (Philadelphia: Westminster, 1976).

62. John Polkinghorne, *One World: The Interaction of Science and Theology* (London: SPCK, 1986), 34.

63. Keith Ward, *Rational Theology and the Creativity of God* (London: Blackwell, 1982), 229.

64. Alister E. McGrath, *Christian Theology: An Introduction* (Oxford: Blackwell, 1994), 227–28.

65. Cobb and Griffin, *Process Theology*, 111–27.

Chapter 6. Chaos Theology: An Alternative Creation Theology

1. Sjoerd L. Bonting, "Chaos Theology: A New Approach to the Science-Theology Dialogue," *Zygon* 34(2) (1999); 323–32; *Chaos Theology: A Revised Creation Theology* (Ottawa: Novalis, 2002).

2. *Tohu* is rare in the Old Testament. Job 12:24 uses it for a "pathless waste" where evil rulers will be sent; Isa 45:18-19 has it in the same sense as Genesis 1; Jer 4:23 uses it for the condition of the earth ("waste and void") after God's judgment on Judah. The difficulty in translating Gen 1:1 is whether to include "when" in "In the beginning when God created the heavens and the earth." Without "when," the verse would suggest that God created first the chaos, which seems unlikely for an almighty Creator. Isa 45:18 already seems to perceive this problem, saying parenthetically, "he did not create it a chaos." See also notes 3, 4, and 5.

3. Robert H. Pfeiffer, *Introduction to the Old Testament* (New York: Harper, 1941), 192–93, 704; T. C. Vriezen, *An Outline of Old Testament Theology* (Newton, Mass.: Branford, 1958), 181; and Claus Westermann, *Genesis 1–11: A Commentary*, trans. John J. Scullion (London: SPCK, 1984), 93–110.

4. Westermann, *Genesis 1–11*, 110.

5. Augustine, *The City of God*, XI.5 and 6.

6. Westermann, *Genesis 1–11*, 110–12.

7. T. J. van Bavel, "De kerkvaders over de schepping" [The Church Fathers' View of Creation], *Tijdschrift voor Theologie* 30(1) (1990): 18–33 (with English summary).

8. Tom Stonier, *Information and the Internal Structure of the Universe* (London: Springer-Verlag, 1990), 38–41, 70–72. Stonier starts with the Boltzmann/Schrödinger equation: $S = k \log 1/\Omega$, where S is the entropy, Ω is order, and k is the Boltzmann constant. Assuming that information content I is linearly related to the order of a system (that is, $I = c\Omega$, where c is a constant), Stonier then finds the following relation between information content and entropy: $I = c \times e^{-S/k}$. Plotting information content (I) against entropy (S) yields a plot of the evolution of the universe. At zero time, entropy approaches infinity (complete disorder or chaos), and information content is zero; this is the big bang. With the evolution of the universe, S decreases (increasing order), and I increases. Eventually S will become zero (complete order), and I will become infinite. Then the evolution process has come to an end.

9. Craig J. Hogan, "Observing the Beginning of Time," *American Scientist* 90(5) (2002): 420–27; "The Beginning of Time," *Science* 295 (2002): 2223–25.

10. "Leviathan," in *Encyclopaedia Judaica*, CD-ROM ed. (Jerusalem, Israel: Judaica Multi-media).

11. Martin Kiddle, in *The Revelation of St. John*, Moffatt New Testament Commentary (London: Hodder and Stoughton, 1940), writes, "The sea personifies the very principle of disorder in the creation. . . . When the sea vanishes we know that all the imperfections of the first creation have gone with it" (p. 411). Alan F. Johnson, in "Revelation," in Kenneth L. Barker and John Kohlenberger, eds., *The NIV Bible Commentary*, vol. 2, *New Testament* (London: Hodder and Stoughton, 1994), writes, "The sea serves as an archetype with connotations of evil. . . . Thus, no trace of evil in any form will be present in the new creation" (p. 1225).

12. Paul Davies, *The Last Three Minutes* (New York: Basic Books, 1994). Recent calculations suggest a collapse of the universe 24 billion years from now. Mark Peplow, "Cosmic Doomsday Delayed," *Nature News Online* (November 5, 2004).

13. John Polkinghorne, *The God of Hope and the End of the World* (London: SPCK, 2002), 141.

14. David A. S. Fergusson, *The Cosmos and the Creator: An Introduction to the Theology of Creation* (London: SPCK, 1998), 77.

15. Kiddle, *The Revelation of St. John*, 409–13.

16. Vriezen, *An Outline of Old Testament Theology* (n. 3 above), 187.

17. Margaret Wertheim, "God of the Quantum Vacuum," *New Scientist* (October 4, 1997): 28–31.

18. Paul Tillich, *The Courage to Be* (Douglas, U.K.: Fontana, 1962), 41–68.

19. Gregory R. Peterson, "The Intelligent-Design Movement: Science or Ideology?" *Zygon* 37(1) (2002): 7–23.

20. Stephen J. Gould, "The Evolution of Life on the Earth," *American Scientist* 271(4) (April 1994): 62–69. Similar views are presented by Michael Ruse, *Monad to Man: The Concept of Progress in Evolutionary Biology* (Cambridge: Harvard University Press, 1996).

21. Dale A. Russell, "The Long-Term Evolution of Life," *American Scientist* 89(5) (2001): 475–76; and D. H. Erwin and S. L. Wing, eds., *Deep Time: Paleobiology's Perspective* (Chicago: Paleontological Society/University of Chicago Press, 2000).

22. Simon Conway Morris, "We Were Meant to Be . . . ," *New Scientist* (November 16, 2002): 26–29.

23. Fergusson, *The Cosmos and the Creator* (n. 14 above), 45.

24. Alan Richardson, *Genesis 1–11* (London: SCM, 1966), 47.

25. John B. Cobb and David R. Griffin, *Process Theology: An Introductory Exposition* (Philadelphia: Westminster, 1976), 65; Ian Barbour, *Religion and Science: Historical and Contemporary Issues* (San Francisco: Harper, 1997), 199–214; and David R. Griffin, *Reenchantment without Supernaturalism: A Process Philosophy of Religion* (Ithaca, N.Y.: Cornell University Press, 2001).

26. Barbour, *Religion and Science*, 300–303.

27. James E. Huchingson, in *Pandemonium Tremendum: Chaos and Mystery in the Life of God* (Cleveland: Pilgrim, 2001), has developed a creation theology with creation from chaos but with a more robust Creator, who battles "recalcitrant matter which keeps relapsing into chaos" (p. 173). He does not describe remaining chaos as the source of evil.

Chapter 7. Chaos Theory and Chaos Events

1. Eugene Polzik, "Flight of the Qubit," *Nature* 428 (March 11, 2004): 129–30; Brian Julsgaard et al., "Experimental Demonstration of Quantum Memory for Light," *Nature* 432 (November 25, 2004): 482–86; and Charles Seife, "Researchers Build Quantum Info Bank by Writing on the Clouds," *Science* 306 (October 22, 2004): 593.

2. Lucia Hackermuller et al., "Decoherence of Matter Waves by Thermal Emission of Radiation," *Nature* 427 (February 19, 2004): 711–14.

3. M. D. LaHaye et al., "Approaching the Quantum Limit of a Nanomechanical Resonator," *Science* 304 (April 2, 2004): 74–77.

4. Alessandro Zavatta et al., "Quantum-to-Classical Transition with Single-Photon-Added Coherent States of Light," *Science* 306 (October 22, 2004): 660–62.

5. Robert J. Russell, Nancey Murphy, and C. J. Isham, eds., *Quantum Cosmology and the Laws of Nature: Scientific Perspectives on Divine Action*, 2nd ed. (Vatican: Vatican Observatory Publications; Berkeley, Calif.: Center for Theology and Natural Sciences, 1999).

6. Robert J. Russell, Nancey Murphy, and Arthur R. Peacocke, eds., *Chaos and Complexity: Scientific Perspectives on Divine Action* (Vatican City: Vatican Observatory Publications; Berkeley, Calif.: Center for Theology and Natural Sciences, 1995).

7. Arthur R. Peacocke, "God's Interaction with the World," in ibid., 263–87. Elsewhere he argues against the possibility of God influencing a chaos event, because God "self-limits" God's omniscience in the case of unpredictable events. Arthur R. Peacocke, *Theology for a Scientific Age* (London: SCM, 1993), 157–60. To this I say that if humans are able to calculate a plot as shown in Figure 7.1, then God can do this. God would, moreover, know all relevant parameters and so would be able to discern when and where a chaos event will occur. Then God can influence the system, making it go along the leg God wants it to take.

8. John Polkinghorne, "The Metaphysics of Divine Action," in Russell, Murphy, and Peacocke, *Chaos and Complexity*, 147–56. He maintains this position in *Traffic in Truth: Exchanges between Science and Theology* (Norwich, U.K.: Canterbury, 2000), 24–27.

9. Ian Stewart, *Does God Play Dice? The New Mathematics of Chaos*, 2nd ed. (London: Penguin, 1997), 342.

10. Stuart Kauffman, *The Origin of Order: Self-Organization and Selection in Evolution* (New York: Oxford University Press, 1993).

11. Peter P. Kirschenmann, "On Self-Organisation, Design, and the Almost Inevitableness of Complex Order," in *Studies in Science and Theology*, vol. 8, ed. Niels H. Gregersen, Ulf Görman, and Hubert Meisinger, 17–42 (Aarhus, Denmark: University of Aarhus, 2002).

12. Christopher M. Dobson, "Protein Folding and Misfolding," *Nature* 426 (2003): 884–90.

13. Kauffman, *The Origin of Order*.

14. Palmyre Oomen, "Divine 'Second Order' Design and Natural Self-Organization," in Gregersen, Görman, and Meisinger, *Studies in Science and Theology*, vol. 8, 4–6.

15. Ibid., 12

16. Niels H. Gregersen, "Beyond the Balance: Theology in a Self-Organizing World," in *Design and Disorder: Perspectives from Science and Theology*, ed. Niels H. Gregersen and Ulf Görman, 83–84 (Edinburgh: T. & T. Clark, 2002).

17. James Gleick, *Chaos: Making a New Science* (New York: Penguin Books, 1987).

18. Wesley J. Wildman and Robert J. Russell, "Chaos: A Mathematical Introduction with Philosophical Reflections," in Russell, Murphy, and Peacocke, *Chaos and Complexity* (n. 6 above), 49–90.

19. Arthur Peacocke, *Theology for a Scientific Age* (London: SCM, 1993), 50–53.

20. Kathleen T. Alligood, Tim D. Sauer, and James A. Yorke, *Chaos: An Introduction to Dynamical Systems* (New York: Springer-Verlag, 1996), reviewed by J. A. Rial, *American Scientist* 85(5) (1997): 487–88.

21. Stewart, *Does God Play Dice?* (n. 9 above), 246–49.

22. John L. Stanford, "Chaotic Dynamics and Implications for Weather Forecasting," in *Encyclopedia of Physics*, ed. Rita G. Lerner and George L. Trigg, 2nd ed. (New York: VCH, 1990), 723.

23. Ross N. Hoffman, "Controlling Hurricanes," *Scientific American* 291(4) (October 2004): 38–45.

24. Stephen J. Gould, "The Evolution of Life on the Earth," *American Scientist* 271(4) (April 1994): 62–69.

25. Peter Smith, *Explaining Chaos* (Cambridge: Cambridge University Press, 1998), 119.

26. Ibid., 143.

27. Juan Cabrera and John Milton, *Physical Review Letters* (October 2002).

28. George Pickett, "Suddenly It's Chaos," *Nature* 424 (August 28, 2003): 1002–3.

29. T. M. Fromhold et al., "Chaotic Electron Diffusion through Stochastic Webs Enhances Current Flow in Superlattices," *Nature* 428 (April 15, 2004): 726–30.

30. Mason A. Porter and Richard L. Liboff, "Chaos on the Quantum Scale," *American Scientist* 89(6) (November–December 2001): 532–37.

31. Russell, Murphy, and Peacocke, *Chaos and Complexity* (n. 7 above); Peacocke, "God's Interaction with the World" (n. 7 above); Polkinghorne, "The Metaphysics of Divine Action" (n. 8 above); Polkinghorne maintains this position in *Traffic in Truth* (n. 8 above), 24–27.

32. Willem B. Drees, "Gaps for God?" in Russell, Murphy, and Peacocke, *Chaos and Complexity* (n. 7 above), 223–37.

33. The Wilkinson Microwave Anisotropy Probe (WMAP) can detect stationary temperature differences of 2×10^{-5} °C in the microwave background radiation. Neil J. Cornish et al., *Physical Review Letters* 92 (May 19, 2004): 201302. Compare this with the influencing of a chaos event: 10^{-8} °C in only 2×10^{-13} second.

34. Stewart, *Does God Play Dice?* (n. 9 above), 345.

35. Ibid., 365.

36. John Barrow, "How Chaos Coexists with Order," in *Design and Disorder: Perspectives from Science and Theology*, ed. Niels H. Gregersen and Ulf Görman, 11–29 (Edinburgh: T. & T. Clark, 2002).

37. Adrian Cho, "A Fresh Take on Disorder, or Disorderly Science?" *Science* 297 (August 23, 2002): 1268–69. See also letters in *Science* 298 (November 8, 2002): 1171–72 and *Science* 300 (April 11, 2003): 249–51.

38. Note that the text of Cho, "A Fresh Take," says wrongly, "when q approaches 1" (rather than 0).

39. William R. Stoeger, "Contemporary Physics and the Ontological Status of the Laws of Nature," in Russell, Murphy, and Isham, *Quantum Cosmology* (n. 5 above), 207–31.

40. Wesley J. Wildman and Robert J. Russell, "Chaos: A Mathematical Introduction with Philosophical Reflections," in Russell, Murphy, and Peacocke, *Chaos and Complexity* (n. 6 above), 83.

41. Taede Smedes, "Chaos: Where Science and Religion Meet? A Critical Evaluation of the Use of Chaos Theory in Theology," in *Studies in Science and Theology, ESSSAT Yearbook, 2001–2002*, ed. Niels H. Gregersen, Ulf Görman, and Hubert Meisinger, 277–94 (Aarhus, Denmark: University of Aarhus, 2002).

42. John Polkinghorne, "The Laws of Nature and the Laws of Physics," in Russell, Murphy, and Isham, *Quantum Cosmology* (n. 5 above), 429–40.

43. Smedes, "Chaos," 283.

Chapter 8. The Problem of Evil

This chapter is an adapted version of a previously published article: Sjoerd L. Bonting, "The Problem of Evil," *Sewanee Theological Review* 47(4) (September 2004): 402–12.

1. Karel van 't Reve, *De ongelooflijke slechtheid van het opperwezen* [The Unbelievable Wickedness of the Supreme Being] (Amsterdam: Van Oorschot, 1987).

2. Full text on the Internet at www.ucc.org/faith/heidel.htm.

3. Maarten 't Hart, *Een vlucht regenwulpen* [A Flight of Curlews] (Amsterdam: Arbeiderspers, 1978), 69–82.

4. Marjoleine de Vos, "Het eindeloze zoeken" [The Endless Search], *NRC Handelsblad* (September 22, 1997).

5. Anton Houtepen, *God, een Open Vraag* [God, an Open Question] (Zoetermeer, The Netherlands: Meinema, 1997), 97.

6. John Hick, *Evil and the God of Love* (Glasgow: Collins, 1979); Harold S. Kushner, *When Bad Things Happen to Good People* (London: Pan, 1982); C. S. Rodd, *Why Evil and Suffering?* (Peterborough, U.K.: Epworth, 1998); Hermann Häring, *Das Böse in der Welt: Gottes Macht oder Ohnmacht?* [Evil in the World: God's Potence or Impotence?] (Darmstadt: Primus Verlag, 1999); Brian Hebblethwaite, *Evil, Suffering and Religion* (London: SPCK, 2000); John A. Sanford, *Evil, the Shadow Side of Reality* (New York: Crossroad, 1989) ("The problem of evil is unresolved in Christian theology," p. 129); and Susan Neiman, *Evil in Modern Thought: An Alternative History of Philosophy* (Princeton, N.J.: Princeton University Press, 2002).

7. Klaus Hemmerle, "Evil," in *Encyclopedia of Theology,* ed. Karl Rahner (London: Burns & Oates, 1981).

8. Hebblethwaite, *Evil, Suffering and Religion.*

9. "Evil," in "Philosophies of the Branches of Knowledge," *Encyclopaedia Britannica,* CD-ROM, 1999.

10. Wouter J. Hanegraaff, "New Age Religion and Western Culture: Esotericism in the Mirror of Secular Thought" (PhD diss., Utrecht University, 1995), 233–53.

11. Hick, *Evil and the God of Love* (n. 6 above), 160–75.

12. Kushner, *When Bad Things Happen* (n. 6 above); and Dorothee Sölle, *Suffering* (Philadelphia: Fortress Press, 1984).

13. Hanegraaff, "New Age Religion," 157–73.

14. Elaine Pagels, *The Origin of Satan* (New York: Random House, 1995), 173–74.

15. Hick, *Evil and the God of Love* (n. 6 above).

16. F. C. Copleston, *Aquinas* (Hammondsworth, U.K.: Penguin, 1955), 143–50.

17. Claus Westermann, *Creation* (London: SPCK, 1974), 60–64.

18. Patricia A. Williams, "The Problem of Evil: A Solution from Science," *Zygon* 36(3) (2001): 563–74.

19. Friedrich Schleiermacher, *The Christian Faith* (Edinburgh: T. & T. Clark, 1986), 337.

20. Wolfhart Pannenberg, *Systematic Theology,* vol. 2 (Grand Rapids: Eerdmans, 1994), 169.

21. Ibid., 171.

22. Edward Schillebeeckx, "Plezier en woede beleven aan Gods schepping" [Experiencing Pleasure and Anger with God's Creation], *Tijdschrift voor Theologie* 33(4) (1993): 325–47.

23. David A. S. Fergusson, *The Cosmos and the Creator* (London: SPCK, 1998), 77–87.

24. H. M. Kuitert, *Het Algemeen Betwijfeld Christelijk Geloof* (Baarn, The Netherlands: Ten Have, 1992), 59–63, 82–97; English translation, *I Have My Doubts: How to Become a Christian without Being a Fundamentalist* (London: SCM, 1993).

25. John F. Haught, "In Search of a God for Evolution: Paul Tillich and Pierre Teilhard de Chardin," *Zygon* 37(3) (2002): 539–53.

26. Pierre Teilhard de Chardin, *Le Milieu Divin* (London: Fontana/Collins, 1964), 74–94.

27. George C. Williams, "Huxley's Evolution and Ethics in Sociobiological Perspective," *Zygon* 23(4) (1988): 383–407.

28. Sarah Blaffer Hrdy, "Comments on George Williams's Essay on Morality and Nature," *Zygon* 23(4) (1988): 409–11.

29. Michael Ruse, "Response to Williams: Selfishness Is Not Enough," *Zygon* 23(4) (1988): 413–16.

30. Ralph W. Burhoe, "On 'Huxley's Evolution and Ethics in Sociobiological Perspective' by George C. Williams," *Zygon* 23(4) (1988): 417–29.

31. Ann Gibbons, "When It Comes to Evolution, Humans Are in the Slow Class," *Science* 267 (1995): 1907–8.

32. John B. Cobb, "Befriending an Amoral Nature," *Zygon* 23(4) (1988): 431–36.

33. George C. Williams, "Reply to Comments on 'Huxley's Evolution and Ethics in Sociobiological Perspective,'" *Zygon* 23(4) (1988): 437–38.

34. Arthur Peacocke, "Theodicy and Suffering: The Cost of New Life," in *The Work of Love: Creation as Kenosis*, ed. John C. Polkinghorne (Grand Rapids: Eerdmans, 2001). Surprisingly, Peacocke does not consider moral evil, either in this essay or in his major works, *Creation and the World of Science* (Oxford: Clarendon, 1979; p. 166) and *Theology for a Scientific Age* (London: SCM, 1993; 125–27).

35. Christopher Southgate, "God and Evolutionary Evil: Theodicy in the Light of Darwinism," *Zygon* 37(4) (2002): 803–24.

36. Sanford, *Evil, the Shadow Side of Reality* (n. 6 above).

37. Paul Ricoeur, *Het Kwaad: Een uitdaging aan de filosofie en aan de theologie* [Evil: A Challenge to Philosophy and to Theology], 2nd ed. (Kampen, The Netherlands: Agora, 1995), 61.

38. John Paul II, *Fides et Ratio*, chap. 6, par. 76 (Catholic Information Network, 1999), www.cin.org/jp2/fides.html.

39. Sjoerd L. Bonting, "Chaos Theology: A New Approach to the Science-Theology Dialogue," *Zygon* 34(2) (1999): 323–32; and Sjoerd L. Bonting, *Chaos Theology: A Revised Creation Theology* (Ottawa: Novalis, 2002), 20–36.

40. Craig J. Hogan, "Observing the Beginning of Time," *American Scientist* 90(5) (2002): 420–27; "The Beginning of Time," *Science* 295 (2002): 2223–25.

41. Tom Stonier, *Information and the Internal Structure of the Universe* (London: Springer-Verlag, 1990), 38–41, 70–72.

42. Peter Smith, *Explaining Chaos* (Cambridge: Cambridge University Press, 1998), 143.

43. Houtepen, *God, een Open Vraag* (n. 5 above), 104–25.

44. Philip Hefner, "God and Chaos: The Demiurge versus the Ungrund," *Zygon* 19(4) (1984): 483.

45. Mark W. Worthing, *God, Creation, and Contemporary Physics* (Minneapolis: Fortress Press, 1996), 146–48.

46. Kushner, *When Bad Things Happen* (n. 6 above).

Chapter 9. God's Action in the World

1. On the nature of God, I remain silent. How can we creatures hope to analyze the divine nature? Scott Cowdell, in *A God for This World* (London: Mowbray, 2000), 37–57, reviews numerous descriptions of the nature of God and finds them all wanting. He concludes that we must consider the actions, rather than the nature, of God. I agree; we can observe and describe God's actions in the world in scientific as well as theological terms, which I try to do in this chapter.

2. John Polkinghorne, *Science and Providence: God's Interaction with the World* (London: SPCK, 1989), 31.

3. John B. Cobb and David R. Griffin, *Process Theology: An Introductory Exposition* (Philadelphia: Westminster, 1976), 65.

4. Arthur Peacocke, *Theology for a Scientific Age* (London: SCM, 1993), 371–72.

5. Cobb and Griffin, *Process Theology.*

6. Keith Ward, *Rational Theology and the Creativity of God* (London: Blackwell, 1982), 229.

7. Irenaeus, *Adversus haerses* 4.20.1.

8. J. N. Sanders, "The Word," in *The Interpreter's Dictionary of the Bible,* vol. 4, ed. George A. Buttrick et al., 868–72 (New York: Abingdon, 1962).

9. "Logos," in *Encyclopaedia Judaica* 14 (Jerusalem: Ketar, 1972), 460–62.

10. The physical concept of energy as a measure of the capacity to do work is a late development. It was first introduced in the seventeenth century by Galileo and further developed by Isaac Newton. Heat was identified as a form of energy by Hermann von Helmholtz and James Joule around 1840. Thus, energy in its present physical meaning was not yet known to Philo and Maximus.

11. Sanders, "The Word."

12. William Temple, *Readings in St. John's Gospel* (London: Macmillan, 1945), 4–5.

13. C. K. Barrett, *The Gospel according to St. John* (London: SPCK, 1958), 125–32.

14. J. W. C. Wand, *The Four Great Heresies* (London: Mowbray, 1957).

15. Leo D. Davis, *The First Seven Ecumenical Councils (325–787)* (Collegeville, Minn.: Liturgical Press, 1983).

16. Lars Thunberg, *Man and the Cosmos: The Vision of St. Maximus the Confessor* (Crestwood, N.Y.: St. Vladimir's Seminary Press, 1985), 137–43.

17. Claus Westermann, *Genesis 1–11* (Minneapolis: Fortress Press, 1994), 106–8.

18. Martin Buber and Franz Rosenzweig, *Zu einer neuen verdeutschung der Schrift, Beilage zum ersten Band, die Fünf Bücher der Weisung* [Toward a New German Translation of Scripture: Addendum to Vol. 1, The Five Books of the Law] (Gerlingen, Germany: Lambert Schneider, 1976); S. V. McCasland, "Spirit," in *The Interpreter's Dictionary,* vol. 4 (n. 8 above), 432–34; Alan Richardson, *Genesis 1–11: The Creation Stories and the Modern World View* (London: SCM, 1953), 48; J. De Fraine, *Genesis,* vol. 1, bk. 1, The Books of the Old Testament (Roermond, The Netherlands: Romen, 1963), 33–35; and H. Berkhof, *Christelijk Geloof* [The Christian Faith] (Nijkerk: Callenbach, 1973), 166.

19. Celia Deane-Drummond, *Creation through Wisdom* (Edinburgh: T. & T. Clark, 2000).

20. S. H. Blank, "Wisdom," in *The Interpreter's Dictionary,* vol. 4 (n. 8 above), 852–61.

21. W. O. E. Oesterley, "The Wisdom of Jesus, the Son of Sirach, or Ecclesiasticus," in *A New Commentary on Holy Scripture*, pt. 2, eds. Charles Gore et al. (London: SPCK, 1928), 79.

22. Eugen Biser, "Wisdom," in *Encyclopedia of Theology,* ed. Karl Rahner, 1817–21 (London: Burns & Oates, 1975).

23. Westermann, *Genesis 1–11* (n. 17 above).

24. Richardson, *Genesis 1–11* (n. 18 above).

25. John Macquarrie, *Principles of Christian Theology* (London: SCM, 1966), 181.

26. Sjoerd L. Bonting, *Chaos Theology: A Revised Creation Theology* (Ottawa: Novalis, 2002), 13–37.

27. Craig J. Hogan, "Observing the Beginning of Time," *American Scientist* 90(5) (September–October 2002): 420–27.

28. Tom Stonier, *Information and the Internal Structure of the Universe* (London: Springer-Verlag, 1990), 38–41, 70–72.

29. George Musser, "A Pixelated Cosmos," *Scientific American* 287(4) (2002): 8–9; and Craig J. Hogan, "The Beginning of Time," *Science* 295 (2002): 2223–25.

30. I agree with Stephen W. Need, who concludes in "Re-reading the Prologue: Incarnation and Creation in John 1:1-8," *Theology* 106(834) (2003): 397–404, "the [non-incarnate] Logos is the pre-existent instrument of creation moving in its own realm of creation *until* its incarnation in Jesus in v. 14." This rules out the idea of a preexistent Christ, who would, moreover, be not fully human and thus unable to be the Savior of humankind.

31. Charles Seife, "Galaxy Maps Support Theory That the Universe Is Flying to Pieces," *Science* 302 (October 31, 2003): 762–63. See also chapter 14.

32. John Gribbin and Martin Rees, *The Stuff of the Universe: Dark Matter, Mankind and Anthropic Cosmology* (London: Penguin, 1995).

33. J. P. Moreland, ed., *The Creation Hypothesis: Scientific Evidence for an Intelligent Designer* (Downers Grove, Ill.: InterVarsity, 1994), 141–64, table 4.4.

34. Are the fundamental constants really constant? In 2001 it was claimed on the basis of an analysis of the light from seventy-two distant quasars that the fine-structure constant (which is related to the speed of light) was 0.001 percent less in the early universe than at present. Charles Seife, "Changing Constants Cause Controversy," *Science* 293 (August 24, 2001): 1410–11. A new analysis shows there is no such change. Lennox L. Cowie and Antoinette Songaila, "The Inconstant Constant?" *Nature* 428 (March 11, 2004): 132–33.

35. Paul Davies, *God and the New Physics* (London: Dent, 1983), 179.

36. Alan H. Guth, *The Inflationary Universe* (Reading, Mass.: Addison-Wesley, 1997).

37. Charles Seife, "With Its Ingredients MAPped, Universe's Recipe Beckons," *Science* 300 (May 2, 2003): 730–31.

38. Philip Ball, "Water, Water, Everywhere?" *Nature* 427 (January 1, 2004): 19–20.

39. Paul Davies, *The Cosmic Blueprint* (London: Unwin, 1989), 131–32.

40. L. Becker et al., "Bedout: A Possible End-Permian Impact Crater Offshore of Northwestern Australia," *Science* 304 (June 4, 2004): 1469–76. But this is still disputed: Rex Dalton, "Comet Impact Theory Faces Repeat Analysis," *Nature* 431 (October 28, 2004): 1027.

41. Yukio Isozaki, "Permo-Triassic Boundary Superanoxia and Stratified Superocean: Records from Lost Deep Sea," *Science* 276 (1997): 235–38.

42. Walter Alvarez, *T. Rex and the Crater of Doom* (Princeton, N.J.: Princeton University Press, 1997).

43. Yves Coppens, "East Side Story: The Origin of Humankind," *Scientific American* 270(5) (May 1994): 62–69.

44. Chris Stringer, "Out of Ethiopia," *Nature* 423 (June 12, 2003): 692–95.

45. Henry C. Harpending et al., "Genetic Traces of Ancient Demography," *Proceedings of the National Academy of Sciences, USA* 95 (1998): 1961–67.

46. L. A. Zhivotovsky et al., "Features of Evolution and Expansion of Modern Humans, Inferred from Genomewide Microsatellite Markers," *American Journal of Human Genetics* 72 (2003): 1171–86.

47. Ann Gibbons, "When It Comes to Evolution, Humans Are in the Slow Class," *Science* 267 (1995): 1907–8.

48. John D. Barrow and Frank J. Tipler, *The Anthropic Cosmological Principle and the Structure of the Physical World* (New York: Oxford University Press, 1986).

49. John Polkinghorne, *Beyond Science* (Cambridge: Cambridge University Press, 1996), 87–89. Less polite was Martin Gardner in his review of Barrow and Tipler's book in the *New York Review of Books* (May 8, 1986, 22–25): "In my not so humble opinion I think the last principle is best called CRAP, the Completely Ridiculous Anthropic Principle."

50. J. Richard Gott, "Creation of Open Universes from de Sitter Space," *Nature* 295 (1982): 306.

51. Lee Smolin, *The Life of the Cosmos* (New York: Oxford University Press, 1997).

52. Joseph Silk, "Holistic Cosmology," *Science* 277 (1997): 644.

53. Max Tegmark, "Parallel Universes: Not Just a Staple of Science Fiction, but a Direct Implication of Cosmological Observations," *Scientific American* 288(5) (May 2003): 31–41.

54. George F. R. Ellis, "The Shape of the Universe," *Nature* 425 (2003): 566–67.

55. Michael Behe, *Darwin's Black Box: The Biochemical Challenge to Evolution* (New York: Free Press, 1996).

56. Detlev Arendt et al., "Ciliary Photoreceptors with a Vertebrate-Type Opsin in an Invertebrate Brain," *Science* 306 (October 29, 2004): 869–71.

57. A. J. Robinson et al., "Hagemann Factor (Factor XII) Deficiency in Marine Mammals," *Science* 166 (1969): 1420–22.

58. C. J. Davidson et al., "450 Million Years of Hemostasis," *Journal of Thrombosis and Haemostasis* 1 (2003): 1487–94.

59. V. K. Nguyen et al., "Heavy-Chain Only Antibodies Derived from Dromedary Are Secreted and Displayed by Mouse B Cells," *Immunology* 109(1) (2003): 93–101.

60. S. I. Aizawa, "Bacterial Flagella and Type III Secretion Systems, *FEMS Microbiology Letters* 202 (2001): 157–64; and Thomas C. Marlovits et al., "Structural Insights into the Assembly of the Type III Secretion Needle Complex," *Science* 306 (November 5, 2004): 1040–42.

61. Gregory J. Velicer and Yuen-tsu N. Yu, "Evolution of Novel Cooperative Swarming in the Bacterium *Myxococcus xanthus*," *Nature* 425 (2003): 75–78.

Chapter 10. The Cosmic Christ: Person and Work

1. Adherents.com, "Major Religions of the World," data as of September 2002, www.adherents.com/Religions_By_Adherents.html.

2. I follow the dating of the New Testament writings proposed by John A. T. Robinson, *Redating the New Testament* (London: SCM, 1976), 336–58.

3. C. F. D. Moule, *The Origin of Christology* (Cambridge: Cambridge University Press, 1978), 11–46.

4. Ibid., 47–96.

5. J. W. C. Wand, *The Four Great Heresies* (London: Mowbray, 1955).

6. Some have ridiculed this doctrine of the two natures of Christ (the "schizophrenic" Christ), but I do not find it quite so unintelligible. Think of a woman who holds a managerial position in business and is also a mother. She will show quite a different nature to her business associates than she will to her children. She may even have to if she wants to be successful in both functions. The Gospels show us the two natures of Christ: hungry and thirsty at some times, yet authoritative in his teaching and healing acts.

7. Sjoerd L. Bonting, *Tussen geloof en ongeloof* [Between Belief and Unbelief] (Zoetermeer, The Netherlands: Meinema, 2000). English translation available upon e-mail request to s.l.bonting@wxs.nl.

8. John A. T. Robinson, *Honest to God* (London: SCM, 1963).

9. J. B. Phillips, *The New Testament in Modern English* (London: G. Bles, 1960), 181.

10. In upholding here that the incarnation of the *Logos* in Jesus of Nazareth conferred full divinity on him, while concluding in chapter 9 that through the *Logos* God introduced the energy necessary for the big bang, am I guilty of either subordinationism (Christ being subordinate to God the Father) or modalism (Christ being merely a mode of the self-revelation of the one God)? I do not think so, and I refer to the phrase of Irenaeus: "The Son and the Spirit are the two hands of God by which he created all things." Using a human image, I note that the hand can at one time grab a sandwich to eat and at another time caress the beloved, leading to their union in a loving relationship of equals. The distinction is not between Father and Son, but between Christ and energy.

11. John Hick, ed., *The Myth of God Incarnate* (London: SCM, 1977).

12. Michael Green, ed., *The Truth of God Incarnate* (London: Hodder and Stoughton, 1977).

13. Michael Goulder, ed., *Incarnation and Myth: The Debate Continued* (London: SCM, 1979).

14. Edward Schillebeeckx, *Jesus, an Experiment in Christology* (London: Fount, 1983).

15. H. M. Kuitert, *Jezus: Nalatenschap van het christendom, schets voor een christologie* [Jesus: Inheritance of Christendom, Sketch of a Christology] (Baarn, The Netherlands: Ten Have, 1998), 239–42.

16. Schillebeeckx, *Jesus*.

17. Arthur R. Peacocke, *Science and the Christian Experiment* (London: OUP, [**Oxford University Press?**] 1971), 167–69.

18. C. J. den Heyer, *Verzoening: Bijbelse notities bij een omstreden thema* [Reconciliation: Biblical Notes on an Embattled Theme] (Kampen, The Netherlands: Kok, 1997).

19. Ibid., 136.

20. Ibid., 17, 33.

21. Hans van Munster et al., *Uit op Verzoening in Praktijk en Theologie* [Going for Reconciliation in Practice and Theology] (Kampen, The Netherlands: Kok, 1997); L. J. van den Brom et al., *Verzoening of Koninkrijk* [Reconciliation or Kingdom] (Kampen, The Netherlands: Kok, 1998); P. Valkenberg, ed., *Begaanbare Wegen: Verzoening tussen de Godsdiensten* [Practicable Roads: Reconciliation between Religions] (Kampen, The Netherlands: Kok, 1998); and C. Houtman, ed., *Ruimte voor Vergeving* [Space for Forgiveness] (Kampen, The Netherlands: Kok, 1998).

22. H. Baarlink, *Het Evangelie van de Verzoening* [The Gospel of Reconciliation] (Kampen, The Netherlands: Kok, 1998).

23. Anselm, *Cur Deus Homo*, full text online at www.fordham.edu/halsall/basis/anselm-curdeus.html.

24. Ibid.

25. Emil Brunner, *Dogmatics*, vol. 2, *The Christian Doctrine of Creation and Redemption*, 4th ed. (London: Lutterworth, 1960), 98–100. He rejects the Augustinian idea of "original sin" as completely foreign to the thought of the Bible (103–7).

26. Sjoerd L. Bonting, *Schepping en Evolutie: Poging tot Synthese* [Creation and Evolution: Attempt at Synthesis] (Kampen, The Netherlands: Kok, 1996), 154–65. English translation available upon e-mail request to s.l.bonting@wxs.nl.

Chapter 11. Human Ambivalence: Genetic Modification

1. Michael J. Reiss and Roger Straughan, *Improving Nature? The Science and Ethics of Genetic Engineering* (Cambridge: Cambridge University Press, 1996), 11–42.

2. Lloyd J. Old, "Immunotherapy for Cancer," *Scientific American* 275(3) (1996): 102–9.

3. Reiss and Straughan, *Improving Nature?* 139–64.

4. Ibid., 165–93.

5. Suzanne Kamel-Reid et al., "Model of Human Acute Lymphoblastic Leukemia in Immune-Deficient SCID Mice," *Science* 246 (1989): 1597–99.

6. Reiss and Straughan, *Improving Nature?* (n. 1 above), 202–16.

7. Ronald G. Crystal, "Transfer of Genes to Humans: Early Lessons and Obstacles to Success," *Science* 270 (1995): 404–10.

8. Reiss and Straughan, *Improving Nature?* (n. 1 above), 216–23.

9. G. D. Schuler et al., "A Gene Map of the Human Genome," *Science* 274 (1996): 536–46; and Denis Duboule et al., "The Evolution of Genomics," *Science* 278 (1997): 555, 564–68, 601–14, 631–37.

10. Bernard D. Davis, "Bacterial Domestication: Underlying Assumptions," *Science* 235 (1987): 1329–35; confirmed by the National Academy of Sciences, *Introduction of Recombinant DNA-Engineered Organisms into the Environment* (Washington, D.C.: National Academy Press, 1987).

11. Erik Stokstad and Gretchen Vogel, "Mixed Message Could Prove Costly for GM Crops," *Science* 302 (2003): 542–43; and R. Freckleton et al., "Deciding the Future of GM Crops in Europe," *Science* 302 (2003): 994–96.

12. Jim Giles, "Transgenic Planting Approved despite Scepticism of UK Public," *Nature* 428 (March 11, 2004): 107.

13. The United Kingdom bans gene manipulation, cloning, and hybridization of the human embryo; it permits in vitro fertilization only by licensed clinicians. David Dickson, "British Government Rekindles Debate on Embryo Research," *Science* 238 (December 4, 1987): 1348.

14. D. A. Williams and C. Baum, "Gene Therapy, New Challenges Ahead," *Science* 302 (October 17, 2003): 400–401.

15. Marina Cavazzana-Calvo et al., "The Future of Gene Therapy: Balancing the Risks and Benefits of Clinical Trials," *Nature* 427 (February 26, 2004): 779–81; and Josh P. Roberts, "Gene Therapy's Fall and Rise (Again)," *The Scientist* 18(18) (September 27, 2004): 22–24.

16. Tomohiro Kono et al., "Birth of Parthenogenetic Mice That Can Develop to Adulthood," *Nature* 428 (April 22, 2004): 860–64.

17. Gretchen Vogel, "Misguided Chromosomes Foil Primate Cloning," *Science* 300 (2003): 225–27. Other reasons why human cloning through nuclear transfer fails so often are discussed by Cathryn M. Delude, "Transfer Troubles," *Scientific American* 291(4) (October 2004): 12.

18. W. S. Hwang et al., "Evidence of a Pluripotent Stem Cell Line Derived from a Cloned Blastocyst," *Science* 303 (2004): 1669–74.

19. G. Schatten et al., "Cloning Claim Is Science Fiction, Not Science," *Science* 299 (2003): 344.

20. Gretchen Vogel, "Dolly Goes to Greener Pastures," *Science* 299 (2003): 1163. A relationship between telomere length and mortality has been reported for humans. Richard Cawthon et al., "Association between Telomere Length in Blood and Mortality in People Aged 60 Years or Older," *The Lancet* 361(9355) (February 1, 2003): 393–95.

21. Carol Ezzell, "Ma's Eyes, Not Her Ways," *Scientific American* 288(4) (April 2003): 14.

22. Smadar Cohen and Jonathan Leor, "Rebuilding Broken Hearts," *Scientific American* 291(5) (November 2004): 22–29.

23. Charles E. Murry et al., "Haematopoietic Stem Cells Do Not Transdifferentiate into Cardiac Myocytes in Myocardial Infarcts," *Nature* 428 (2004): 664–68; James M. Weimann

et al., "Stable Reprogrammed Heterokaryons Form Spontaneously in Purkinje Neurons after Bone Marrow Transplant," *Nature Cell Biology* 5 (November 1, 2003): 959–66; Yuval Dor et al., "Adult Pancreatic β-Cells Are Formed by Self-Duplication Rather than Stem-Cell Differentiation," *Nature* 429 (2004): 41–46.

24. Robert Lanza and Nadia Rosenthal, "The Stem Cell Challenge," *Scientific American* 290(6) (June 2004): 60–67; and Gretchen Vogel, "More Data but No Answers on Powers of Adult Stem Cells," *Science* 305 (July 2, 2004): 27.

25. John Habgood, *A Working Faith: Essays and Addresses on Science, Medicine and Ethics* (London: Darton, Longman & Todd, 1980), 109–15.

26. However, in 2004, 90 percent of the farmers worldwide growing GM crops operated in developing countries, according to the trade organization ISAAA (International Service for the Acquisition of Agri-biotech Applications). The high percentage probably reflects the small farm size in developing countries.

27. Nina Fedoroff and Nancy M. Brown, *Mendel in the Kitchen: A Scientist's View of Genetically Modified Foods* (Washington, D.C.: Joseph Henry Press, 2004).

28. Rachel Nowak, "Genetic Testing Set for Takeoff," *Science* 265 (1994): 464–67; letters 1509–10.

29. Kathy L. Hudson et al., "Genetic Discrimination and Health Insurance," *Science* 270 (1995): 391–93; and Karen Rothenberg et al., "Genetic Information and the Workplace," *Science* 275 (1997): 1755–57.

30. The President's Commission for the Study of Ethical Problems in Biomedical and Behavioral Research, *Splicing Life: A Report on the Social and Ethical Issues of Genetic Engineering in Human Beings* (Washington, D.C.: Government Printing Office, 1982).

31. National Bioethics Advisory Commission (NBAC), *Cloning Human Beings: Report and Recommendations* (Rockville, Md.: NBAC, 1997).

32. Angelika E. Schnieke et al., "Human Factor IX Transgenic Sheep Produced by Transfer of Nuclei from Transfected Fetal Fibroblasts," *Science* 278 (December 19, 1997): 2130–33. Sheep producing human factor IX (against hemophilia) were obtained by cloning.

33. Report of Human Fertilisation and Embryology Authority (HFEA) and Human Genetics Advisory Commission (HGAC), December 8, 1998.

34. Karen Kaplan, "Existing Stem Cells Unsafe for Humans, Study Says," *Los Angeles Times*, January 25, 2004. All approved stem cell lines appear to be contaminated with mouse cell proteins, which could cause harm to patients being treated with these cell lines.

Chapter 12. Disease: Punishment for Sin or Chaos Event?

1. Karl Rahner, *Hominisation: The Evolutionary Origin of Man as a Theological Problem* (Freiburg: Herder; London: Burns & Oates, 1965).

2. Emil Brunner, *Dogmatics*, vol. 2, *The Christian Doctrine of Creation and Redemption* (London: Lutterworth, 1952), 79–88.

3. This ambiguity is visible in Wolfhart Pannenberg's speaking about the soul as immortal and mortal, divine and created, preexistent and created at conception and created directly, as vital principle and ensouled body itself, as creaturely element and divine part of creature, only in humans and in all living beings. *Systematic Theology*, vol. 2 (Grand Rapids: Eerdmans, 1994), 181–89. Similarly in Keith Ward, *In Defence of the Soul* (Oxford: Oneworld, 1998).

4. W. Eichrodt, *Theology of the Old Testament*, vol. 2, trans. J. A. Baker (London: SCM, 1967), 131–50.

5. N. W. Porteus, "Soul," in *The Interpreter's Dictionary of the Bible*, vol. 4 (Nashville: Abingdon, 1962), 428–29. It is interesting to note that the Athanasian Creed says, "The reasonable soul [equivalent to my definition of mind as the seat of intelligence and spirituality] and flesh is one man."

6. Arthur R. Peacocke, *Science and the Christian Experiment* (London: Oxford University Press, 1971), 141–44.

7. Sora Song, "The Price of Pressure," *Time*, July 26, 2004, based on Suzanne C. Segerstrom and Gregory E. Miller, "Psychological Stress and the Human Immune System: A Meta-Analytic Study of 30 Years of Inquiry," *Psychological Bulletin* 130(4) (July 2004).

8. R. K. Harrison, "Medicine," in *The Interpreter's Dictionary of the Bible*, vol. 3, 331–34.

9. R. K. Harrison, "Healing," in *The Interpreter's Dictionary of the Bible*, vol. 2, 541–48.

10. E. Andrews, "Gifts of Healing," in *The Interpreter's Dictionary of the Bible*, vol. 2, 548–49.

11. Harrison, "Healing."

12. R. K. Harrison, "Disease," in *The Interpreter's Dictionary of the Bible*, vol. 1, 847–54.

13. Harrison, "Healing."

14. Andrews, "Gifts of Healing."

15. John Rennie and Ricki Rusting, "Making Headway against Cancer," *Scientific American*, 275(3) (1996): 28–30; "Cancer Warriors Claim a Victory," *Science* 279 (1998): 1842–43.

16. Robert A. Weinberg, "How Cancer Arises," *Scientific American* 275(3) (1996): 32–40. Recent insights are presented in six Cancer Reviews, *Nature* 432 (November 18, 2004): 294–337.

17. R. Scott Hawley, "Unresolvable Endings: Defective Telomeres and Failed Separation," *Science* 275 (1997): 1441–43.

18. Judah Folkman, "Fighting Cancer by Attacking Its Blood Supply," *Scientific American* 275(3) (1996): 116–19; Rakesh K. Jain and Peter F. Carmeliet, "Vessels of Death and Life," *Scientific American* 285(6) (December 2001): 26–33.

19. Erkki Ruoslahti, "How Cancer Spreads," *Scientific American* 275(3) (1996): 42–47; Jennifer Couzin, "Tracing the Steps of Metastasis: Cancer's Menacing Ballet," *Science* 299 (February 14, 2003): 1002–6.

20. Lance A. Liotta, "Cancer Cell Invasion and Metastasis," *Scientific American* 266(2) (1992): 54–63.

21. Samuel Hellman and Everett E. Vokes, "Advancing Current Treatments for Cancer," *Scientific American* 275(3) (1996): 84–89.

22. Karen Antman, "When Are Bone Marrow Transplants Considered?" *Scientific American* 275(3) (1996): 90–91.

23. Eliot Marshall, "Tamoxifen: Big Deal but Complex Hand to Play," *Science* 280 (1998): 196.

24. Paula Kiberstis et al., "Frontiers in Cancer Research," *Science* 278 (1997): 1035–77.

25. Folkman, "Fighting Cancer" (n. 18 above). Recent excitement over angiogenesis inhibition is premature, since mice are different from humans. Eliot Marshall, "The Power of the Front Page of the *New York Times*," *Science* 280 (May 15, 1998): 996–97.

26. Lloyd J. Old, "Immunotherapy for Cancer," *Scientific American* 275(3) (1996): 102–9. Preparations that will reduce the number of T-cells are being developed to decrease the immune-inhibiting effect of these cells. Amy Adams, "Cancer Immunotherapy Inches Forward," *The Scientist* 18(14) (July 19, 2004): 37–39.

27. Steven Dickman, "Antibodies Stage a Comeback in Cancer Treatment," *Science* 280 (1998): 1196–97.

28. Allen Oliff et al., "New Molecular Targets for Cancer Therapy," *Scientific American* 275(3) (1996): 110–15.

29. Deborah Fitzgerald, "Antibody Drug Development: On Target," *The Scientist* 17(22) (November 17, 2003): 29–31.

30. B. M. Rothschild et al., "Epidemiologic Study of Tumors in Dinosaurs," *Naturwissenschaften* 90(11) (2003): 495–500.

31. Randolph M. Nesse and George C. Williams, "Evolution and the Origins of Disease," *Scientific American* 279(5) (1998): 58–65.

32. Eugen Drewermann, *Exegese en Dieptepsychologie* [Exegesis and Depth Psychology] (Zoetermeer, The Netherlands: Meinema, 1993), 27.

33. Surprisingly, Dame Cicely Saunders, the eminent founder of the hospice movement, still held to this view when she wrote: "Disease and all our other ills were caused in the first instance by the sin of man. These things are permitted by God because He can use them to serve His own purposes and bring about an even greater good in the end." *Care of the Dying* (London: Macmillan, 1962), 2.

34. Greta Riemersma, "In Blessuretijd" [Time Out for Injury], *Volkskrant* (November 15, 1997).

35. B. Garssen and K. Goodwin, "Psychological Factors and Cancer Progression," in *Psychoimmunology of Cancer: Mind and Body in the Fight for Survival,* ed. C. E. Lewis et al. (Oxford: Oxford University Press, 1994).

36. Bill Moyers, *Healing and the Mind* (New York: Bantam Doubleday Dell, 1993); Dutch translation, *Gezondheid en Geest* (Houten: Van Holkema & Warendorf, 1994), 349–93.

37. Helmut Hark, *Jesus der Heiler: Vom Sinn der Krankheit* [Jesus the Healer: On the Meaning of Illness] (Olten, Germany: Walter, 1988), 225.

38. Dale A. Matthews and David B. Larson, *The Faith Factor: Annotated Bibliography of Clinical Research on Spiritual Subjects,* 3 vols. (Rockville, Md.: National Institute for Healthcare Research, 1993–95). For an excellent case study, see D. Oman et al., "Religious Attendance and Cause of Death over 31 Years," *International Journal for Psychiatry in Medicine* 32(1) (2002): 69–89.

39. In a 1996 Time/CNN poll, 82 percent of Americans professed a belief in the healing power of personal prayer. In a Yankelovich poll, 99 percent of the 269 physicians present at the annual meeting of the American Academy of Family Physicians were convinced that religious belief can contribute to healing.

40. A. Rendle Short, *The Bible and Modern Medicine* (Exeter, U.K.: Paternoster, 1966), 124–33.

41. Episcopal Church USA, *The Book of Common Prayer* (New York: Church Hymnal Corp., 1979), 456: "I lay my hands upon you in the name of the Father, and of the Son, and of the Holy Spirit, beseeching our Lord Jesus Christ to sustain you with his presence, to drive away all sickness of body and spirit, and to give you that victory of life and peace which will enable you to serve him both now and evermore."

42. Martyn Percy, "The Gospel Miracles and Modern Healing Movements," *Theology* 99(793) (1997): 8–17.

Chapter 13. Are We Alone? Theological Implications of Possible Extraterrestrial Intelligent Life

Adapted with permission from the author's article in *Zygon* 38(3) (September 2003): 587–602. Copyright 2003 by Joint Publication Board of *Zygon*.

1. William Markowitz, "The Physics and Metaphysics of Unidentified Flying Objects," *Science* 157 (1967): 1274–80. Sociologist William S. Bainbridge notes that the New Paradigm in the sociology of religion states, "Religion is an inevitable feature of all human societies and . . . secularization merely weakens old religious movements to the advantage of new ones—rather than marking the triumph of science over religion." William S. Bainbridge, "Extraterrestrial Tales," *Science* 279 (1998): 671.

2. Michael J. Crowe, "A History of the Extraterrestrial Life Debate," *Zygon* 32(2) (1997): 147–62.

3. Donald Goldsmith, *The Quest for Extraterrestrial Life* (Mill Valley, Calif.: University Science Books, 1980), 4.

4. Ibid., 6.

5. Ibid., 17–19.

6. Ibid., 24–27.

7. Stephen Webb, *If the Universe Is Teeming with Aliens . . . Where Is Everybody?* (New York: Springer, 2002).

8. Jack Cohen and Ian Stewart, *Evolving the Alien: The Science of Extraterrestrial Life* (New York: Wiley, 2002).

9. Richard A. Kerr, "Rainbow of Martian Minerals Paints Picture of Degradation," *Science* 305 (August 6, 2004): 770–71.

10. Jack J. Lissauer, "Extrasolar Planets," *Nature* 419 (2002): 355–58.

11. Bernard M. Oliver, "Search Strategies," in *Life in the Universe,* ed. John Billingham, 351–76 (Cambridge: MIT Press, 1982).

12. John H. Wolfe et al., "SETI, the Search for Extraterrestrial Intelligence: Plans and Rationale," in Billingham, *Life in the Universe,* 391–417.

13. G. R. Coulter et al., "Searching for Intelligent Life in the Universe," in *Advances in Space Biology and Medicine,* vol. 4, ed. S. L. Bonting, 189–224 (Greenwich, Conn.: JAI, 1994).

14. Richard A. Kerr, "No Din of Alien Chatter in Our Neighborhood," *Science* 303 (February 20, 2004): 1133.

15. Ellen Van Wolde, *Stories of the Beginning* (London: SCM, 1996).

16. Crowe, "A History of the Extraterrestrial Life Debate" (n. 2 above); and W. B. Drees, "Theologie over Buitenaardse Personen" [Theology of Extraterrestrial Beings], *Tijdschrift voor Theologie* 27 (1987): 259–76 (Dutch with English summary).

17. Goldsmith, *The Quest for Extraterrestrial Life* (n. 3 above), 6.

18. Ibid., 8.

19. Ibid., 10–16.

20. Drees, "Theologie over Buitenaardse Personen" (n. 16 above), 264.

21. Ibid., 264–68.

22. Sjoerd L. Bonting, "Teilhard de Chardin en Buitenaards Leven" [Teilhard de Chardin and Extraterrestrial Life], *Gamma* 5(2) (1998): 41–43.

23. Drees, "Theologie over Buitenaardse Personen" (n. 16 above), 268–72.

24. Steven J. Dick, ed., *Many Worlds: The New Universe, Extraterrestrial Life, and the Theological Implications* (Philadelphia: Templeton, 2000).

25. Ernan McMullin, "Life and Intelligence Far from Earth: Formulating Theological Issues," in Dick, *Many Worlds*, 151–75; and George V. Coyne, "The Evolution of Intelligent Life on the Earth and Possibly Elsewhere: Reflections from a Religious Tradition," in Dick, *Many Worlds*, 177–88.

26. Steven J. Dick, "Cosmotheology: Theological Implications of the New Universe," in Dick, *Many Worlds*, 191–210.

27. A claim for a direct observation of a "hot Jupiter" has recently been made. Mark Peplow, "Hubble Photographs Extrasolar Planet," News@Nature.com (May 14, 2004), www .nature.com/news/.

28. Lissauer, "Extrasolar Planets" (n. 10 above)

29. Robert Irion, "Planet Hunting Gets Rocky as Teams Clash over Small Worlds," *Science* 305 (September 3, 2004): 1382.

30. Martin E. Beer et al., "How Special Is the Solar System?" Astrophysics archive (July 22, 2004), http://arxiv.org/abs/astro-ph/0407476.

31. J. P. Moreland, ed., *The Creation Hypothesis: Scientific Evidence for an Intelligent Designer* (Downers Grove, Ill.: InterVarsity, 1994), 165–70.

32. Robert Irion, "Are Most Life-Friendly Stars Older Than the Sun?" *Science* 303 (January 2, 2004): 27.

33. David Bradley, "The Genome Chose Its Alphabet with Care," *Science* 297 (2002): 1789–91.

34. Jeffrey L. Bada, "Extraterrestrial Handedness?" *Science* 275 (1997): 942–43; and John Horgan, "The Sinister Cosmos," *Scientific American* 276(5) (1997): 16–18.

35. S. L. Jaki, *Cosmos and Creator* (Edinburgh: Regnery Gateway, 1980), 124.

36. Sjoerd L. Bonting, *Schepping & Evolutie: Poging tot Synthese* [Creation and Evolution: Attempt at Synthesis] (Kampen, The Netherlands: Kok, 1996), 94–96. English translation available by writing to s.l.bonting@wxs.nl.

37. "Systems of Religious and Spiritual Belief," in *Encyclopaedia Britannica*, 15th ed.

38. Van Wolde, *Stories of the Beginning* (n. 15 above); and Bonting, *Schepping & Evolutie*, 154–61.

39. W. O. E. Oesterly and T. H. Robinson, *Hebrew Religion, Its Origin and Development* (London: SPCK, 1935); and Karen Armstrong, *A History of God: From Abraham to the Present, the 4000 Year Quest for God* (London: Heinemann, 1993).

40. Bonting, *Schepping & Evolutie*, 161–65.

41. Frans De Waal, *The Ape and the Sushi Master: Cultural Reflections of a Primatologist* (New York: Basic Books, 2001).

42. Drees, "Theologie over Buitenaardse Personen" (n. 16 above), 263.

43. Ibid., 262.

44. Ibid., 263.

45. E. L. Mascall, *Christian Theology and Natural Science* (London: Longmans Green, 1956), 40–45.

46. Brian Hebblethwaite, "The Impossibility of Multiple Incarnations," *Theology* 104(821) (2002): 323–34.

47. William Temple, *Nature, Man and God* (London: Macmillan, [1934] 1960), 473–95. Paul Tillich also recognized a sacramental aspect of nature. Henry Carse, "Simple Water, Consuming Flame: Nature, Sacrament and Person in Paul Tillich," *Theology* 99(787) (1996): 22–27.

Chapter 14. Future and Destiny: Eschatology and Chaos Theology

1. Mark Peplow, "Cosmic Doomsday Delayed," News@Nature.com (November 5, 2004), www.nature.com/news/; refers to Yun Wang et al., "Current Observational Constraints on Cosmic Doomsday," *Journal of Cosmology and Astroparticle Physics* (November 30, 2004), available online at http://arxiv.org/astro-ph/0409264.

2. Charles Seife, "Galaxy Maps Support Theory That the Universe Is Flying to Pieces," *Science* 302 (October 31, 2003): 762–63.

3. Philip Ball, "Universe Can Surf the Big Rip," News@Nature.com (June 9, 2003), www.nature.com/news/.

4. Tom Gehrels, "Collisions with Comets and Asteroids," *Scientific American* 274(3) (1996): 34–39. The impact of a 1-kilometer asteroid (equivalent to 100,000 nuclear bombs) could destroy all or nearly all life on Earth; the chance of this is estimated at once every 600,000 years. Project Spacewatch now locates and tracks all "Near Earth Objects." Methods are being studied for deflecting an asteroid heading for Earth. One idea is to use a ballistic missile with a chemical or nuclear charge. Steve Nadis, "Planetary Protection," *Scientific American* 287(4) (October 2002): 12. Another method is to use spacecraft to push it into another orbit. R. L. Schweickart et al., "The Asteroid Tugboat," *Scientific American* 289(5) (November 2003): 34–41.

5. Steven Weinberg, *The First Three Minutes: A Modern View of the Origin of the Universe* (Glasgow: Fontana/Collins, 1978).

6. Data from U.S. Census Bureau, www.census.gov/ipc. Worldwide annual growth is 1.15 percent. The fastest growth is in sub-Saharan Africa (2.22 percent) and the Near East (2.07 percent). The slowest growth is in North America (0.92 percent), Western Europe (0.23 percent), and Eastern Europe (–0.06 percent, that is, a decline). As reported in Chris Wilson, "Fertility below Replacement Level," *Science* 304 (April 16, 2004): 207–9, for 50 percent of humanity, the global human fertility level has now decreased to below the long-run replacement level of 2.1 children per woman.

7. Stephen J. Zipko, *Toxic Threat* (New York: Messner, 1986). Toxic substances in water may be amplified some 10 million times through the food chain (plankton, fish, birds, to humans).

8. F. Sherwood Rowland, "Chlorofluorocarbons and the Depletion of Stratospheric Ozone," *American Scientist* 77 (1989): 36–45. Initially, Rowland and Molina were merely studying the mechanism of photochemical reactions in the laboratory, but later they realized the mechanism's relevance for ozone depletion.

9. Daniel P. Schrag and Richard B. Alley, "Ancient Lessons for Our Future Climate," *Science* 306 (October 29, 2004): 821–22. The present carbon dioxide level is higher than it has ever been in the past 430,000 years. Their conclusion: "The release of greenhouse gases through human activities represents a large perturbation, sending our atmosphere to a state unlike any seen for millions of years."

10. Bernard A. Maher, "Building Meaningful Climate Models," *The Scientist* 18(13) (July 5, 2004): 25.

11. Richard A. Kerr, "Three Degrees of Consensus," *Science* 305 (August 13, 2004): 932–34.

12. Edward R. Cook et al., "Long-Term Aridity Changes in the Western United States," *Science* 306 (November 5, 2004): 1015–18; and Richard B. Alley, "Abrupt Climate Change," *Scientific American* 291(5) (November 2004): 40–47. The European heat wave in summer 2003 cannot be explained as a random event, but must be part of this trend. C. Schär, "The Role of Increasing Temperature Variability in European Summer Heatwaves," *Nature* 427 (January 22, 2004): 332–36.

13. Philip Ball, "Climate Change Set to Poke Holes in Ozone," News@Nature.com (March 1, 2004), www.nature.com/news/.

14. Laury Miller and Bruce C. Douglas, "Mass and Volume Contributions to Twentieth-Century Global Sea Level Rise," *Nature* 428 (March 25, 2004): 406–9; Jocelyn Kaiser, "Warmer Ocean Could Threaten Antarctic Ice Shelves," *Science* 302 (October 31, 2003): 759; Philip Ball, "Glaciers Are Flowing Faster," News@Nature.com (September 20, 2004), www.nature.com/news/; Matthew Sturm et al., "Meltdown in the North," *Scientific American* 289(4) (October 2003): 42–49, on *Impacts of a Warming Arctic*, Arctic Climate Impact Assessment overview report (Cambridge: Cambridge University Press, November 8, 2004), available at www.amap.no/acia/index.html. The polar areas warm up twice as fast as the rest of Earth, as predicted by the climate models. The ACIA report predicts disappearance of ice from the Arctic Sea by 2100 with a local temperature increase of 4°C to 7°C; thawing of permafrost with damage to houses, pipelines, and roads; and a tripling of the ozone depletion.

15. Ruth Curry et al., "A Change in the Freshwater Balance of the Atlantic Ocean over the Past Four Decades," *Nature* 426 (December 18, 2003): 826–29. However, the northward flow is getting more saline, which may reduce the climate effect. Bogi Hansen et al., "Already the Day after Tomorrow?" *Science* 305 (August 13, 2004): 953–54.

16. Masao Fukasawa et al., "Bottom Water Warming in the North Pacific Ocean," *Nature* 427 (February 26, 2004): 825–27.

17. Anthony J. Richardson and David S. Schoeman, "Climate Impact on Plankton Ecosystems in the Northeast Atlantic," *Science* 305 (September 10, 2004): 1609–12. For similar findings, see Martin Edwards and Anthony J. Richardson, "Impact of Climate Change on Marine Pelagic Phenology and Trophic Mismatch," *Nature* 430 (August 19, 2004): 881–84.

18. Camille Parmesan and Gary Yohe, "A Globally Coherent Fingerprint of Climate Change Impacts across Natural Systems," *Nature* 421 (January 2, 2003): 37–42.

19. Terry L. Root et al., "Fingerprints of Global Warming on Wild Animals and Plants," *Nature* 421 (January 2, 2003): 57–60.

20. Elizabeth Pennisi, "Naturalists' Surveys Show That British Butterflies Are Going, Going . . . ," *Science* 303 (March 19, 2004): 1747.

21. Chris D. Thomas et al., "Extinction Risk from Climate Change," *Nature* 427 (January 8, 2004): 145–48. In an extensive comment, J. Alan Pounds and Robert Puschendorf conclude that the actual percentages may be even higher due to factors not included in Thomas et al.'s calculations. "Clouded Futures," *Nature* 427 (January 8, 2004): 107–8.

22. James A. Lake et al., "Next-Generation Nuclear Power," *Scientific American* 286(1) (January 2002): 70–79.

23. Sjoerd L. Bonting, "The Solar Power Satellite Scenario," unpublished report to NASA, May 1989 (text available upon request to the author at s.l.bonting@wxs.nl). See also Dennis Normile, "Japan Looks for Bright Answers to Energy Needs," *Science* 294 (November 9, 2001): 1273. After an unwarranted delay of twenty-five years since the initial proposal, the United States is finally considering this option. *Laying the Foundations for Space Solar Power: An Assessment of NASA's Space Solar Power Investment Strategy* (Washington, D.C.: National Academy Press, 2001).

24. N. T. Wright, *For All the Saints: Remembering the Christian Departed* (London: SPCK, 2003).

25. Sjoerd L. Bonting, "Why Bother with Near-Death Experiences?" *ESSSAT-News* 13(2) (June 2003): 12–14. Full text available at www.chaostheologie.nl under publications.

26. Ibid.

27. Doctrine Commission, Church of England, *The Mystery of Salvation: The Story of God's Gift* (London: Church House Publishing, 1996).

28. P. van Lommel et al., "Near Death Experience in Survivors of Cardiac Arrest: Prospective Study in the Netherlands," *The Lancet* 358 (2001): 2039–42.

29. Frank J. Tipler, *The Physics of Immortality* (New York: Doubleday, 1994). For a more extensive critique, see Sjoerd L. Bonting, "Resurrection: In Discussion with Tipler and Pannenberg," *Bulletin of the Society of Ordained Scientists*, no. 32 (2003): 4–12; full text available at www.chaostheologie.nl.

30. Wolfhart Pannenberg, "Moderne Kosmologie: God en de Verrijzenis van de Doden" [Modern Cosmology: God and the Resurrection of the Dead], *Gamma* 10(1) (February 2003): 14–19 (lecture presented at Innsbruck, 1997).

31. Wolfhart Pannenberg, *Systematic Theology*, vol. 2 (Grand Rapids: Eerdmans, 1994), 136–61.

32. John Polkinghorne, *The God of Hope and the End of the World* (London: SPCK, 2002).

33. Ann Gibbons, "When It Comes to Evolution, Humans Are in the Slow Class," *Science* 267 (1995): 1907–8.

34. Keith Ward, *Religion and Human Nature* (Oxford: Oxford University Press, 1998), chaps. 11–14.

35. Helen Oppenheimer, *The Hope of Heaven* (Cambridge, Mass.: Cowley, 1988), 52–59.

36. Michael Perry, *The Resurrection of Man* (London: Mowbrays, 1975), 123–33.

37. Oppenheimer, *The Hope of Heaven*, 114–25.

Index